BREAKING THE POWER OF EVIL

Expanded Edition

BREAKING THE POWER OF EVIL

Expanded Edition

Rick Joyner

Study Guide compiled by Jan Sherman.

Destiny Image® Publishers, Inc.

P.O. Box 310

Shippensburg, PA 17257-0310

"Speaking to the Purposes of God for This Generation and for the Generations to Come."

ISBN 0-7684-2618-9

ISBN 978-0-7684-2618-2

For Worldwide Distribution

Printed in the U.S.A.

This book and all other Destiny Image, Revival Press, MercyPlace, Fresh Bread, Destiny Image Fiction, and Treasure House books are available at Christian bookstores and distributors worldwide.

For a U.S. bookstore nearest you, call 1-800-722-6774.

For more information on foreign distributors, call 717-532-3040.

Reach us on the Internet: www.destinyimage.com.

1 2 3 4 5 6 7 8 9 10 / 12 11 10 09 08

CONTENTS

PART I

THE BATTLE FOR THE SOUL

CHAPTER 1

THE FREEDOM FIGHTERS

There is a battle raging for the soul of every human being. It is a battle between life and death, and we are the territory that is being fought over. Understanding this conflict will mean nothing less than our own life and death—for eternity. Every day we are either taking ground or losing it in this fight. There is no demilitarized zone that we can flee to on this earth. Therefore, the only reasonable course that we have is to understand the battle, fight it, and win.

This battle is not being fought because there is a question of who is the most powerful in the universe, God or satan. Without question God could end the battle at any time and dispense with satan. The reason He has not done this yet is because of His fundamental commitment to freedom for His creation. Without understanding His commitment to freedom, we cannot fully understand the conflict in the world, the conflict in our own soul, or even in a real sense the nature of God.

We Must Be Free

God created man to be free. We cannot be who we were created to be without freedom. If all that the Lord wanted was perfect, harmonious worship, He would have done better to create computers instead of man so He could just program them to worship Him in perfect harmony. Certainly our God is worthy of more than that, but in order to have more than that there must be freedom.

The Scriptures state in Second Corinthians 3:17, "Now the Lord is the Spirit, and where the Spirit of the Lord is, there is liberty." This could have been translated as, "Where the Spirit is Lord, there is liberty." This reflects one of the most basic differences between the kingdom of darkness and the Kingdom of God. In the domain of darkness there is fear, oppression, and bondage. In the Kingdom of God there is faith and freedom.

It is for this reason that the Lord put the Tree of the Knowledge of Good and Evil in the Garden. This was not done to cause our first parents to sin; rather, there could be no true obedience without the freedom to disobey. This tree was placed in the Garden to give Adam and Eve a way to prove their obedience and love for God. Every temptation allowed in our life has the same purpose.

Fundamental to understanding the truth is understanding that man was created to be a free moral agent. This does not in any way infringe on the sovereignty of God; rather, it illuminates His sovereignty. The greatest, most noble authority is always demonstrated by the freedom it allows its subjects. The Lord wants us to worship Him and reject evil because we love Him and love His truth, not just because we are afraid of punishment. There are consequences for disobedience that we cannot overlook, yes, but our main goal must be to obey because we love God and because He is worthy of our devotion.

Freedom and Responsibility

Freedom involves choices that we must make. With our choices there are consequences. This means that with freedom comes responsibility. Why? Man is called to rule with God, and there can be no true authority without a corresponding responsibility. So the greater the authority is, the greater the potential for good when making the right choice—but also the greater potential for bad when we make the wrong one. Because Adam was given authority over the whole world, when he fell the whole world suffered. To the degree that we are given authority, we also can release good or evil into that domain.

This is the world system that man was put in, and that we live in today. Granted, it is much more difficult because of the poor choices of many who have gone before us, but it is still a system that promotes the pursuit of wisdom and truth. To navigate through life on this planet today, we must be able to discern between good and evil. Even so, there remains a wisdom that is higher than just knowing good and evil. It is the knowledge of life, and this knowledge is simply knowing God. There remains a Tree of Life whose fruit alone will release man into his ultimate potential and purpose. The Lord will feed us with the true life of the knowledge of Him if we will simply pursue it.

Truth Sets Us Free

The purpose for this study is to illuminate some of the strongest chains of bondage that yoke the human soul and keep humankind in darkness. The illumination of these strongholds is half the battle to defeating them. As the apostle Paul wrote in Second Corinthians 2:11, he was forgiving those whom they had forgiven "so that no advantage would be taken of us by satan, for we are not ignorant of his schemes." When we become knowledgeable of the devil's schemes, he can no longer use them to take advantage of us.

We have many clear, biblical examples of the schemes of satan, yet he continues to take advantage of the Church because of our neglect to understand them. It is true that our main purpose must always be to seek life, to partake of the fruit of the Tree of Life, but we, too, will fall if we do not discern the devil's constant attempts to lure us to the evil tree. We must discern these schemes and place true watchmen on the walls who have this knowledge and discernment. As we are told in Second Corinthians 10:3-6:

For though we walk in the flesh, we do not war according to the flesh, for the weapons of our warfare are not of the flesh, but divinely powerful for the destruction of fortresses. We are destroying speculations and every lofty thing raised up against the knowledge of God, and we are taking every thought captive to the obedience of Christ, and we are ready to punish all disobedience, whenever your obedience is complete.

The Church is not here just to defend against the attacks of the devil and establish our own safe havens; we are here on earth to attack and tear down his strongholds, releasing as many souls from his grip as possible. We are not supposed to just be on the defensive; we are here to take back ground that was surrendered to the devil by our ancestors who succumbed to his schemes and to follow up on the victories of our ancestors who took ground before us. We have been given divinely powerful weapons for this purpose. Next to knowing and worshiping God, we should be occupied with assaulting the devil, setting his captives free, and tearing down his evil religions and philosophies through which he keeps humankind in darkness.

Why He Came

Of course, the Lord came to save us from our sin. The Scriptures also say in First John 3:8b that, "The Son of God appeared for this purpose, to destroy the works of the devil." When Jesus prayed for His people on the night before His crucifixion, He said concerning us, "As You sent Me into the world, I also have sent them into the world" (John 17:18). So we are sent for the same basic purpose that He was—to destroy the works of the devil. That is why we are on the earth—to be His Body through which He can continue His work.

Therefore every Christian is called to be a freedom fighter—to set the captives free, to see every human soul set free of bondage to the devil and released into the glorious liberty of the children of God. Because of this, the love of freedom must be basic to our spiritual genetic code.

The whole earth may presently lie within the power of the evil one, and we may now therefore be living behind enemy lines, but we will prevail. We will be victorious in the end. Every soul that is set free is a victory that conquers more territory for the Kingdom of God. Even so, we must look beyond setting just individuals free toward setting whole nations free from the bondage they are in, in this present evil age.

CHAPTER 2

THE REASON FOR THE BATTLE

The entire Church Age has been one of spiritual warfare, and that warfare is increasing as we approach the end of this age. Jesus said, "The harvest is the end of the age" (Matt. 13:39b). The harvest is the reaping of what has been sown because it has become mature. At the end of this age there will be a full maturity and reaping of all that has been sown in man, both the good and the evil. Therefore the Scriptures verify that the greatest conflict of all will be at the end.

It is for this reason that the bride who comes out of the wilderness in the Song of Solomon is like "an army with banners" (Song of Sol. 6:4). When the Church emerges from the wilderness in this age, she will be the glorious, beautiful Bride that Solomon describes here, and she also will be a mighty army. We are called to be not only passionate worshipers of God, but also warriors. King David is one of the great examples of this duality. He was both a great warrior and a great worshiper. In the same way, we are called to be great lovers of God as well as haters of evil. We are a bride dressed in the full armor of God. These two natures seem to be in conflict to some, but they are the basic, essential nature of the Body of Christ. They are also the basic nature of God.

God is love, yet the most common title given to God in Scripture is "the Lord of hosts," which literally means "the Lord of armies." This title is actually used for God more than ten times as much as any other title given to Him in Scripture. If we are following the Lord, we are in an army. There is a battle raging right now in the heavens and on the earth. To not see this battle raging is certainly one of the ultimate delusions that one can be in at this time.

The ultimate outcome of this battle is not in doubt; the enemy was completely defeated by the cross of Jesus. Jesus could have bound satan and cast him into the lake of fire immediately after His resurrection, but He did not do so for our sake. The entire Church Age has been allowed as "training for reigning" for those who are called to be joint heirs with Him. This is our greatest opportunity. Nothing reveals the true character of a person like conflict.

The Enemy Called "Easy"

To the degree that our lives are difficult or embattled usually reflects the high calling that we have been given. I say "usually" because many are in constant conflict because of the evil that they allow to have dominion over them. However, we must understand that many of the conflicts that Christians experience are because of what they are doing right, not what they are doing wrong.

In every field, those who reach the greatest heights will inevitably be those who have the greatest training. Likewise, the Lord wants His joint heirs to have the best training. He is using the age that we live in to give it to us. It should therefore not be our goal to have it easy, but to accept and overcome the challenges. If our life is always easy, it is only because we are called to a lesser purpose. Just as those considered to be the greatest generals in history are those who won the most desperate battles, the trials and battles of this age are the forge by which the Lord is raising His sons and daughters to be worthy heirs whom even the angels will acknowledge.

The bride of the first Adam lived in a perfect world and chose to sin. This has enabled satan to boast that, given freedom, even man—God's crowning creation—will choose evil. Before the end of this age the "last Adam," Christ Jesus, will have a

Bride that lived in a most imperfect, evil world and, against the entire onslaught of hell, chose to obey. For all of eternity thereafter, all of creation will boast in the Lord and His ways, with the knowledge that good will ultimately always triumph over evil. The whole creation also will consider His Bride worthy to rule with Him because she proved her devotion to Him and His truth.

Even though we should certainly appreciate any respite from conflict when it comes, we must understand that we are not here on this earth to enjoy ourselves. We are here to stand for truth and proclaim the gospel of His Kingdom to those who are caught in the shackles of evil and on the path to destruction. We need rest when it is given to us, but how can any soldier of the cross want to rest for long while there is yet even a single soul in bondage to the evil one? Every Christian is sent out as a knight of the Kingdom, to slay the dragons, fight for the poor and oppressed, and establish the domain of the King.

A Strong Delusion

Those who refuse to acknowledge the reality of the spiritual warfare we are in are inevitably overcome by it. Even so, we need not fear—He who is in us is much greater than he who is in the world. (See First John 4:4.) He who is least in the Kingdom of God has more power than all the antichrists who have ever lived. However, just as even the greatest military power today is vulnerable if it does not recognize the nature of the enemy's attack, we too are vulnerable if we do not recognize satan's schemes. The only way that he can defeat us is by our own ignorance or complacency. As we maintain our position in Christ, take on the full armor of God, and remain vigilant, we will not only stand, but also prevail against the gates of hell.

Peter warned the Church to "be of sober spirit, be on the alert. Your adversary, the devil, prowls about like a roaring lion, seeking someone to devour. But resist him, firm in your faith" (1 Pet. 5:8-9a). The enemy's schemes have not really changed since The Garden. He uses the same attacks and traps for each new spiritual generation. The reason he does so is because they continue to work. They work because the Church still has difficulty recognizing them. This has caused almost every new revival, movement, or precedent-setting church to be sidetracked by the same traps as the previous generation. It is time to break this tragic cycle.

The Greatest Freedom

It is the Lord's purpose for our life that we be free from every yoke but one—His yoke. He then wants to use us to set others free. The ultimate freedom comes from knowing the truth—the truth of who He is and where He sits above all rule and authority and dominion. To know the truth is to live by it, and to live by it is to demonstrate it. If we say that we believe the truth but do not live by it, we have only deceived ourselves. Every truth that we really believe, we live by. That is why His people are not known by their words, but by their fruit.

We are called to walk in authority and dominion so that evil flees from us wherever we go. Light is more powerful than darkness. When you open your shades at night, darkness does not pour into the room; rather, light shines out into the darkness. Our goal is to grow in the light to the degree that it shines ever brighter and overcomes darkness wherever we go.

In this book we are going to shine the light on some of the most basic evil strongholds that trap people in bondage. Our first goal must be to get free of their influences ourselves. Our next goal is to sharpen our swords so that we can strike the devil and free others of these same shackles. In this way we will set our families free...then our churches...then our neighborhoods...then our cities.... Our goal must be nothing less than taking over the world—possessing it for the Kingdom of God.

We will not be able to accomplish this entirely before the Lord's return. However, when He returns He will find a faithful army that has refused to retreat before His enemies, even against the ultimate enemy that will be revealed at the end. This we see in Daniel 11:31-32:

> *Forces from him will arise, desecrate the sanctuary fortress, and do away with the regular sacrifice. And they will set up the abomination of desolation.*
>
> *By smooth words he will turn to godlessness those who act wickedly toward the covenant,* **but the people who know their God will display strength and take action.**

We see here that even when the "abomination of desolation" is being set up, "the people who know their God will display strength and take action." The people who know God will never bow the knee to the evil one, and they will not sit by and do nothing while the devil leads the world astray. However, can we be those who display strength and take action right in the face of the abomination of desolation if we do not confront the evil in our own lives, our families, our churches, or our cities? If we truly have the light, we will confront the darkness. Just as the young David could not tolerate the boasting of Goliath against the armies of God, we too will be just too provoked to stand by and let evil prevail.

Worship and Warfare

The Lord Jesus Himself often is referred to in Scripture as "the Son of David." When the Jews came to Jesus claiming to be the "sons of Abraham," the Lord replied to them, "If you are Abraham's children, do the deeds of Abraham" (John 8:39b). We can deduce from this that Jesus was not just the Son of David by lineage, but also because He was here to do the deeds of David.

David was the first one to conquer and possess the entire land that Israel had been promised through Abraham and then confirmed through Moses. Jesus came to fully posses the Kingdom. David also was both the greatest worshiper and greatest warrior in Israel's history. Though many people have trouble reconciling our calling to both worship and warfare, they actually go together. In this age you cannot do one without the other. Even so, we will be great warriors only to the degree that we are great worshipers. This is why we are told in Psalm 149:5-6:

> *Let the godly ones exult in glory; let them sing for joy on their beds.*
>
> *Let the high praises of God be in their mouth, and a two-edged sword in their hand.*

Our first calling is to worship, but we must do so with a sword in our hands. Even though this book is mostly about warfare, any Christian who is mostly devoted to warfare will certainly be imbalanced, and he or she can be open to some of the greatest deceptions of all.

As we are told in First Timothy 1:5, "But the goal of our instruction is love from a pure heart and a good conscience and a sincere faith." Our goal in this life is to grow in love and faith. We can do this only by drawing closer to the Lord Himself. True love comes from seeing Him as He is, and true faith comes from the same—seeing Him as the One who is above all rule and authority and dominion.

As Peter Lord likes to say, "The main thing is to keep the main thing the main thing." The main thing in our life is loving God, not fighting evil. It is because we love God that we stand for truth and fight evil. Even so, our strength in the fight is directly related to our love for Him, which always overflows into a love for people. Love and truth are the divinely powerful weapons.

In my opinion, one of the greatest Christian movements during the 1980s and '90s was the Vineyard Movement led by John Wimber. Though I was never officially a member of this movement, I did get to know John Wimber quite well, and I ministered in some of his conferences and churches. I marveled many times at the extraordinary authority that John, his leaders, and so many people in Vineyard churches had over demons. I witnessed some of the strongest evil spirits I had ever seen come out of people with a word—from an usher! Yet, almost no one thought of the Vineyard as a major deliverance ministry. Rather, they were best known for their worship and for healing. That is the way it should be.

True worship does not come in order to see the Lord; it comes from seeing the Lord. If we see Him, we will worship! To the degree that we see Him with the eyes of our hearts, we will worship. We need many times as much worship in our life as warfare. We have too many examples of people who become overly focused on fighting demons who have taken on the nature of the demons they are casting out of people. Those who spend too much time studying cults often start to take on a more foul spirit than the cults they study. That is because of the spiritual principle highlighted in Second Corinthians 3:18, which states that we will become what we are beholding.

I have sown therefore throughout this book counterbalancing truths of the Kingdom and of the nature of our King, in relationship to the evil strongholds and schemes of the enemy we are seeking to overthrow. We are here to fight battles on the earth, but let us always heed the exhortation of Colossians 3:1-2:

> *Therefore if you have been raised up with Christ, keep seeking the things above, where Christ is, seated at the right hand of God. Set your mind on the things above, not on the things that are on earth.*

The primary way that we will win our battles on the earth is by dwelling in the heavenly places with Christ and bringing evidence of Heaven—the Kingdom of God—to the earth.

CHAPTER 3

FIGHTING THE RIGHT WAR

Individuals have a composite of factors that make up who they are. These would include such things as their basic gifts and talents, their knowledge and experience, as well as their fears and social wounds that affect the way they think and perceive others. We'll call this composite of who a person is his "soul" for the basis of this study.

Groups also have a soul that is the composite of all the above characteristics combined to form how the group thinks, perceives, and acts. Churches, businesses, sports teams, and clubs all have a composite soul that one needs to discern in order to relate to that group effectively. The same is true of nations and even larger cultural entities such as religions and races. There is also what we might call "the soul of man," which is the composite of humankind in general.

Just as people change as they mature or have different experiences, social groups such as churches, teams, corporations, and others also change. They can change quite radically with the addition or loss of single individuals. Even quite large entities such as an army or a large industry can change a great deal with the change of a single leader. They also may change after just one experience, such as a battle, or for a corporation, something that affects its economy.

Discerning the soul of an individual is important to ministering to that individual. Discerning the soul of a group can be important for ministering to that group. Of course, discerning the larger, more ambiguous "soul of humankind" is crucial for the ministry of the Church during our times. True, the larger the group is, the more general the characteristics of its soul will be, which will make it easier to over-generalize at times. Even so, the discernment of the soul is crucial for those whose calling in this world is to save souls. We also should consider that the "Great Commission" was to disciple all nations, not just individuals. So it is important that we discern the *nations* that we are called to minister to.

The Foundational Stronghold

In these last days, the battle raging for the soul of man is intensifying. This battle is being fought in every individual, every church, every city, and every nation. Those who do not understand this conflict will be defeated by it. Before we go on to address the other major strongholds that the evil one has over humankind, we must recognize and understand the basic power that he uses to keep men in bondage to do his will—and that power is *fear*!

The devil uses fear to keep the world under his power just as the Lord uses faith to set men free to serve Him. Faith will lead us to the Lord's domain, which is His Kingdom. There we find the liberty that releases us to be who we were created to be. This battle between faith and fear that rages in every soul will determine whether we live a successful life or not—and whether we are able to do what we were created and gifted to do.

The course of our lives will be dictated by either faith or fear. We must choose which it will be. Then we must choose to fight. One basic definition of faith might be to fight fear. Obviously there is more to faith than this, but it is certainly a fundamental ingredient. We must strengthen our hands for this battle and resolve to overcome every fear that seeks dominion in our life. We must replace the fears in our life with a faith that climbs irresistibly toward the fulfillment of our individual purpose.

Though the basic course of our life is dictated by our submission to either fear or faith, there are degrees to this dictatorship. We are under the control of evil to the degree that fear is allowed to control our life. That is why we are told in Romans 14:23b, "Whatever is not from faith is sin." If fear controls us, then fear is our lord. To walk in obedience to the Lord requires us to walk in faith. As we are told in Hebrews 10:38-39 (NKJV),

> *Now the just shall live by faith; but if anyone draws back, My soul has no pleasure in him. But we are not of those who draw back to perdition, but of those who believe to the saving of the soul.*

It should be a basic goal in our life to grow in faith and to resist the control that fear has over us. This is a process that requires the renewing of our minds, or changing the very thinking by which we perceive and understand ourselves and the world around us. We will be the one who determines whether fear or faith in God will control our actions and beliefs.

One vs. the Many

We should note that faith in God is always singular, but there are a multitude of fears that seek dominion over us. There is a simplicity to the faith walk that is liberating. Fear is much more complicated.

One of the most basic fears that seeks to control us is the fear of man. Under this category a multitude of fears can be found, such as the fear of rejection, the fear of failure, the fear of embarrassment or humiliation, etc. This is why the more we grow in faith in God, the more peace, rest, and fulfillment we will have in our life.

Most of our failures, rejections, and even humiliations are actually the result of fear we have in those areas and that controls us. Fear causes us to do things that we would not have done if we were living by faith in that area. As someone once said, "Fear is faith for the things you don't want." In this way fear actually causes the release of the things we fear.

Even the beasts can discern fear and react to it. Studies have shown that almost every form of animal predator senses fear in its prey, which alerts it to the vulnerability of its victims. Most of us have probably witnessed how a person who has a fear of dogs seems to arouse a desire to attack in even the most docile of pets. This is to be expected because it is natural for animals that sense fear to be aroused to catch their prey.

There is an order in the present fallen world that is prevalent throughout nature, including humankind. That order is often called "the pecking order." The pecking order is the determination of who will be in control, of who will be under who, right down to the last one. You can take a group of almost any animal—horses, dogs, sheep, or geese—or people and put them together, and there will be a major striving and conflict until the pecking order is established. Then there will be a continual battle to maintain position by suppressing the ambitious ones below us, or to go higher by nosing out those above us. This is a main reason for the continual, basic human conflicts.

This tendency to establish position within a group is the result of both the called purpose of humankind, which was to rule over the earth, and the perversion of that purpose, which was to use our rule for selfish reasons instead of serving those whom we are to rule over. Even so, it is natural in people that when one senses fear in another, he will almost inevitably move to dominate that person. This is the very thing that the enemy of our souls does to us spiritually. Fear arouses demonic forces to swarm to the vulnerable. Likewise, faith repels them.

For this reason, it is a basic purpose of every Christian to walk in the faith that resists the enemy's attempts to dominate us. We then must grow in our dominion and faith for the purpose of serving others, setting them free and not dominating them.

Pecking Order in the Church

I am convinced that one of the reasons there is such a modern addiction to sports is because it is such a blatant battle to establish the pecking order. Whoever is ahead in the standings is determined by teams facing each other in the fight for supremacy. Then we find a number of other ways to measure individuals—batting averages, number of home runs, pass completions, interceptions, rebounds, even minutes played per game. We are in a continual pursuit to determine who is at the top and where everyone else fits in. We need to understand that competition is *always* about establishing the pecking order.

The same is true in business. Profit, market share, and such are the ways that we keep score in business. As stated, this tendency in us is the result of good characteristics that were given to man so that he could fulfill his purpose, but that have been corrupted. I have found from years of playing basketball, golf, or any sport with my employees or staff that those who are the most competitive on the court tend to be the ones who will accomplish the most. However, we must understand that our competitive nature must be redeemed and focused rightly or we will end up building another tower of Babel instead of being used to preach and bring the Kingdom.

I have been privileged to know some of the great spiritual leaders of our times. I am convinced that some of the greatest Christian leaders who ever lived are alive today. Even so, it has been interesting to observe the way some of the most influential Christian leaders will react when they are all thrown into a room together for a period of time. Even if it is very subtle, the battle for the pecking order will quickly begin.

Those who have built their ministries on good promotional abilities will immediately start trying to establish their place in the group and seek to be dominant. These are obviously uncomfortable in a position in which they may not be the one in control, and there can be an almost desperate attempt by them to gain that control in such situations.

Contrary to this, those who have true spiritual authority will tend to have a very distinguishable peace about them. They spend their time trying to get to know others, asking about what others are doing, rather than just trying to establish that they are the greatest in the room. The dignity and nobility of true spiritual authority is truly marvelous to behold when there is such a contrast. One of the most important texts in the Bible on this fundamental issue is Second Corinthians 10:8-12:

> *For even if I boast somewhat further about our authority, which the Lord gave for building you up and not for destroying you, I will not be put to shame,*
>
> *for I do not wish to seem as if I would terrify you by my letters.*
>
> *For they say, "His letters are weighty and strong, but his personal presence is unimpressive, and his speech contemptible."*
>
> *Let such a person consider this, that what we are in word by letters when absent, such persons we are also in deed when present.*
>
> *For we are not bold to class or compare ourselves with some of those who commend themselves; but when they measure themselves by themselves and compare themselves with themselves, they are without understanding.*

It is a natural thing in this present world to be competitive for the purpose of establishing our positions and being successful in the world. However, this same tendency carried over into our spiritual life will be a stumbling block that can disqualify us from growing in true spiritual authority. Comparing himself with others is the most basic way that we can know that someone really does not have a true understanding of the Kingdom. Those who have a true understanding rejoice in the promotion of the Kingdom whomever it comes through, and even if it means the decrease of their own ministry, as John the Baptist demonstrated.

Ministries that are competing with other ministries are not promoting the Kingdom but their own domains. Churches, denominations, or movements that are in competition with others are not building the Kingdom; rather, they have fallen to the snare of the devil and are trying to build on their own fallen nature and not by the Spirit of God.

I am often asked by those who are in such churches, ministries, or denominations that have such an obvious spirit of competition whether they should stay in it or not. My position on this matter has never changed. We must ask which kingdom we want to be a part of building. Unless you have received a very clear and specific call to be a part of such a work as a missionary to it, don't waste yourself building the wrong kingdom. If we are going to be the freedom fighters that we are called to be, then we must fight in the right army and by the right Spirit.

Our competitive nature can be used for good or evil. In some ways competition can be used to stimulate one another to love and good deeds. Two of my best friends are Ricky Skaggs and Wellington Boone. They were together in a meeting in Nashville when Ricky felt that he should wash the feet of some Baptist leaders who were present. Wellington immediately said, "I can't let Ricky out humble me!" So Boone got down and tried to wash more feet than Ricky did.

I was very curious about the fruit from this, as this was a new form of competition to me. It seems to have been so powerful that I kept hearing about this meeting years later. It also seems that all who were present were convicted and loving relationships were established where leaders started to esteem each other as more important than themselves—relationships that I think have continued to this day.

What would happen if churches decided that they would spend more time talking about the great things God was doing in other churches than in talking about themselves? What would happen if we started a competition among the churches in our community for who could do the most to build up the other churches? What would happen if we started measuring our success by how others whom we helped succeeded? I can tell you what would happen. We would start to love each other, and then we would come into such a unity that the whole world would start to believe because of the great miracle of Christians loving each other.

Like it or not, there is rank in Heaven. Like it or not, there is a competition on the earth right now for where we are going to be positionally for eternity. That may seem to contradict what I have written here, but it doesn't. There is good competition and there is bad competition. What I am saying is clear in the Scriptures. What is bad, and what the Lord rebuked His disciples for doing, is arguing about it when we should be out there working.

It is also apparent that the Lord has so established things at this time that we cannot know our position while on the earth. That is why the apostle Paul said near the end of his life that he did not consider that he had yet attained, but he pressed on toward the mark of the high calling of God in Christ Jesus. (See Philippians 3:12-14.)

Just as Aaron, the high priest, had to carry the stones of all the tribes on his heart, if we are going to walk in the high calling of God, we must carry all of God's people on our heart, not just our own little tribe. I therefore want to challenge other churches and movements to a friendly competition. I realize that we won't be able to determine the score until that great Judgment Day, but we, The MorningStar Fellowship Church, intend to be known in Heaven as the movement that did the most to help other movements and churches prevail and be victorious in their calling. I challenge you to beat us out of this.

CHAPTER 4

FROM DEMONS TO WORLD RULERS

There are levels of demonic forces that are assaulting the world. These range from demonic attacks on individuals, to principalities that seek dominion over regions or nations, to "world rulers" that seek dominion over the entire earth.

When the terrorist leader Osama bin Laden prophesied that America would fear from north to south and east to west, he was issuing a demonic prophecy that was a clear indication of the enemy's strategy against America. Because the enemy is always seeking to counter the work of God, we can know for sure that it is God's plan for faith to be released in America from north to south, east to west. We are in fact close to another Great Awakening sweeping over America.

As the enemy steps up his assault across the world to dominate foreign policy with fear and terror, we can be assured that it is the greatest opportunity for faith to be released in every place the enemy attacks. Faith is much more powerful than fear, and faith will ultimately prevail.

Earthly governments must fight the war against terror on the level of natural weapons, but only the Church can achieve the ultimate victory over this enemy. As we are told in Ephesians 6:12, "For our struggle is not against flesh and blood, but against the rulers, against the powers, against the world forces of this darkness, against the spiritual forces of wickedness in the heavenly places." This is not a war against flesh and blood; it is a spiritual battle that must be fought with spiritual weapons if we are going to have a true and lasting victory.

Demons assault individuals in the same manner that a principality attacks a city or region. They both begin simply by seeking to gain influence. They increase their influence until they have control over the actions of those they are seeking to dominate. When this happens to an individual, it is called being "possessed" by demons. Lesser levels of control by them are usually referred to as demonic oppression. In the same manner, cities, regions, and even nations can be possessed by the more powerful forces of evil.

Christians are given authority over demons. No Christian who has come to know the authority of our Lord Jesus Christ should have a fear of being possessed by demons. If a Christian is walking in faith, it releases God's authority that will cause demons to fear us and flee from us. Recognizing, confronting, and casting out demons is normal, biblical Christianity.

Another level of evil addressed in Scripture is called "principalities and powers." As stated, these are more powerful than demons, and they seek dominion over regions or nations, not just individuals. Though every Christian has the authority to cast out demons, we do not cast out principalities and powers; instead, we must "wrestle" with them to displace them. This level of warfare is addressed in other books I have written such as *Epic Battles of the Last Days*, *Mobilizing the Army of God*, and *A Prophetic Vision for the 21st Century*.

Then there is another, higher realm of evil called "world rulers." These do not just affect individuals or regions, but can dominate much of the earth. This level of evil I address in my book *Shadows of Things to Come*. Above this level is the evil lord, satan himself. Christians are called to fight evil on all these levels. However, we only have true spiritual authority to the degree that the King lives within us, or to the degree that we abide in the Lord. As we grow in authority, which is evidenced by our increased faith, we will be called to fight battles on higher levels.

Generally, only demons will possess individuals, and the battle that most Christians face is a personal battle. This is mostly with the evil that tries to gain entrance to our own life. As we are victorious on this level and are trusted with more spiritual authority, we may be called on to confront evil on a higher level, seeking the liberation of a region or even a nation from the enemy's domain. As my friend Francis Frangipane likes to say, "With new levels come new devils." This may not be too encouraging, but one of the ways that we know we have been promoted in spiritual authority is by the bigger demons that we have to fight.

Francis has written what many consider to be the greatest book ever on spiritual warfare, *The Three Battlegrounds*. In this classic message he explains how our battle against evil starts with the battle in our own minds. As we gain victory there, we must then fight for victory of the Church. Only when the Church is victorious in a region will it displace the principalities over it. This book is a very practical step-by-step advance toward such victories.

If we are going to be given national or international spiritual authority, we can count on attacks from principalities and powers. If we have been given authority that will have an impact on the whole earth, we will have to face a world ruler at some point. Paul the apostle was such a man, which is why he had to face Caesar. Because Jesus is the highest authority in the Kingdom, He had to be confronted by satan himself and prevail.

Because of Caesar's scope of authority, he was not being manipulated by a mere demon, but by a world ruler. Satan has to use men to do his will just as the Lord works through His people. Therefore, as one grows in spiritual authority, they will be buffeted by those who are controlled by more powerful demonic forces. This is not something that we should fear, as the One who is in us is much greater than all of the power of the evil one. To be attacked on a higher level should actually be an encouragement to us.

There are watershed events that cause sweeping changes over the whole earth. If these events are evil, you can count on a world ruler being behind them. We witnessed such an event on September 11, 2001. This was the beginning of another strategic assault of fear that was on the level of a world ruler. This did not just affect the United States; the whole world was shaken that day. It is right that the civilized governments of the world have now made terrorism the world's foremost enemy— it is. However, this is a spiritual enemy that cannot be defeated by mere bombs and bullets. Christians must overcome the fears that dominate their own lives, and then the Church must over- come the same. Then we must rise to the place of faith and authority where we confront the world ruler that is assaulting the whole world.

The Two Mandates

For us to understand that the real war is spiritual and not natural is not to negate the righteousness of the war in which our earthly governments are now engaged. As we are told con- cerning them in Romans 13:1-4 (NKJV):

> *Every person is to be in subjection to the governing authorities. For there is no authority except from God, and those which exist are established by God.*
>
> *Therefore whoever resists authority has opposed the ordinance of God; and they who have opposed will receive condemnation upon themselves.*
>
> *For rulers are not a cause of fear for good behavior, but for evil. Do you want to have no fear of authority? Do what is good, and you will have praise from the same; for it is a minister of God to you for good. But if you do what is evil, be afraid; for it does not bear the sword for nothing; for it is a minister of God, an avenger who brings wrath on the one who practices evil.*

As this passage states, civil governments have a mandate from God to avenge evil and bring wrath on those who practice evil on the earth. For this reason civil governments have been given the sword, or military power. We always should pray for our governments and for their success in bringing the wrath of God on those who practice evil. Throughout the Bible we see that most of the time when the Lord fulfilled His Word by bringing judgment upon a nation or people, it was done by using the military power of other nations.

Civil government is essential for keeping order to the degree that it is possible until the Kingdom of God comes to restore righteousness and justice on the earth. Because fallen men exercise this authority, it will never be exercised perfectly. However, it does at least restrain the forces that would bring about a complete meltdown of order and authority. Civil authority is ordained by God, but we must not mistake it for the authority of the Kingdom of God.

A Different Spirit

As Christians we have a different mandate of authority. We are not here in this age to avenge evil, but in fact are required to love our enemies and pray for them. Our warfare is not against people, but against whatever has people in bondage. The greatest victory of all would be the repentance and salvation of our enemies. Many Christians have a difficult time understanding the two different mandates given to civil governments and to the Church. However, this is something important that we must settle in our hearts if we are going to be effective in our job of tearing down the spiritual strongholds that keep men in bondage.

Our civil governments are fighting a righteous war against evil as they combat terrorism or governments that promote terrorism. Even so, the Church is called to a much different battle. We are called to fight the unseen war that is being waged in the heavenly places. Ours is a spiritual war.

This does not mean that Christians cannot join the military forces of nations to fight the war on the level of civil authority. However, they should understand that while marching under the orders of civil governments, their authority will be exercised through their physical weapons, not their spiritual ones. This does not mean that Christian soldiers should not pray and try to use their spiritual authority too, but when you're in battle, don't drop your gun to do so! If you are under orders from a civil government, you must not hesitate to use the weapons that the government has given to you for fighting.

Likewise, if we are operating under the mandate given to the Church, we do not have authority to use the weapons that are used for fighting flesh and blood for our battle. This is why "Christian militias" that arm themselves with guns or other physical weapons will always be motivated by fear and paranoia. They are actually controlled by evil since they are not properly under either of the mandates of authority that God has given to men.

Fighting the Good Fight

Spiritual authority is something that we grow into. We are given more authority as we mature spiritually and are given higher commissions by the Lord. This will be evidenced by an increase of faith to new levels. We see in the Book of Acts that Paul the apostle was called as an apostle many years before he was actually commissioned to that ministry. With that commissioning came authority on a higher level. However, "…many are called, but few are chosen" (Matt. 22:14). One interpretation of this is that many are called but few persevere through all that is required to receive their commission.

Being called to a high position does not automatically give one authority. Maturity and the faithfulness that goes on to possess the promises is what will release true authority in us. However, we must understand that spiritual authority is not given so that we get more respect from people, but so we can fight effectively against the powers that are destroying people.

Our first goal must be to confront and overcome our personal demons and our personal fears, so that we can grow in the authority to take on bigger demons and set other people free. Because there is a faith that overcomes the world, nothing less than this can be our goal. We may not see evil fully displaced until the King Himself returns to Earth, but there is a biblical mandate for us to do all we can to prepare the way for His coming Kingdom by overcoming evil in every way that we can now.

I have heard many express fear that this can be carried too far. I am quite sure that if we get carried away with too much faith and tear down some strongholds of evil that we were not called to tear down, (and saving more souls than we were actually called to set free), I think the Lord will forgive us!

One of the ways the enemy has kept much of Evangelical, Pentecostal, and Charismatic Christianity in bondage has been to impart a belief that since it is inevitable the entire world is going to fall to the antichrist, it is useless to fight the evil in the world, and therefore we should just try to be faithful ourselves and wait for the Rapture. There are a number of Scriptures that challenge this deception, such as the one we quoted in an earlier chapter, Daniel 11:31-32.

We know from the Scriptures there are certain ways in which evil will increase and that it will prevail over the earth for a time, but hasn't that always been the case? The apostle John wrote in the first century that "... the whole world lies in the power of the evil one" (1 John 5:19). It may lie in the power of the evil one now, but it does not belong to him! It is a usurped dominion that will be restored to its rightful owner—the Lord, who paid the ultimate price with His own life to redeem it. As Psalm 24:1 declares, "The earth is the Lord's, and all it contains, the world, and those who dwell in it." That is the truth that we must determine to live by.

Summary

The primary inroad that the enemy has into our lives, our families, our schools, and our world, is through fear. We must take a stand against the fear the enemy is seeking to increase over the whole world in order to enhance his control. We must determine right now that we will not let fear dictate the course of our lives or our present actions. We are at war with fear.

As President Roosevelt said, "We have nothing to fear but fear itself." We can win this war if we grow in faith. True faith is not an ambiguous confidence in ourselves; it is the result of a living relationship with the God who loves us, has called us, and will empower us to do all that He created us to do.

The Lord Jesus said that the end of the age is the harvest (see Matt. 13:39). The world is presently experiencing the greatest ingathering of souls into the Kingdom in history. However, the harvest is also the time when everything that has been sown in man will come to full maturity, both the good and the evil. This is why we see in such Scripture passages as Isaiah 60:1-5 that the light and glory will appear upon the Lord's people at the very time when "darkness" and even "deep darkness" cover the earth. Therefore, at the end of this age we can expect to see the ultimate yoke of bondage—fear—coming to its full maturity at the same time the Lord's people are experiencing the greatest levels of faith and peace.

We are about to experience the greatest fear and the greatest faith ever released on the earth. These will be taking place at the same time. If we are not growing in faith, which is also evidenced by growing in the peace of God, we will be growing in fear and the anxiety that will ultimately even cause men's hearts to fail. Therefore, the ultimate answer to combating fear is to be growing in faith and the peace of God that goes beyond understanding.

We must first illuminate the evil nature of fear and how it is used to place a multitude of shackles on our life. This illumination alone will begin to break that fear off of our lives. The enemy dwells in darkness, and whenever the light exposes him it quickly begins unraveling his power. Then we want to replace every fear in our life with a biblical, step-by-step strategy for growing in the faith, love, and peace of God.

PART II

THE ROOTS OF OUR BONDAGE;
THE SOURCE OF OUR FREEDOM

CHAPTER 5

GOOD FEAR

Before we proceed further to illuminate the fears that yoke the human soul, we must understand the nature of the one good fear—the fear of the Lord. "The fear of the Lord is the beginning of wisdom," we are told in Psalms chapter 111:10, Proverbs chapter 9:10, and Job chapter 28:28. When the pure and holy fear of the Lord reigns in our life, we will not have to fear anything else. Our goal is to have only one fear in our life that is so great that it casts out all other fears.

To wake up somebody who is sleeping usually requires an alarm. Alarm is also a kind of fear, as we say that people are "alarmed" if they are worried or fearful about something. It is good for the Church to become alarmed about the increase of evil in our times. This is the kind of alarm that we need to help wake us up. However, after we wake up we do not want to be controlled by a fear of the evil, but by the fear of the Lord, which is really a profound trust and faith in the Lord.

The fact that the fear of the Lord is actually a kind of trust in Him seems to be a paradox. Such paradoxes in Scripture are often the places where the greatest treasures of wisdom and knowledge are found. Consider that we are told that jealousy is a work of the flesh in Galatians 5, and yet we also are told that God is a jealous God. (See Joshua 24:19, for example.) Is God therefore subject to a work of the flesh by being jealous? Of course not. God's jealousy is not like man's, for it is not based on self-ishness but on concern for us. Neither is the fear of the Lord the same kind of fear that the devil is trying to darken the world with.

Biblical paradoxes are not contradictions; rather, they are a view of something from different perspectives. There are also some apparent paradoxes that are created by the inadequacy of our language. These can usually be overcome with a little more effort or just a little expansion of our biblical vocabulary.

The fear of the Lord is the beginning of wisdom, but it is not the ultimate wisdom or the ultimate of spiritual maturity. We begin our path to maturity with a healthy fear of the Lord, but as we mature it turns to love, as we read in First John 4:16-19 (NKJV):

> *And we have known and believed the love that God has for us. God is love, and he who abides in love abides in God, and God in him. Love has been perfected among us in this: that we may have boldness in the day of judgment; because as He is, so are we in this world. There is no fear in love; but perfect love casts out fear, because fear involves torment. But he who fears has not been made perfect in love. We love Him because He first loved us.*

Our goal should be to have the perfect love of God in our life that will cast out all evil fear. The fear of God is the beginning, or the foundation, of wisdom. A foundation is something that the whole building stands on. If it is not built correctly, the entire structure will be weak or even dangerous. If our understanding of the love of God is not first built on a solid foundation of the pure and holy fear of God, our understanding of His love will be perverted into a subtle form of man-centric idealism that is really a form of humanism.

A Good Foundation

To perceive the love of God is the higher wisdom, but those who try to construct the higher floors of the building without laying a good foundation will be building something that is quite shaky. At best, the greatness of what can be built will be limited. At worst, the whole structure will be in jeopardy of collapsing. A primary weakness of modern, Western Christianity is the tendency of many believers to have a weak foundation of the fear of the Lord. Only when we have a strong foundation here will we be able to really comprehend the true love of God on the level that casts out all evil fear.

This is why the apostle Paul exhorts in Romans 11:22a, "Behold then the kindness and severity of God." Many who can see the kindness of God cannot see His severity, and many who see His severity cannot see His kindness. However, if we are going to see Him as He is, we must be able to behold both His kindness and His severity together. These are not contradictory characteristics; He is kind in His severity and severe in His kindness.

The Purity of Love

The Bride of Christ is not going to purify herself to be without spot or wrinkle because she is afraid that her Bridegroom will smite her if He finds her dress soiled. Rather, she is going to be without spot or wrinkle because she is so in love with Him that she wants to be perfect for Him, and she puts forth the supreme effort to be clean and pure in every way. If you have ever been around a bride who is getting ready for her wedding, you can glimpse the kind of focus and determination that the Church will have in this before the Lord returns! Woe to anyone who gets in her way!

The Bride of Christ began like a dirt-poor, filthy little girl. When she first beheld the King in His glory, she was rightly appalled and fearful because of her condition. For her to be called into His great palace is an understandably fearful thing. At first it is this awe and fear of the King that causes her to clean herself up to be near Him, but gradually she is so captured by His irresistible love that she will fall in love with Him. Then she will want to be pure and ready for Him because of her love. As her love grows, so does this devotion. That is the nature of true holiness.

To be actually called into the very family of God may be doctrinally understandable to a new believer, but in fact it is almost incomprehensible. To be simply brought into the presence of the King is a fearful thought, as well it should be. He is God! But our fears will eventually be overcome by His love. It is a part of the process of our minds being renewed that transforms us into an ever-deepening lover. However, as much as we grow in love, we will never forget that He is God!

Love Is the Cross

If we do not go through this kind of process and transition, we will not realize how filthy we are, where we have come from, and how desperately we need the forgiveness of the cross. Or, just as bad, we will not really comprehend His holiness and His grace toward us to first accept us as we are and then change us. The deeper the realization of our sin and the deeper the revelation of His holiness, the more we will be in the fear of the Lord for a time. This is right and necessary. Neither does this diminish just because we get cleaner. It is a foundation that we build on with the realization of His unconditional love.

To use God's love and forgiveness as an excuse to continue in our sin is an ultimate affront to the cross and to His love. If we are touched by the true fear of the Lord and the true love of God, we will begin to hate sin just as He does. Sin separates us from God, and after we come to truly know Him there is nothing more fearful than being separated from Him. Then, as we grow to love Him, there is nothing more terrible than the pain that our sin causes Him.

We also must remember that when the Lord used the allegory comparing His Church to being His Bride, it was from the perspective of marriage in biblical times, not what it has become today in the West. In those times the king was the ultimate, absolute authority, and every man was the head of his household. Jesus is not calling us into some kind of loose partnership—it is an absolute commitment to His Lordship, as well as the most wonderful, intimate, and fulfilling relationship to the King of Glory.

The apostle John was the most intimate friend of the Lord's when He walked the earth. John then outlived all the other apostles so when he had the revelation on the Isle of Patmos, he had known the Lord Jesus longer than anyone. Yet, as he beheld the glorified Lord Jesus whose breast he had once leaned against, he fell at His feet like a dead man! Our God is truly an awesome God and a much greater King than any king who has ever reigned on the earth! If we ever forget this, we have fallen into a serious delusion.

Summary

The first step in the deliverance from fear is to have the right kind of fear—the fear of the Lord. That is why Solomon wrote in Proverbs 2:1-5 (NKJV),

> *My son, if you receive my words, and treasure my commands within you,*

> *So that you incline your ear to wisdom, and apply your heart to understanding;*

> *Yes, if you cry out for discernment, and lift up your voice for understanding,*

If you seek her as silver, and search for her as for hidden treasures;

Then you will understand the fear of the Lord, and find the knowledge of God.

The fear of the Lord is a greater treasure than anything else we could possess on this earth. It is worth pursuing more than any earthly treasure. Consider just a few of the great promises for those who have the fear of the Lord:

Oh how great is Thy goodness, which Thou hast laid up for them that fear Thee; which Thou hast wrought for them that trust in Thee before the sons of men! (Psalm 31:19 KJV).

Behold, the eye of the Lord is on those who fear Him, on those who hope for His lovingkindness, To deliver their soul from death and to keep them alive in famine (Psalm 33:18-19).

The angel of the Lord encamps around those who fear Him, and rescues them (Psalm 34:7).

O fear the Lord, you His saints; for to those who fear Him there is no want.

The young lions do lack and suffer hunger; but they who seek the Lord shall not be in want of any good thing (Psalm 34:9-10).

For as high as the heavens are above the earth, so great is His lovingkindness toward those who fear Him (Psalm 103:11).

Just as a father has compassion on his children, so the Lord has compassion on those who fear Him (Psalm 103:13).

He will fulfill the desire of those who fear Him; He will also hear their cry and will save them (Psalm 145:19).

The Lord favors those who fear Him, those who wait for His lovingkindness (Psalm 147:11).

The fear of the Lord prolongs life, but the years of the wicked will be shortened (Proverbs 10:27).

In the fear of the Lord there is strong confidence, and his children will have refuge. The fear of the Lord is a fountain of life, that one may avoid the snares of death (Proverbs 14:26-27).

The fear of the Lord leads to life, so that one may sleep satisfied, untouched by evil (Proverbs 19:23).

The reward of humility and the fear of the Lord are riches, honor and life (Proverbs 22:4).

Then those who feared the Lord spoke to one another, and the Lord gave attention and heard it, and a book of remembrance was written before Him for those who fear the Lord and who esteem His name. "They will be Mine," says the Lord of hosts, "on the day that I prepare My own possession, and I will spare them as a man spares his own son who serves him" (Malachi 3:16-17).

CHAPTER 6

IDOLS AND FEARS

Our goal after tearing down the evil strongholds that keep us in bondage is to replace them with fortresses of truth. Every time that we can do this, we basically will be turning a fear into the faith that allows us to advance further toward our purpose.

As we proceed, we therefore should become a less fearful person and start becoming more secure and bold. "The righteous are bold as a lion" (Prov. 28:1b). The more right that we make things in our life, the more bold and confident we will be. There is no greater confidence that we can have on this earth than knowing that we are right with God, and that is always our ultimate purpose—to be right with God.

The same power of God that was used to deliver Israel from her bondage also destroyed the idols of Egypt. This was because the spiritual yokes and fears that keep us in bondage are often linked to our idols. By this example we also can be sure that the power of God that sets His people free will threaten those who seek to keep people in bondage to them and their idols. They know that when we lose our devotion to their idols, they will lose their influence and control over us.

Religious Idols

We also must understand that the idols of Egypt were religious objects. Many of the idols that are keeping Christians in bondage today are religious devotions that are used to keep people in the control of religious authorities. One of the great spiritual deceptions of our times is highlighted in Jeremiah 50:6:

My people have become lost sheep; their shepherds have led them astray. They have made them turn aside on the mountains; they have gone along from mountain to hill and have forgotten their resting place.

Many of the Christians who are led astray today are being led astray by their own shepherds. They are doing it in the same way that Jeremiah addresses here. They try to keep them moving from one high place to the next, from project to project, but they are not leading the people to their true resting place, which is the Lord Jesus Himself. We must keep in mind that one of the primary strategies of the enemy is to wear out the saints, and this is one of the most effective ways that he has been able to do it.

We must keep in mind that fruit from the good side of the Tree of Knowledge of Good and Evil is just as deadly as the fruit from the evil side—it is from the same tree. Good works that are not initiated by God can be just as much of a trap to us as the more obvious evils in the world. Our goal is to partake only of the Tree of Life, of that which is life. The only way that we have true life is to abide in the Lord Himself. When we take off to do our own works, even good ones, we have departed from Him.

So, how do we distinguish between the works of the Lord and those that are motivated by men? We do this by following the Lord. That sounds too simple, but it is the most profound truth we can ever know for those who do know it. We must learn not to judge things just by whether they are good or not, but whether they are initiated by God or not. The father of faith, Abraham, was seeking the city that God built, not men, and so are all of those who are walking by true faith.

If we are going to walk on the path of true faith, we are going to be rejected by some, and we are going to have to learn to reject some, including their works. We will not stay on the path if we do not learn this truth. That is why the apostle Paul asserted, "If I were still trying to please men, I would not be a bond-servant of Christ" (Gal. 1:10b).

If we are controlled by the fear of man, then we will be serving man and not Christ. The fear of man is one of the primary fears that we must cast off if we are going to be a true worshiper of God. To be a true worshiper of God is to do His works, and His alone.

For a Christian who is seeking to live right and do the works of God, then religious good works that have originated out of someone's good intentions rather than been initiated by God will be one of the most dangerous traps. In this way, many spend their entire lives doing things God has not called them to do. It is for this reason that the Lord Jesus gave us one of the most sobering warnings in Matthew 7:21-23:

> *Not everyone who says to Me, "Lord, Lord," will enter the kingdom of heaven, but he who does the will of My Father who is in heaven will enter.*

> *Many will say to Me on that day, "Lord, Lord, did we not prophesy in Your name, and in Your name cast out demons, and in Your name perform many miracles?"*

> *And then I will declare to them, "I never knew you; depart from Me, you who practice lawlessness."*

Think about it. "Many," not just some, who call Him "Lord" and do many great works in His name will be told to depart from Him because they practiced lawlessness. How did they practice lawlessness? By primarily doing their own thing rather than doing the will of the Father. In the previous chapter we discussed good fears, and it is certainly a good fear to be concerned about doing many great things but not doing the will of the Lord.

Graven Images

Another idolatrous trap, especially for Christians, is the worship of graven images. Israel was commanded not to make such images, even of God, because the people would begin to worship those images. A graven image of an object, a beast, or a person that was worshiped was obviously a serious departure from the worship of God, but to worship even a man-made image of God was also a sin.

Of course, to worship an image of God rather than God is a serious departure from true worship, but there is a way in which many, if not most, Christians do this and are not aware of it. We can come up with our own image of God in our minds and worship it in place of God. I am not talking here about a physical representation of what we think God looks like, but our concept of who God is and what He is like that is born out of our own idealism rather than revealed truth.

Human idealism is one of the greatest obstacles to truth. Again, human idealism is born out of the good side of the Tree of Knowledge and will have all of the appearances of being good, but its fruit is deadly. Much of the teaching and theology that is prevalent in the Church today has its source in man rather than in the Scriptures. This is what happened to the Pharisees, who were the most devoted to the Scriptures in biblical times, but they still allowed the traditions of men to eclipse the revealed truth of the Scriptures.

We not only do this with God, but we do it with men and women of God as well. Paul the apostle was probably very different from the picture that most Christians have of him, as were most of the men and women of God in Scripture...as are most men and women of God who are alive today! We can form our own image of what someone is like from their television programs, books, and tapes, or even from sitting under their preaching personally. It is not that we always make them out to be better than they really are; they may in fact be much better than we perceive them to be, but it is still our own image of them rather than who they really are. This is a form of deception.

There are several reasons why making our own image of someone is destructive. First, it is not the truth, and we must build our lives on truth. Second, any image that man can form of God is still going to be a tragic reduction of who He really is. When we build our own image of God, we have greatly reduced our potential to see His glory and be changed into His true image.

It is only the worship of God that promotes true faith. When we worship an image that we have constructed, we will become most protective of it, which means we will be motivated by a fear of our image being damaged rather than by the teachableness that the seeker of truth must always have. God is much bigger than any one person can ever perceive. That is why we are told in First Corinthians 13:9 that we "know in part." Therefore, if we are to have a complete knowledge, we must put what we know together with that which others have been given. This requires a perpetual openness to others who have a different perspective than we have.

We must admit that most Christians have built protective walls and barriers around their perceptions of the truth—and guard them furiously. This only reveals that they are in fact worshiping a graven image. Even if the part that they have is completely accurate and true, we all "know in part," and therefore it is at best incomplete.

I am not talking in this regard about the basic doctrines of the faith that we all should agree on. However, those are almost never what Christians divide over. If we are going to be a true worshiper of God, we must rise above our image worship, especially worshiping the images that we have made of God.

Other Idols

We may think that few in the modern world worship idols, but in truth, everyone who does not serve the Lord worships idols. Many who do worship the Lord still have other idols in their hearts besides the graven images that we discussed above. An idol is not just an object; it is something that we trust in place of God. This can be anything from our professions, the stock market and bank accounts to our own abilities and other people. Our ministry can even become an idol if we are more devoted to it than we are to God Himself.

This does not mean that we cannot trust anything but God. However, when we allow our faith in anyone, or anything, to eclipse our faith in God, it has become an idol. Any bond will grow into bondage if it surpasses our love for, and trust in, God. If this happens, our misplaced trust will turn into irrational fears that bind us.

The idolatry of humankind is one of the reasons that the great time of trouble is coming upon the earth in these last days. These troubles will reveal for all time just how shaky our misplaced trust in anything but God really is. This is spoken of in Hebrews 12:25-29 (NKJV):

> *See that you do not refuse Him who speaks. For if they did not escape who refused Him who spoke on earth, much more shall we not escape if we turn away from Him who speaks from heaven,*

> *whose voice then shook the earth; but now He has promised, saying, "Yet once more I shake not only the earth, but also heaven."*

> *Now this, "Yet once more," indicates the removal of those things that are being shaken, as of things that are made, that the things which cannot be shaken may remain.*

Therefore, since we are receiving a kingdom which cannot be shaken, let us have grace, by which we may serve God acceptably with reverence and godly fear.

For our God is a consuming fire.

The whole world is going to be shaken to reveal how weak are the things that humankind has devised and puts his trust in instead of God. Man was created to rule over the earth, but we also were created to do so in relationship with God. To try to rule without Him will always ultimately lead to catastrophe. However, Christians have a Kingdom that "cannot be shaken." If we have built our lives on the Kingdom that cannot be shaken, we will remain unshaken through whatever comes. If we have built our lives primarily on the ways of this world, we will be shaken every time the world shakes.

A Coming Conflict

A problem that is about to face many Christians was dramatically portrayed in one of the subplots in the movie *The Ten Commandments*. One of the characters was a Hebrew who had so ingratiated himself with the Egyptians that they had elevated him to a position of prominence. As a result, he had more invested in Egypt than he did Israel. He therefore felt compelled to resist Moses and Aaron, and he became a stumbling block to those who had come to set God's people free. When the liberation of Israel was accomplished, it brought judgment upon him, as he lost everything. Likewise, those who have more invested in this present world than in the Kingdom are likely to be the primary resistors of every true move of God.

Where do we have the most invested? Where our treasure is, there will our hearts be also (see Matt. 6:21). Are our hearts more with this present world than in the Kingdom? If so, we will have all the fears that this world has. If so, we will be shaken when the earth shakes. The Lord is coming back to liberate the entire earth. For Him to do this, the entire earth must be shaken loose from its trust in idols.

When His Kingdom comes, it will shake and bring down all the dominions and idols that have been built on the fallen nature of man. We should fear this shaking only if we have built our lives more on the kingdoms of men than on the Kingdom of God. Those who have rightly built their lives on faith in God and the principles of His Kingdom will not be shaken by what is coming, and neither will they fear it.

Not Even a Bump

I had a prophetic experience a few years ago in which I was suddenly standing in what appeared to be the radar room of a warship. Before me was a radar screen, and the Lord was standing next to me. Suddenly a blip appeared on the screen directly ahead and was coming rapidly closer. I called for the ship to turn 90 degrees to the right to avoid it. The blip remained directly ahead and drew steadily closer. I called for the ship to be turned back to the left, but the blip remained directly ahead and was coming right at us. I braced myself for the impact, but there was not even a bump. I asked the Lord what had happened. He said that what I had seen on the radar screen was the time of great trouble, or what many call "the great tribulation." He said that it was coming and was unavoidable, but that those who stayed close to Him would not even feel it!

Summary

We can discern the idols that now control us in a number of ways. One way is if something has our affections, or our attention, more than God does. Another is if we are continuously burdened by the fear of losing that thing. Another is by how our protection of it causes conflicts with others in a way that is contrary to the fruit of the Spirit.

Because Abraham had supreme faith in God, he was willing to sacrifice even his promised son to God. He held on to nothing, and therefore he could not be controlled by any affection more than his affection for God. This test of Abraham was to see if Isaac had become an idol that would control him more than his devotion to God. The ultimate key to our freedom from idols, or any other fear, is the true worship and love for God above all other things.

Paul wrote in Second Corinthians 13:5, "Test yourselves to see if you are in the faith; examine yourselves! Or do you not recognize this about yourselves, that Jesus Christ is in you—unless indeed you fail the test?" To test ourselves in this way is something that we should do on a regular basis. The way that we know we pass this test is when Jesus Christ is truly the One ruling our heart and our affections. Is this true of us now, or have we failed the test?

The consequence of failing it is to hear the most tragic words ever uttered on the Day of Judgment: "Depart from Me!" The Lord Himself made it clear that many who call Him "Lord" will hear those words. Are you going to be one of them? To pass the test is to hear the most glorious words on that day: "Well done, good and faithful servant. Enter into the joy of your Master."

This is a most serious test. We should fear not passing it. However, when we truly pass it, when Jesus really is our Lord, ruling us and having possession of our heart, there is no greater freedom, joy, and peace that we will ever have.

CHAPTER 7

BUILDING ON THE HIGH GROUND

The primary way that we combat fear is to grow in faith. We grow in faith by beholding the Lord and drawing closer to Him. When we see Him, when we see where He sits and the power that He has, we believe. The more that we are able to behold the glory of His plan, the more we will trust Him.

It is right that we "behold...the kindness and severity of God" (Rom. 11:22a) if we are going to see Him as He is. It is therefore right that we understand His love as well as His wrath and His judgments. We know clearly from the Scriptures that the end of this age is going to be a time of great trouble on the earth. We are deceived if we cannot see this. Even so, we have for too long allowed the enemy to take the high ground of hope for the future.

There is no religion or philosophy on earth that has a utopia as great as the promise we have received for the age to come. When I had the prophetic experience that I wrote about in the previous chapter, standing in the radar room of the warship, I was told to stop living for the end of this age and start living for the beginning of the age that is to come—the age in which He will reign over the earth in righteousness and justice. There will be such peace in His Kingdom that the lion will lie down with the lamb, children will be able to play with cobras, and no one will hurt anyone else. A joy that is presently incomprehensible on the earth will then prevail over the earth.

Some have made even their doctrines of the end times into an idol. This is what they have put their trust in even more than the Lord. When we do this, it is unlikely that we will be able to understand accurately the biblical prophecies about these times. Even if we do understand them, we are likely to be deceived because we are being led by a doctrine in place of the Lord Himself.

Deception is more than just misunderstanding doctrines or prophecies. An even more serious deception is not being in the will of God, or not doing the will of God. Could this be the reason for the warning that the Lord gave to those who did many things in His name, but were not doing the will of the Father? We must always keep in mind that when the Lord gives us gifts or authority, He will not take them back, even if we fall into sin or idolatry. He remains faithful even if we become unfaithful. That is why the gifts may still work even though someone has departed from the will of God. We therefore cannot take the continued ability to walk in the gifts of the Spirit, or power, to be evidence of the Lord's approval of our life, our ministry, or our doctrines.

Those who have built their hope on their own ability to figure out the biblical prophecies will miss, or even resist, God's work because it will not fit into their understanding of things. Studying the biblical prophecies is important, but not knowing how the end times are going to unfold is not as bad as being deceived about His will for our lives. If we are following Him and abiding in Him, we will be in the right place doing the right thing regardless of whether our eschatology is correct or not.

The Lord did not say that it was the gospel of salvation that had to be preached to all nations before the end came, but rather the gospel of the Kingdom (see Matt. 24:14). In order to preach that gospel, we must live in that Kingdom. We declare it as ambassadors. Ambassadors are citizens whose true home is the country that they represent. Where is our true home?

This is not to imply that we cannot enjoy material things. However, if we are going to be submitted to the Kingdom of God and represent it, we must rule over material things and not allow them to rule over us. Any wrong or exces-sive attachment that we have is an open door for the enemy, who will usually come through that door in the form of a fear. Any wrong or excessive attachment to our eschatology also will mis-lead us likewise.

To date it is rare in Church history to find anyone who understood a biblical prophecy before it happened. There were some who got one or two things right. For example, there were some who understood that the Jewish people had to be re-gath-ered to their land and become a nation again before the end could come. Yet, there are many unfulfilled prophecies about the end of the age that must still come to pass, some of which seem to be imminent, like Isaiah 11:11-16 and Isaiah 19:19-25.

As you have probably perceived throughout this book so far, I have tried to establish a vision for the positive reasons for overcoming the strongholds that bind us, but then including the negatives, or consequences, for allowing evil to control us. In this way we build on faith, but include in the foundation an accurate understanding of the fear of the Lord. We must behold both His kindness and His severity if we are going to get it right.

There are devastating times coming upon the earth. However, the main focus of our attention should not be on the troubles, but on the glorious Kingdom that they are preparing the way for. The world is already sinking into this time of trou-ble, and what it needs to hear now is about the Kingdom that is coming in which all of these troubles cease.

The world needs to know the reason for the troubles, which is man's rebellion against God, the idolatry of man, etc., but in order for the world, which has been so devastated by evil, to trust anyone, including God, it needs to hear about the good-ness of God. As we are told in Romans 2:4, it is the kindness of God that leads to repentance. The world desperately needs to hear of His plan that redeems us from our sin, delivers us from the sin, and then restores us to the condition that we were created to be in. As the prophets foretold, the ultimate end of this matter is that Eden again will be restored to the whole earth.

The Crucial Freedom for the Times

Part of our ability to preach the Kingdom of God is for us to live in it ourselves, now. One of the ultimate idols of the human heart is money. Therefore, to represent the Lord and His Kingdom without compromise, we must be free of this idol. We must be financially independent.

"Financial independence" means different things to different people, but the way that I am applying this term does not have to do with being wealthy or poor. It means that we should never be in a place where our decisions are determined by financial considerations, but simply whether the matter is the will of God or not. We must be ruled by God's will, period. If we are abiding in His Kingdom, there are unlimited resources. However, these are not to be drawn on at our whim, but to do His will.

In Romans 1:5 and 16:26 Paul talks about the "obedience of faith." True faith is directly linked to obedience. We obey the one we truly worship. For this reason we are warned in First Timothy 6:10-12 (KJV),

> *For the love of money is the root of all evil: which while some coveted after, they have erred from the faith, and pierced themselves through with many sorrows.*
>
> *But thou, O man of God, flee these things; and follow after righteousness, godliness, faith, love, patience, meekness.*
>
> *Fight the good fight of faith, lay hold on eternal life, whereunto thou art also called, and hast professed a good profession before many witnesses.*

To repeat again, the love of money is the root of all evil because it can be the ultimate idol that we put our trust in by allowing it to take God's rightful place. As this passage declares, this always results, for those who fall to it, in piercing themselves with many sorrows. This is because they fall to the bondage of many fears. Now, this does not mean that no one can be trusted with great wealth. The issue is, do we have it, or does it have us?

If we have tasted the true wealth of the Kingdom and beheld the true riches of God, having a lot of money or a little money will not be of great concern to us. We just want enough to do His will. When we are in obedience to Him whose account we can never exhaust, we will not have either great fears or great desires for money or other forms of natural wealth. The more free we are in this area, the more we can then be trusted with.

The Lord needs people whom He can trust with resources for the great work of His Kingdom. The way His people handle money will be one of the distinguishing characteristics of the Kingdom. As we have discussed, this is why the mark of the beast is an economic mark, determining whether we can buy, sell, or trade. This mark will be the ultimate test of where our trust really is.

Remember, the freedom of the Kingdom is to walk in faith, and the bondage of this world is through fear. Our freedom from one of the ultimate yokes of bondage at the end of the age, the love of money, is actually to walk in the ultimate liberty that comes from being a slave of Christ. Understanding this paradox is one of the great truths that will set us free from this ultimate yoke of bondage.

This is the theme that we will continue in the next chapter, with our goal to become those who can be trusted with the resources of the Kingdom. It is essential that we reach this goal, as we read in one of the most poignant texts in the Scriptures on these times, which the Lord spoke concerning His people in Isaiah 60:1-5:

> *Arise, shine; for your light has come, and the glory of the Lord has risen upon you.*
>
> *For behold, darkness will cover the earth and deep darkness the peoples; but the Lord will rise upon you, and His glory will appear upon you.*
>
> *Nations will come to your light, and kings to the brightness of your rising.*
>
> *Lift up your eyes round about, and see; they all gather together, they come to you. Your sons will come from afar, and your daughters will be carried in the arms.*
>
> *Then you will see and be radiant, and your heart will thrill and rejoice; because the abundance of the sea will be turned to you, the wealth of the nations will come to you.*

Here we see that at the very time that deep darkness is covering the peoples, the Lord's glory will be appearing upon His people. This will lead to the wealth of the nations being brought to the house of the Lord. This is both an encouragement and a warning. We will be entrusted with unprecedented wealth, but we must be in the place spiritually where it will not become a stumbling block to us.

A lust for money and material things is being widely promoted in the Body of Christ during our times. We must distinguish between that which is true discipleship that leads to the worship and service of the Lord, and that which is feeding our flesh so as to cause us to stumble. Just as the devil tempted Jesus by offering Him what He was already called to have, but without having to go to the cross, a primary scheme of the devil is to offer to the heirs of salvation the riches and benefits of the Kingdom without their having to go to the cross. It's a trap!

However, just as Jesus received much more than satan ever could have offered Him by going to the cross, so we, if we will obey and follow the Lord, will ultimately receive far more than the tempter could ever give us.

CHAPTER 8

THE ULTIMATE IDOL AND
THE ULTIMATE FREEDOM

As we have discussed, money can be the ultimate idol of
the human heart. This is why stewardship is the emphasis of a
substantial portion of Scripture. If we do not understand how to
handle money rightly, we will do it poorly.

It is noteworthy that every one of the warnings and
counsel that John the Baptist gave to those who questioned him
was economic in nature (see Luke chapter 3:10-14). Teaching
how to handle the practical matters of this life rightly was an
important way that John helped prepare the people for the
Lord. The same is still true today. Therefore, sound, biblical
financial teaching must become an important emphasis for the
Church in our times.

The Mark of the Beast

As I will repeat often, it is no accident that one of the
ultimate tests at the end will be whether or not people will take
the mark of the beast, which is an economic mark. We will look
at this in some detail later, but first let us underscore some basic
financial teachings in Scripture, always remembering that it is
the truth that sets us free.

As the Lord made clear in the parable of the talents (see
Matthew chapter 25:14-30), we should seek to use everything
the Lord has entrusted to us in the most profitable way. It is
right that we give more emphasis to our spiritual gifts than to
our natural resources. Even so, we must understand that in this
parable of the talents the Lord was talking about money. In biblical times, "talents" were a form of currency. Recorded in Luke
16:10-13 is another related exhortation from the Lord:

71

He who is faithful in a very little thing is faithful also in much; and he who is unrighteous in a very little thing is unrighteous also in much.

Therefore if you have not been faithful in the use of unrighteous [mammon], *who will entrust the true riches to you?*

And if you have not been faithful in the use of that which is another's, who will give you that which is your own?

No servant can serve two masters; for either he will hate the one, and love the other, or else he will hold to one and despise the other. You cannot serve God and [mammon].

That we "cannot serve God and mammon" means that we cannot combine the motive of serving God with the motive of making money. We must balance godly and wise financial management with keeping our primary motives true, which is seeking the purposes of the Kingdom of God in everything we do. There is abundant evidence in our times that the love of money, or poor financial management, will corrupt ministry as well as individuals. This does not necessarily have anything to do with how much we have, since the poor can be more controlled by the love of money, or the desire for it, than the wealthy.

The Lord makes it clear in this text that we must learn to be faithful with worldly goods before we can be entrusted with the true riches of the Kingdom. Learning to properly handle unrighteous mammon while maintaining a right spirit is important for every Christian. If prosperity is our primary goal, then we will serve the one who gives it to us. Just as satan promised Jesus, if you will bow down to worship him, which is to live by his ways, then he will give you everything God has promised you, he will give it to you much quicker, and he will give it without the pain of the Cross.

Satan will offer us the easy way to attain the promises without going to the cross, and many take his offer because they fail to recognize who they are dealing with. Many ministries fall into this trap and are sidetracked from that point on. They can still have a lot of activity, make a lot of noise, and even bear fruit, but not be doing the will of the Father.

Taking the mark of the beast is not the sin that brings judgment—the sin is to worship the beast. The mark is simply evidence that one has been worshiping him. Will we escape judgment if we refuse to take a mark, but go on living our lives according to the ways of the beast? Of course not. Rather than being so concerned about the mark, we should be concerned about how we may be serving the beast or living according to his ways.

The mark of the beast is probably far more subtle than many have been led to believe, just as the mark of God is not literal, but spiritual. Even if the mark of the beast is a literal mark, the only way we will not take it is to already have the mark of being God's bond servants. This is highlighted in Revelation 7:1-3:

> *After this I saw four angels standing at the four corners of the earth, holding back the four winds of the earth, so that no wind would blow on the earth or on the sea or on any tree.*
>
> *And I saw another angel ascending from the rising of the sun, having the seal of the living God; and he cried out with a loud voice to the four angels to whom it was granted to harm the earth and the sea,*
>
> *saying, "Do not harm the earth or the sea or the trees until we have sealed the bond-servants of our God on their foreheads."*

Since World War II there has been a restraining that has kept the world from another world war. The events began that led to the recovery "a second time" of the remnant of Israel to their land, as well as the marking of God's bond servants. This is presently going on. We must in these times understand the yoke of the beast, the mark of God, and what it means to be a bond servant.

Breaking the Yoke of the Beast

The main reason Christians today are not free to respond to the call of God on their life is debt or other financial encumbrances. When there is a call to do anything—from entering the ministry full-time to going on a mission trip—if our main consideration is whether or not we can afford it, then our financial condition rules us more than the will of God. It is also a revelation of just how much we have built our lives upon the foundations of this present age rather than on the Kingdom of God.

If we are caught in this deadly trap, we still can get free. We build our lives on the Kingdom of God, the Rock, by hearing and obeying the Word of God. Regardless of how disobedient we were, how foolish we have been, or how bad our situation is now, if we repent the Lord will deliver us. Our God really is all-powerful. When He helps, there is no limit to what can be done. When His people are trapped with the hordes of the enemy bearing down on them, He delights in doing some of His greatest miracles. However, true faith begins with true repentance for whatever we have been doing that is wrong. Repentance does not mean just that we are sorry, but that we turn away from our wicked ways.

As C.S. Lewis pointed out, in Christ, once we miss a turn and start down the wrong road, it will never become the right road. The only way we can get back on the right road is to go back to where we missed the turn. The Lord does not want to deliver us just to have us slip right back into bondage because we did not change our ways. Therefore, true repentance is evidence of the true faith that compels Him to respond.

Financial Freedom

There is a clear biblical procedure for getting out of and staying out of debt and for becoming and remaining financially independent. The definition that I am using for financial independence is being in the place where you never have to make a decision based on financial considerations, but simply on the revealed will of God. This is the condition in which every Christian should live. This should be our first and most important financial goal. We must always keep in mind, regardless of how bad our present financial condition is, that there is a very simple biblical formula that will provide a sure way of escape:

Repentance + Obedience = Freedom

We must start by recognizing and repenting of any ways in which we have departed from the clear mandates of Scripture. Then we must begin to obey the clear and simple biblical instructions for financial management. If we do, we will escape our present situation and begin to live a life of freedom that is better than we have ever dreamed.

The Answer

Most of us think that the way out of our situation is to make more money. That is seldom the answer to financial problems, and it can even make matters worse. What we need is true faith in God, which is always demonstrated by obedience to Him. God's plan for our financial freedom does not require us to make more money, and He probably will not give us a revelation so that we can win the lottery. We may not think there is any other way, but there is. If God can multiply bread and fish, He can make whatever we are now earning go just as far as He wants it to. Most of us would be in good shape if we just had "the devourer" rebuked from our lives so that the losses and waste are stopped. Regardless, we will be on solid financial ground if we will obey the simple and clear instructions in the Scriptures for managing what we are entrusted with.

We know that "the love of money is a root of all sorts of evil" (1 Tim. 6:10a) and that money can test the ultimate issues of the human heart. Idolatry is one of the ultimate offenses against God, and the way that we put our trust in money is one of the primary forms of idolatry in the world today. Money in itself is not evil, but how we relate to it can be a factor that determines the entire course of our life for good or evil. It is therefore imperative that we confront this issue in our lives now, determine that we will obey God first and foremost, and discipline ourselves in this area where needed. How can we do this?

We saw in Revelation chapter 7:1-3 that four angels are sent to hold back the four winds of the earth until the bond slaves of God have been marked on their foreheads. We must get this mark. Believers have spent a great amount of time trying to figure out how the mark of the beast will come so they will not be fooled by it, but almost no attention to how to take the mark of God. The only way we will not take the mark of the beast is to have the mark of God. If God marks us, we will never have to fear taking the enemy's mark.

The key to understanding the seal of God is understanding the bond servant—just as the key to understanding the mark of the beast is to understand the beast. As we discussed earlier, the Lord created us for freedom. This may seem to conflict with the concept of a bond servant, who is literally a slave, but we can become a bond servant only if we freely choose to be one. Even though the Lord purchased us with His blood, He will not force anyone to be His bond servant. So, what is a bond servant?

In Scripture a bond servant was one who was able to go free, but loved his master so much that he chose to be his master's slave for the rest of his life. We too are free to choose whether we will be bond servants or not. Not all believers are bond servants. Many come to an understanding of the sacrifice of Jesus for their sins, but they still go on living their lives for themselves. Before, we were the slaves of sin. The cross purchased us, and we are Christ's. We are no longer our own, but we belong to Him. A bond servant does not live for himself, but for his master. This is the commitment to a radical lifestyle of obedience.

A true bond servant does not have any money of his own, so he cannot spend freely what he has been entrusted with because it is not his. Does this mean that we must pray and get an answer from Heaven to buy a can of beans? No. As we see throughout the parables that the Lord taught, He is a master who freely delegates authority to His slaves. However, He does so expecting us to have the maturity, responsibility, and wisdom to manage *His* resources well.

Neither does a bond servant have any time of his own. His time belongs to his master. A bond servant does not waste his free time because it does not belong to him. Time is one of the most precious gifts that we can be given on this earth, and how we use our time, especially our "free" time, is usually a good indication of who we are really serving on this earth—ourselves, the world, or the Lord. One common characteristic of those who will be the faithful ones who hear, "Well done, good and faithful servant," will be that they did not waste their time.

Even the family of a bond servant belongs to his master. Our children are not "our" children, but have been entrusted to us. The Lord wants them overseen with the devotion of a governor or governess who is entrusted with the child of a king, an heir to the throne.

To voluntarily become a slave is the ultimate commitment that can be made in this world. That is what it really means to embrace the cross. Those who are truly bond servants do not live for themselves, but for their Master. These are the ones who receive the Lord's mark.

We are free to go on living for ourselves and receive many blessings from the Lord, but it is the ultimate folly. Those who are truly wise and mature in the ways of the Kingdom do not just seek blessings—they seek to be the habitation of the *manifest presence* of the Lord. The Lord blesses many things that He will not inhabit.

The Benefits of Bond Service

The Lord is the best Master that one could ever have; He is better even than we are as masters of our life. The life of a bond servant is the most fulfilling, the most interesting, and the easiest life that we could ever live on the earth. The fact that it is the "easiest" does not necessarily mean that it will be easy, but it will certainly be much easier than if we try to run things ourselves.

When we become a bond servant, we trade our meager bank accounts for His inexhaustible resources. This does not mean that we can go on a spending spree. Rather, when we have fully entered into the life of a bond servant, all of our financial worries will be forever over—unless we drift from this commitment. As our Master, He will take care of us. He will lead us through times when we need to grow in faith, but as long as we know we are being led by Him, these trials truly are joy because we know that they are leading us to greater authority and responsibility in His Kingdom. Only as His bond servants can we truly come to know the Lord as our Source. The key to our survival in this time is being a bond servant to the Lord. Every master is obligated to provide for his slaves, and we have the most dependable Master of all. He will take care of His own.

Being a bond servant of the Lord is to become His slave, but it is also the greatest freedom we can ever know in this life. When we are united with Him, by taking His yoke, we die to this world just as He did. When we are truly dead to the world, there is nothing the world can do to us. It is impossible for a dead man to fear, to be offended, or to feel remorse because he loses some of his possessions. To the degree that we fear the loss of our possessions or positions is the degree to which we are still not dead to these things. Again, the enemy uses fear to bind us just as the Lord uses faith to set us free.

When we are dead to this world but alive to Christ, we have Him, so all the treasures of this earth seem petty and insignificant. When we are seated with the King of kings on His throne, what pull can an earthly position have for us? This does not mean we do not have a genuine care for our jobs or ministries here, but we care for them because He has entrusted them to us, and we do them as worship unto Him. If our positions here are taken from us, we are still seated with Him, and we will worship Him in whatever way He calls us to next. We are His slaves, and we must be content with whatever job He gives us.

When Christ is our life, our trust, and the true desire of our heart, He can then trust us with earthly possessions and positions that we are called to rule over. But if He is not our life, our trust, and the desire of our heart, our possessions and positions will inevitably rule over us. Whoever or whatever rules over us is in fact our lord. We are entering a time when the Lordship of Jesus must be more than a doctrine—it must be the profound and continuing reality in our life. Then we will be free indeed. When we are fully yoked to Him, having cast off all the yokes of this present evil age, He will then be free to trust us with the unlimited resources of His Kingdom.

The only answer to the radical fears that bind us is radical discipleship to the Lord.

CHAPTER 9

SOCIAL FREEDOM

The very first thing that God said was not good was for man to be alone. This is quite interesting because man had an intimate relationship with God when the Lord said this. We may wonder why God was not enough for man, but the truth is God created us so that we would need other people as well. It is therefore not wrong to be strongly attached to our families, churches, and other social groups as long as we keep our relationship to the Lord first. We all need community.

Our relationship to God should be the most fulfilling part of our life, but we must have fellowship with others too. Relationships are crucial in our life. The fear versus faith principle works in relationships as well. Developing good social skills is crucial to developing good relationships. Having good social skills gives us a considerable amount of confidence in life, which dispels many fears that can otherwise have devastating control over us.

I remember well the confusion of my teenage years. Because of serious family problems, these times were probably more confusing for me than most. I remember how amazed I was at the peace that came into my life when I entered the military. I was trained, equipped, and given a specific job to do. Great security came into my life when I knew where I fit in. My social confidence grew when I learned what my relationship was to others in the organization. I had a rank and knew exactly who I had authority over and who had authority over me. This gave me a secure place, and I could advance to the degree that my skills developed.

In a similar way this is what the Body of Christ is supposed to be to a world that is sinking into increasing social confusion. Every new believer quickly should come to know his or her calling and spiritual gifts and be given the training and equipping that would enable the person to take his or her rightful place. As these new believers begin to function with wisdom and grace as that part of the Body they are called to be, the Lord will promote them.

Studies have shown that up to 95 percent of the people who make decisions for Christ fail to ever be added to the Church. In the first century 100 percent of those who came to Christ were added to the Church. Biblically, we could question the salvation of anyone who is not added to the Church after committing his life to the Lord. If we are truly joined to the Head, we also will be properly joined to His Body. However, many who want to serve the Lord don't know how to become connected to His Body. Most know instinctively that there must be more to Christianity than sitting in boring meetings a couple of times a week, but few can find in present church life what their hearts yearn for.

The failure of so many who make decisions to serve the Lord to ever become members of a church is an indictment on the church, not the converts or the evangelists. When the Church becomes the Body that it is called to be, with the proper functioning of every individual part, we also will see those who make commitments to Christ become added to His Church and quickly begin to find their place. When they are this strongly attached, the enemy will not be able to draw them away. The Church, as it was intended to be, fulfills the deepest social needs of every human heart like no other entity on earth will ever be able to do.

Presently the Church is very far from being what it was intended to be. Some are making progress, but generally church is like a spectator sport where the many come to watch a few perform and cheer them on. The real basis of many church services is more entertainment than anointing, and the best entertainment that a church can come up with is going to be boring compared to what the world can do. We are not called to compete with the world in that arena, and we do not have the grace or anointing to do it. However, there is nothing more interesting, more captivating, more desirable, or more wonderful than the Lord. If we spent more time trying to get the Lord to come to our meetings than we did trying to get people to come, we would have more people than we can handle.

The Freedom of Learning to March

Now, back to the army that we're called to be as members of His Body. The prophet Joel had a vision of a mighty army of God that was coming upon the earth. A force is about to be released like the world has never seen, which is described in Joel 2:1-11:

> *Blow a trumpet in Zion, and sound an alarm on My holy mountain! Let all the inhabitants of the land tremble, for the day of the Lord is coming; surely it is near,*
>
> *A day of darkness and gloom, a day of clouds and thick darkness. As the dawn is spread over the mountains, so there is a great and mighty people; there has never been anything like it, nor will there be again after it to the years of many generations.*
>
> *A fire consumes before them and behind them a flame burns. The land is like the garden of Eden before them, but a desolate wilderness behind them, and nothing at all escapes them.*
>
> *Their appearance is like the appearance of horses; and like war horses, so they run.*

With a noise as of chariots they leap on the tops of the mountains, like the crackling of a flame of fire consuming the stubble, like a mighty people arranged for battle.

Before them the people are in anguish; all faces turn pale.

They run like mighty men, they climb the wall like soldiers; and they each march in line, nor do they deviate from their paths.

They do not crowd each other; they march everyone in his path; when they burst through the defenses, they do not break ranks.

They rush on the city, they run on the wall; they climb into the houses, they enter through the windows like a thief.

Before them the earth quakes, the heavens tremble, the sun and the moon grow dark and the stars lose their brightness.

The Lord utters His voice before His army; surely His camp is very great, for strong is he who carries out His word. The day of the Lord is indeed great and very awesome, and who can endure it?

There is a fire in the army of God that will march in the last days. It will be a fire on the earth because our God who is a consuming fire will be in their midst. As this army goes forth, it will destroy all the wood, hay, and stubble that it comes near. It also will purify gold, silver, and precious stones. It will consume what man has built, but it will reveal what was indeed built by God. What is coming will be either terrible or glorious depending on what we have built our lives upon. The earth will literally quake at the presence of the Lord in the midst of this army that is now being mobilized. The Word of God that will be in their mouths will shatter the idols of this world like a hammer shatters rocks. The Spirit that is in them will be an irresistible force.

Finding our place in God's army, which is His Church, is becoming increasingly critical. We cannot make it alone. As the breakdown of the social order in the world continues, the Body of Christ will become a much more clearly defined, disciplined, and powerful social force in the earth. We will ultimately be as disciplined as the best army that ever marched. Every one will know his or her specific place in this army, and each will march in line, not crowding one another, but supporting one another in the great advance that is coming. Those who are in this army will know increasing peace and security. Those who are not in their place will be subject to increasing fear.

There is a freedom that comes from knowing our place that is essential if we are going to fulfill our purpose on this earth. Just as a train must have the tracks that restrain it in order for it to do what it was created to do, we need specific guidelines in our lives that set us free to move forward with boldness and confidence. Without such clear guidelines, we will be perpetually hesitant.

Without the tracks to restrain, the train might go cutting across the countryside. And if it did, it would quickly get bogged down so that it could not function. This is what is happening with the unrestrained "freedom" that the spirit of lawlessness is now promoting in the world. If we cast off all restraints, we will be the most bound and pitiful of people. It is the guidelines that God has given to us that set us free. He is our Maker and knows us better than we know ourselves. His goal for us is freedom. That is a basic principle of the Kingdom, but it is the freedom to be what we were created to be and to do what we were called upon this earth to do.

The Tragic Failure of Ministry

For a couple of years I asked almost every large group of Christians that I spoke to how many of them knew their calling, ministry, gifts of the Spirit, or place in the Body of Christ. I came to the conclusion that those who did were around 5 percent of the believers. How well could you function if just 5 percent of your body was working? That is the present state of the Church. It also should be interesting to us that this seemed to be about the same percentage of those who make decisions for Christ who become a part of the Church. It is because of this that Ephesians 4:11-16 may be one of the most crucial biblical texts for our times:

> *And He gave some as apostles, and some as prophets, and some as evangelists, and some as pastors and teachers,*
>
> *for the equipping of the saints for the work of service, to the building up of the body of Christ;*
>
> *until we all attain to the unity of the faith, and of the knowledge of the Son of God, to a mature man, to the measure of the stature which belongs to the fullness of Christ.*
>
> *As a result, we are no longer to be children, tossed here and there by waves and carried about by every wind of doctrine, by the trickery of men, by craftiness in deceitful scheming;*
>
> *but speaking the truth in love, we are to grow up in all aspects into Him, who is the head, even Christ,*
>
> *from whom the whole body, being fitted and held together by what every joint supplies, according to the proper working of each individual part, causes the growth of the body for the building up of itself in love.*

Here we see that the equipping ministries listed in verse 11 are not called to do the work, but to equip the believers to do the work of the ministry. This is done "to the building up of the body of Christ," and the true Body of Christ cannot be built any other way. This is to be done until:

1. We attain to "the unity of the faith."

2. We have "the knowledge of the Son of God."

3. We become "a mature man" (singular).

4. We have grown up into "the measure of the stature which belongs to the fullness of Christ."

Is there a congregation on the earth that has done this? If so, I would love to know because I would pay any price just to see it. The following verses in this text tell us how we must do this:

1. We speak "the truth in love."

2. We grow up "in all aspects" into Christ.

3. We become "fitted and held together by that which every joint supplies."

4. It is the proper functioning of each individual part that causes the building up of the Body in love.

Now let's break each of these down a bit. First, we must speak the truth, but we must speak it in love. One reason some churches and Christians repel unbelievers is because they do not speak the truth. The second reason is that those who speak the truth often do not speak it in love. Speaking the truth without love will not work.

Next we must have a vision of growing up in "all aspects into Him." How do we do this? First, we must understand that no one can do this alone. No one person is going to have all the gifts and ministries of the Lord. It is as a body of believers together that we can manifest "all aspects" of Christ. This requires that we come into unity.

Then we are to be "fitted and held together by that which every joint supplies." A joint is not a part, but the place where two parts come together. Every part cannot be joined to every other part of the body. The hand has to be joined to the wrist, etc. We must understand that some members of the body must become closer to certain members. We must allow special bonding between certain members as long as they are bonding around their function in the body.

Lastly we see that it is the proper functioning of every individual part that causes the building up of the Body in love. Therefore we must be devoted to seeing every individual part of the Body begin to function if we are to expect the Body to be truly built up the way it is supposed to be, or the Church will remain as ineffective as any body would be if only 5 percent of its members were functioning.

Summary

So, what does all this have to do with spiritual warfare and our becoming free? We will never be free until we become what we were created to be and do what we were created to do. We will never be the victorious army that we are called to be without the proper training, equipping, and deploying of the saints into their purpose on this earth.

In general, the Church is right now more like a huge mob that has been mobilized for war, but no one is training them, much less equipping them (putting the weapons in their hands) and then sending them out to battle. The Church, in general, is like a giant sheep pen where shepherds throw food at the sheep a couple of times a week, but that is about all the sheep can expect. That is why the majority of those who want to come to the Lord end up drifting away.

There are many positive signs that at least some of the leaders of the Church are grasping the fact of this problem. Few have yet understood what to do about it, and fewer still are addressing it, but this condition will change. The Home Group movement is one of God's answers, but the biggest one of all is the changing of our very concept of what the Church is. We have got to see ourselves as the Church just as much Monday morning as Sunday morning. We must realize that the ministries and gifts of the Spirit are for everyday life, not just meetings. Some of the great pastors are pastoring their fellow employees; some of the greatest teachers are teaching a handful around the lunch table. Isn't that how Jesus did it? His ministry took place in everyday life and in every place that He went. Ours must do the same.

CHAPTER 10

THE WEAPONS OF GOD'S ARMY

It may seem like another paradox, but we cannot function properly as part of this great army that we are called to be until we are firmly established in the peace of God. One of the most powerful spiritual weapons that has been given to God's people is peace. We may think that peace is not a weapon, but it is such a weapon that Paul did not write that it was the Lord of hosts, or the Lord of armies, who would crush the enemy, but that "the *God of peace* will soon crush Satan under your feet" (Rom. 16:20). When we abide in the peace of God, it is both a fortress and a weapon that the enemy has no power against.

If we abide in the peace of God in a situation, it unravels the enemy's power over that situation. That is why most attacks of the enemy upon believers are intended to first rob them of their peace. The peace of God is the linchpin fruit of the Spirit that must be in place in order to hold all the others in their places. Once we lose the peace of God, we quickly lose our patience, love, self-control, etc. This causes us to fall from our position of abiding in Christ. If we are truly abiding in Christ, the fruit of the Spirit will always demonstrate it.

Because we represent the Prince of Peace and because it is the peacemakers who are called the sons of God (see Matthew 5:9), it is the Church that the world should be turning to for the solutions to its conflicts. Our victory over evil is accomplished by overcoming it with good. We destroy the enemy's power of destruction by standing in and imparting peace.

However, instead of the world turning to the Church for solutions to its conflicts, the Church is now viewed more as a source of conflicts. This will change. The Church is called to judge the world, and as conflicts and anxiety grow in the world, peace and wisdom are going to grow in the Church to such an extent that even the heathen will start coming to Christians for help. Through this the Church's spiritual authority will grow stronger and stronger as lawlessness erodes human authority.

The Church is the "Jerusalem above," the spiritual Jerusalem that Paul mentions in Galatians 4:26. *Jerusalem* means "city of peace." Like the earthly Jerusalem, the Church is now embroiled in almost continuous strife with war within herself as well as war against the forces of the world without. Even so, she soon will be victorious over the strife within, and then she will be able to turn all of her great weapons on the forces without. When she does, she will bring peace in place of conflict.

The Church will arise to fulfill her purpose in all that she is called to do and be. As stated, it will be as foretold in Isaiah 60:1-2, when darkness will increase, deep darkness will come upon the people, and the Lord's glory will rise and appear upon His people. When human conflict and strife reach unprecedented levels, the Church will know unprecedented peace. This peace will be a fortress that will be impregnable to the enemy. Then the Church will become the true sanctuary on earth.

Presently, just as there is no human solution to the conflict in the Middle East, there is no human solution to the conflict within the Church. The solution must come from God. The peace of God is rooted in knowing that God is God and that Jesus is the King above all kings, rulers, and authorities. When we see that He is in control, we come to understand deep in our hearts that Romans 8:28 is true: "And we know that God causes all things to work together for good to those who love God, to those who are called according to His purpose." When we know in our hearts that this is true, there is no power on earth that can steal our peace.

When we abide in the peace of God regardless of what the circumstances are, it crushes satan's attempts to turn and use those circumstances, and it also allows us to see God's purpose in them. The Lord is not in Heaven wringing His hands over a single problem on earth. He knows the end from the beginning, and He already knows what He is going to do to make things right. If we are abiding in Him, seated with Him in the heavenly places as we are called, we too will dwell in perfect peace. As we are promised in Isaiah 26:3, **"The steadfast of mind You will keep in perfect peace, because he trusts in You."** That is why Paul uttered the great prayer recorded in Ephesians 1:18-23:

> *I pray that the eyes of your heart may be enlightened, so that you may know what is the hope of His calling, what are the riches of the glory of His inheritance in the saints,*
>
> *and what is the surpassing greatness of His power toward us who believe. These are in accordance with the working of the strength of His might*
>
> *which He brought about in Christ, when He raised Him from the dead and seated Him at His right hand in the heavenly places,*
>
> *far above all rule and authority and power and dominion, and every name that is named, not only in this age, but also in the one to come.*
>
> *And He put all things in subjection under His feet, and gave Him as head over all things to the church,*
>
> *which is His body, the fullness of Him who fills all in all.*

The "eyes of your heart" refer to our spiritual eyes. When they are open, we will see Jesus where He sits, *far above* all authority, power, and dominion on the earth. As we begin to see Him there and walk in His truth, living our lives in the unfathomable peace this brings, it crushes the influence of satan in our life. This is what King David understood when he wrote Psalm 46:10-11: "'Cease striving and know that I am God; I will be exalted among the nations, I will be exalted in the earth.' The Lord of hosts is with us; the God of Jacob is our stronghold."

When we really know that He is God, we will cease striving. When His people come to this knowledge and walk in it, He will be "exalted among the nations." The peace of God will be in such profound contrast to the fears that are coming upon the world and causing people's hearts to fail. Peace will be one of the greatest witnesses of the Lord in the midst of His people. It is through abiding in His peace that we will be able to crush every manifestation of the enemy in our life. Peace itself is the victory.

CHAPTER 11

THE ULTIMATE TRAP

Pride caused the fall of satan and almost every fall since. We know that "God is opposed to the proud, but gives grace to the humble"(James 4:6b), and we are told in First Peter 5:6-7, "Therefore, humble yourselves under the mighty hand of God, that He may exalt you at the proper time, casting all your anxiety on Him, because He cares for you." This implies that one of the ways we humble ourselves is to cast our anxiety upon the Lord. This is because anxiety is a form of pride; it actually asserts that we think the matter is too big for God so we have to handle it ourselves. If we really believe that He is God, however, we will cease striving, cast off our anxiety, and live in the peace that comes from knowing that He is in control.

It is no accident that "panic attacks" have now reached epidemic proportions almost throughout the earth. Anxiety is rising dramatically in the world, but peace will rise correspondingly in those who are true followers of Christ. The anxiety that is coming upon the world is the direct result of man trying to live without God and do everything on his own. That is why the original temptation of man was to get him to try to become what God had in fact called him to be, but to do it without God. Peace can come only by returning to Him.

The more humankind turns from God, the more striving and confusion there will be, which will result in even more fear. This increases impatience, self-centeredness, and other "deeds of the flesh" that cause conflict. Christians must not live as the world lives. We must grow in the knowledge of the Lord's authority and control. We must grow in the peace of God.

Walking in Truth

If we are going to crush satan under our feet, then we need to understand that this metaphor of "crushing satan under our feet" is used for a purpose. This speaks of his power being broken through our "walk." If you are walking, you are going somewhere. Christianity is not static; it is always moving forward, always growing. That is why the River of Life is a river and not a pond or a lake. A river is always flowing, proceeding toward its destination.

When we walk in the peace of God in our home, it will ultimately crush the enemy's influence there. If we walk in the peace of God at work, it will soon crush the enemy's influence there. If the Christians in a city would walk in the peace of God, the Church there would soon come into unity, and the enemy's influence over that city would be crushed. When Christians in any nation truly begin to walk in the peace of God, they will crush the enemy's influence over that nation.

God's Barometer

God's prophetic barometer of the condition of humanity is the nation of Israel. Almost everyone who visits Israel reports that it is one of the most intense places on earth. The citizens of Israel live under unceasing pressure and anxiety. It now seems that the nation of Israel will do almost anything for peace—even give up precious land that they paid such a high price for in blood and hardship. However, no amount of change in the external conditions will bring Israel the peace that she seeks. Nevertheless, God has a remedy.

After years of inquiring of the Lord to know what we could do as a ministry for Israel, I was told to send "missionaries of peace" to live there. Their main calling is to walk in the peace and rest of God so that their joy and peace in the midst of the stress would stand out as an oasis in contrast to the spirit now prevailing over that nation. When the believers who live there are delivered of anxiety and begin to walk in the peace of God, it will be the most striking witness of the Prince of Peace that Israel has had since the first century. When this is demonstrated, it will make this peace of heart even more desirable than peace with the nations around them. There is no peace like the peace of God, and this alone can lead to a true peace among those neighbors.

The enemy has sent onslaught after onslaught to disturb Israel, but peace will be victorious. True peace is the condition of heart that trusts God regardless of the circumstances. When this happens we are close to receiving the marching orders for the greatest army of God that will ever have been released upon the earth.

If we are going to understand the times, we must heed the Lord's own exhortation in Mark 13:28-29: "Now learn the parable from the fig tree: when its branch has already become tender, and puts forth its leaves, you know that summer is near. Even so you too, when you see these things happening, recognize that He is near, right at the door." Because the fig tree is a symbol of Israel, this is an exhortation to understand this nation as a sign of the times. It is wisdom to be concerned about the events in Israel and to seek to understand what they mean.

It is also noteworthy that when Agabus prophesied in the first century that a famine was coming upon the whole earth, the way the Christians prepared for it was to take up an offering for the believers in Israel. They understood God's promise to bless those who bless Abraham's seed. They also understood that God had established an eternal law in the beginning that a seed could reproduce only after its own kind. If we want to be blessed in the natural, we should bless the natural seed of Abraham. If we are seeking spiritual blessing, we should bless the spiritual seed of Abraham, which is the Church. By blessing the natural seed, which are the believers, we are blessing both together.

CHAPTER 12

THE ROAD TO THE KINGDOM

Who are you now warring with? What is the source of the greatest conflict in your life? Have you cast this anxiety upon the Lord? When you do this exercise of faith, it will release Him to move into the situation. That is why we are told in Hebrews 12:14-15, "Pursue peace with all men, and the sanctification without which no one will see the Lord. See to it that no one comes short of the grace of God; that no root of bitterness springing up causes trouble, and by it many be defiled."

There is no reason for a Christian to ever be bitter at anyone or anything. If we are bitter we are being defiled, and we also will defile others with that bitterness. I've heard it said, "Bitterness is like drinking poison and hoping someone else gets sick." We are called to something much higher than this. We are called to the ultimate nobility of soul that is reflected in forgiveness and to the ultimate dignity that comes from walking in the peace of God.

Define the sources of conflict and agitation in your life, repent of your lack of faith, and trust in the Lord in relation to them. Cast this anxiety upon the Lord. Determine that, regardless of appearances or situations, you are going to trust the Lord to deal with these matters. He will do it, but usually after He has dealt with something even more important—your own heart.

The lack of peace in our lives is directly related to the lack of faith that we have in the Lord. A fundamental calling on our lives is simply to trust God. That is why the Lord said, "This is the work of God, that you believe in Him whom He has sent" (John 6:29b). Simply trusting Him every day will accomplish much more than many of the works and projects that we try to do for Him. The Church and the Kingdom that Jesus is building are in our hearts, and they will be manifested in our daily lives. The Lord does not judge the quality of a church by how good the meeting is Sunday morning, but by how good the people are on Monday morning.

The peace of God is the power that will lead us to victory over ourselves and the strongholds of the enemy. We all are called to be missionaries of the peace of God. This peace is not the result of peaceful conditions but is a profound confidence in God even in the midst of the most trying conditions. The more stressful or violent the conditions, the more the peace of God is a demonstration of the true faith in God. This faith is what moves the Lord to take action on our behalf in those conditions. Peace is therefore an accurate barometer of the true level of our faith.

Our Fortress

How do we build our lives upon this Kingdom that cannot be shaken? Romans 14:17 states, "For the kingdom of God is not eating and drinking, but righteousness and peace and joy in the Holy Spirit." Those who do not know God are always in an endless pursuit of joy and happiness, but these can never be attained outside of Christ. We will never know true peace without building our lives on a foundation of righteousness, which is simply having a right relationship with God.

When we are living lives that are obedient to the Lord and His ways, peace will be the result. With this peace, which comes from knowing that we are right with God, comes the true joy that is beyond anything that we can experience in the world. This is because man was created to have fellowship with God and nothing but intimacy with Him will ever satisfy the deepest longing of our soul.

Because the Lord made us and knows what we need, the righteousness of God is simply living the way we were created to live, doing that which is in fact the best for us. What is best for us is walking with God, dwelling in His presence, following the King, and being obedient to Him in all things. That is righteousness, and it brings peace that cannot be shaken and a joy that is eternal.

It is now time to be armed with the peace of God. Those who are armed in this way will go forth conquering in His name. The peace of God is an impregnable fortress. Never, ever, lose your peace, and you will always know victory.

In First Thessalonians 5:23 Paul prayed, "Now may the *God of peace* Himself sanctify you entirely; and may your spirit and soul and body be preserved complete, without blame at the coming of our Lord Jesus Christ." It is "the God of peace" who will sanctify us, for it is by abiding in the peace of God that we abide in the Lord. Sanctification is not just a state of not sinning; it is abiding in the Lord. When we abide in Him, we will not just renounce sin, but we will love and will have faith for the true works of God.

CHAPTER 13

PEACE AND PROPHECY

We are told in Philippians 4:7, "And the peace of God, which surpasses all comprehension, will guard your hearts and your minds in Christ Jesus." It is interesting that the Greek word translated as "guard" in this text is *phroureo*, which comes from a compound word that means to be a watcher in advance, that is, to mount guard as a sentinel (post spies at gates); figuratively, to hem in, protect, keep as with a garrison. The peace of God not only keeps our hearts and minds in Christ, but it also helps us to see in advance and to know what to do to protect against the attacks of the enemy.

This is one of the primary lessons the Church should have learned from those who got caught up in the Y2K scare. Every prophecy that I personally witnessed about the imminent doom that Y2K would bring had an air of anxiety and fear attached. As we read in James 3:17-18:

> But the wisdom from above is first pure, then peaceable, gentle, reasonable, full of mercy and good fruits, unwavering, without hypocrisy.
>
> And the seed whose fruit is righteousness is sown in peace by those who make peace.

If the peace of God is going to guard our hearts and minds in Christ Jesus, we must learn not to receive that which comes without the peace of God attached to it. I realize many people can hear a pure word from the Lord that is sown in peace and still be afraid. So before we can discern in this way, our own hearts must be at peace. Having the peace of God rule in our hearts, our families, and our churches must be a high priority if we are going to be free from deception.

The Scriptures are clear that difficult times are coming upon the world, but at the same time the glory of the Lord will be coming upon His people. Hearing the prophecies about difficulties should not disturb us; rather, they should awaken us and help to prepare us. This will be true only as we abide in the peace of God, which keeps us abiding in God.

The Lord is not sitting in the heavens worrying about anything, and neither will those who are abiding in Him. If we are abiding in Him, the whole world can collapse around us and we will be in perfect peace because we have built our lives on a Kingdom that cannot be shaken.

When Jesus was tempted by the devil, He answered every temptation with Scripture. The Word of God is stronger than any power that we will ever be faced with. Now is the time to search the Scriptures, taking our stand on that which will stand forever—the Word of God. Consider the following promises of His peace that provide the believer assurance that, if we abide in His peace, we will prevail against any fortress the evil one can build.

> *The Lord will give strength to His people; the Lord will bless His people with peace* (Psalm 29:11).

If we are abiding in the Lord, we will be abiding in His peace as well. If anxiety is growing in our life, it is because we have somehow become separated from Him. If this has happened to us, it is always on our part, not His. Therefore, we should ask the Holy Spirit to convict us of our sin, repent of what is revealed to us as the cause of the separation, and resolve to grow in both peace and faith. It is the Lord's will to bless us with His peace and for us to abide in it. As we are told in Psalm 85:8-9,

I will hear what God the Lord will say; for He will speak peace to His people, to His godly ones; but let them not turn back to folly.

Surely His salvation is near to those who fear Him, that glory may dwell in our land.

Our dwelling place should be full of the glory of the Lord. If it is not, make finding out why the top priority in your life. First Peter 3:10-11 NKJV reveals a primary reason many do not have peace in their lives and are not walking in the glory:

For "He who would love life and see good days, let them refrain his tongue from evil and his lips from speaking deceit.

"Let him turn away from evil and do good; let him seek peace and pursue it."

Are our words and actions sowing peace and unity? Remember, we all will reap what we are sowing. A primary reason many, and possibly most, are not walking in the peace of God or experiencing His glory in their lives is because of what comes from their own tongues. For this reason let us heed the words of King David in Psalm 34:14: "Depart from evil and do good; seek peace and pursue it." As Peter wrote, "Therefore, beloved, since you look for these things, be diligent to be found by Him in peace, spotless and blameless" (2 Pet. 3:14).

Why Did He Come?

Of course we know that Jesus came into this world to redeem humankind, but it is by our walking in His peace that we have evidence of His salvation, as we read in Luke 1:76-79:

And you, child, will be called the prophet of the Most High; for you will go on before the Lord to prepare His ways;

to give to His people the knowledge of salvation by the forgiveness of their sins,

because of the tender mercy of our God, with which the Sunrise from on high will visit us,

to shine upon those who sit in darkness and the shadow of death, to guide our feet into the way of peace.

He came "to guide our feet into the way of peace." Are we following Him? If we are, we should be growing in faith and peace and experiencing less fear and anxiety. It is for this reason that Isaiah declares that the increase of His government will also result in an increase of peace.

For a child will be born to us, a son will be given to us; and the government will rest on His shoulders; and His name will be called Wonderful Counselor, Mighty God, Eternal Father, Prince of Peace. There will be no end to the increase of His government or of peace... (Isaiah 9:6-7).

Therefore, to the degree that the Kingdom of God grows in us, we also will grow in peace. Please consider carefully these other promises concerning the peace of God. Each one is worth more than any treasure on this earth.

Peace I leave with you; My peace I give to you; not as the world gives, do I give to you. Let not your heart be troubled, nor let it be fearful (John 14:27).

*How lovely on the mountains are the feet of him who brings good news, **who announces peace** and brings good news of happiness, who announces salvation, and says to Zion, "Your God reigns!"* (Isaiah 52:7).

*So will My word be which goes forth from My mouth; it will not return to Me empty, without accomplishing what I desire, and without succeeding in the matter for which I sent it. For you will go out with joy, **and be led forth with peace**; the mountains and the hills will break forth into shouts of joy before you, and all the trees of the field will clap their hands* (Isaiah 55:11-12).

Pray for the peace of Jerusalem: "May they prosper who love you.

"May peace be within your walls, and prosperity within your palaces."

*For the sake of my brothers and my friends, I will now say, "May peace be within you." **For the sake of the house of the Lord our God, I will seek your good*** (Psalm 122:6-9).

The Lord is my light and my salvation; whom shall I fear? The Lord is the defense of my life; whom shall I dread?

When evildoers came upon me to devour my flesh, my adversaries and my enemies, they stumbled and fell.

Though a host encamp against me, my heart will not fear; though war arise against me, in spite of this I shall be confident.

One thing I have asked from the Lord, that I shall seek: that I may dwell in the house of the Lord all the days of my life, to behold the beauty of the Lord, and to meditate in His temple.

For in the day of trouble He will conceal me in His tabernacle; in the secret place of His tent He will hide me; He will lift me up on a rock (Psalm 27:1-5).

Light arises in the darkness for the upright; he is gracious and compassionate and righteous. It is well with the man who is gracious and lends; he will maintain his cause in judgment. For he will never be shaken; the righteous will be remembered forever. He will not fear evil tidings; his heart is steadfast, trusting in the Lord. His heart is upheld, he will not fear, until he looks with satisfaction on his adversaries. He has given freely to the poor; his righteousness endures forever; his horn will be exalted in honor (Psalm 112:4-9).

Do not be wise in your own eyes; fear the Lord and turn away from evil.

It will be healing to your body and refreshment to your bones.

Honor the Lord from your wealth, and from the first of all your produce;

So your barns will be filled with plenty and your vats will overflow with new wine.

My son, do not reject the discipline of the Lord, or loathe His reproof,

For whom the Lord loves He reproves, even as a father corrects the son in whom he delights.

How blessed is the man who finds wisdom, and the man who gains understanding.

For her profit is better than the profit of silver and her gain better than fine gold.

She is more precious than jewels; and nothing you desire compares with her.

Long life is in her right hand; in her left hand are riches and honor.

Her ways are pleasant ways **and all her paths are peace.**

She is a tree of life to those who take hold of her, and happy are all who hold her fast. The Lord by wisdom founded the earth; by understanding He established the heavens. By His knowledge the deeps were broken up, and the skies drip with dew. My son, let them not vanish from your sight; keep sound wisdom and discretion, So they will be life to your soul and adornment to your neck.

Then you will walk in your way securely and your foot will not stumble.

When you lie down, you will not be afraid; when you lie down, your sleep will be sweet.

Do not be afraid of sudden fear nor of the onslaught of the wicked when it comes;

For the Lord will be your confidence and will keep your foot from being caught.

Do not withhold good from those to whom it is due, when it is in your power to do it (Proverbs 3:7-27).

PART III

DEFEATING THE THIEF OF HUMAN POTENTIAL

CHAPTER 14

OVERCOMING THE SPIRIT OF POVERTY

The spirit of poverty is one of the most powerful and deadly strongholds satan uses to keep the world in bondage. This stronghold is closely related to many of the fears that we just addressed, and it will help us to identify their connections in our life. Most evil strongholds, which are basically deceptive patterns of thinking, are interrelated and can be overcome completely only as we unravel their entire web. Therefore, there will be some review in this and all future chapters. This is crucial because repetition not only greatly increases the retention of our knowledge, but also each time a truth is repeated it can help us to see more of the web that the enemy has sown in our lives to keep us from walking in truth.

Keeping God's people oppressed and in poverty is the intent of many of the fears that the enemy of our soul sends against us. Every church and every believer must fight and overcome this spirit of poverty in order to walk in the purposes for which they are called. This stronghold is one of the enemy's most successful weapons against believers, which means that by overcoming it we gain some advances and spiritual successes. We also can gain a place of spiritual authority from which we can be used to meet some of the world's most pressing needs. Wherever this stronghold is overthrown, it is like casting off the darkness of the most terrible spiritual winter and seeing the world blossom into spring again.

Defining the Spirit of Poverty

When we think of poverty, we usually think of money, but the spirit of poverty may or may not have anything to do with money. *The spirit of poverty is a stronghold established for the purpose of keeping us from walking in the fullness of the victory gained for us at the Cross and of the blessings of our inheritance in Christ.* This can relate to everything from the quality of our marriages to the anointing we have for ministry, as well as any other resources we need for what we have been called to do.

The goal of the spirit of poverty is not just to keep things from us, but to keep us from the will of God. To do this, satan may even give us great riches, but our lives will be nevertheless just as empty and full of worries as if we were destitute.

Our goal for being free from the spirit of poverty is not just so we can have things that we need or want, but so that we can do the will of God without hindrance from either physical or spiritual depravity. This spirit is a yoke that manifests in both the natural and spiritual realms. Therefore, when we are freed from the yoke of the spirit of poverty, our freedom will be manifested in the natural as well as in the spiritual. Since the Lord Jesus was completely free of the influence of this spirit, He healed the sick, raised the dead, or even multiplied food as the situation required. He always was able to draw on the resources of Heaven, which should be our goal as well. The apostle Paul refers to this kind of walk that should be normal Christianity in Second Corinthians 9:8:

> *And God is able to make all grace abound to you, so that always having all sufficiency in everything, you may have an abundance for every good deed.*

We must settle it in our hearts and minds that as children of God He wants to make "all grace abound" to us. This must be a basic goal of our life—to walk in all the grace of God that is available through the Cross and His present position that is above all rule, authority, power, and dominion. However, a key to receiving this is to understand that it is through grace, and not something that we can earn. It is released simply by having faith in who He is and what He has done.

The goal of our faith should be to live a life of "always having all sufficiency in everything," The two key words here are *always* and *everything*. As Christians living in the Kingdom, we should always represent the life and power that are available to every citizen of the Kingdom. That does not mean that we are called to live lives that never know need. As we are told in Psalm 34:10, "The young lions do lack and suffer hunger; but they who seek the Lord shall not be in want of any good thing."

As Second Corinthians 9:8 continues, we should have "an abundance for every good deed." Jesus did not meet every need because it was not the Father's will for Him to do so. However, there was never one that He could not meet because of a lack of supply. In fact, just as when He multiplied the bread and fish, He always had such an abundance that there was plenty left over. It is in fact a manifestation of the spirit of poverty that wants just enough to get by. The Lord wants our lives to overflow.

If this abundance and overflow is not true in our life, it is because something is awry—we have an evil stronghold that is robbing us called the spirit of poverty. One of the key ways that we break this spirit of poverty is highlighted in the preceding two verses of Second Corinthians 9:

> *Now this I say, he who sows sparingly will also reap sparingly, and he who sows bountifully will also reap bountifully.*
>
> *Each one must do just as he has purposed in his heart, not grudgingly or under compulsion, for God loves a cheerful giver* (2 Corinthians 9:6-7).

A spirit is often another term for an attitude. We release the generosity of God in our life by being generous ourselves. If we have an attitude of just getting by, then that is probably how we sow into the Kingdom—doing just enough to get by—and that attitude is directly related to how Kingdom authority is released in our own life. The Lord did not just give enough; He gave an abundance, more than was needed. That is the attitude that controls those who are abiding in Him, who live by His Spirit.

Freedom

One evidence that we have been truly freed from the yoke of the spirit of poverty is the financial independence we discussed previously. This means that we are free of every financial yoke so that we can make decisions based on the will of God, not on how much money we have. It may be the will of God for us to have a lot or to have a little. Now, didn't we just say that God wanted us to have an abundance, to have enough to overflow for every good deed? Yes. However, sometimes what we think of as a little is more than we need. We can expect to go through ups and downs for the purpose of our own training and expansion in faith.

Like the apostle Paul, we must be content if we are either abased or abounding, as long as it is the will of God for us. That is the key phrase: *if it is the will of God for us.* We do not want to be either abased or abounding if it is not His will. Therefore the key for liberation from any evil stronghold in our lives is to know God's will.

It is important for the Church to be prepared to handle unprecedented wealth. There are a number of prophetic Scriptures that indicate that the wealth of the nations will be brought into the Church, as we have already covered. This will *not* be a great opportunity *for* the advancement of the Kingdom; rather, it will come as a result *of* the advancement of the

Kingdom. We must remember that some of the greatest tests at the end of this age will be economic.

We must seek financial independence, but we must always keep in mind that it is a means and not the end in itself. To be financially independent without knowing our purpose in God would be like getting all dressed up with no place to go. Getting free of this stronghold is for the purpose of enabling us to do His will. Knowing His will is more valuable than all the treasures we could ever have, and we must always esteem knowing His will as the true treasure, and therefore make it the primary thing that we seek. If we start seeking the treasure more than His will, we are in jeopardy of a most terrible tragedy.

God's general will for us is clearly revealed in the Scriptures. We don't need a secret code or an angel from Heaven to explain it to us. If many would just spend the time in the Scriptures that they now spend watching worthless television shows, their lives would be radically different and far more prosperous. So now we want to take some time to review the things that are clearly written in the Word of God about this issue. This truth will set us free.

Get Out of Jail Free!

As stated, one of the most basic conflicts between the Kingdom of God and this present age is that the former is a place of freedom and the latter is built on slavery. The Lord came to set men free. Everything that satan does is intended to increase the yoke of bondage upon us. Everything that the Lord does is intended to set us free. As we proceed toward the end of the age, the differences between these two kingdoms will become increasingly pronounced. In our battle we must always remember that the conflict is between slavery and freedom. If you belong to Christ Jesus, you are called to be free! Because of this, we will not be forced to do His will. We must choose to be faithful, which is a true demonstration of the faith that releases God's authority and provision into our life. Again,

It was for freedom that Christ set us free; therefore keep standing firm and do not be subject again to a yoke of slavery (Galatians 5:1).

The Lord purchased us with His own blood. We belong to the King of kings. He has called us to be sons of God and joint heirs with Him. We are called to represent His Kingdom as ambassadors, walking as members of the highest nobility, royalty of the highest order, and God's own family. To do this, we must be free from the yokes of this present evil age and carry only His yoke.

Come to Me, all who are weary and heavy-laden, and I will give you rest.

Take My yoke upon you and learn from Me, for I am gentle and humble in heart, and you will find rest for your souls.

For My yoke is easy, and My burden is light (Matthew 11:28-30).

Yokes represent bondage. There are yokes of bondage through which men are kept in darkness and oppression. These yokes usually appear to be a form of freedom, but they result in the most terrible burdens. In contrast, the Lord's yoke appears at first to be bondage, but it results in the greatest freedom we can ever know.

We all will carry someone's yoke—either the yokes of this present evil age or the yoke of the Lord. If we are to carry the Lord's yoke, we must cast off every yoke of the enemy. We cannot serve two masters. The one whose yoke we carry will be the one we serve and represent in this world. We can make every claim to be a Christian, but if we live our lives according to the ways of this present evil age, we are serving the powers of evil. James 4:4-8 addresses this issue straightforwardly:

You adulteresses, do you not know that friendship with the world is hostility toward God? Therefore whoever wishes to be a friend of the world makes himself an enemy of God.

Or do you think that the Scripture speaks to no purpose: "He jealously desires the Spirit which He has made to dwell in us"?

But He gives a greater grace. Therefore it says, "God is opposed to the proud, but gives grace to the humble."

Submit therefore to God. Resist the devil and he will flee from you.

Draw near to God and He will draw near to you. Cleanse your hands, you sinners; and purify your hearts, you double-minded.

There can be no compromise. If we are yoked to the world, we are serving the world. If we are yoked to the Lord, we will serve Him only. As we proceed to the end of this age, the differences are going to become more pronounced and the battle between the two kingdoms more fierce. All this is happening for the purpose of setting us free! All that happens will result in the Lord having a Bride that is prepared for Him, without spot or blemish.

Our preparation for our purpose of representing the Kingdom is to have a life that always seeks first the Kingdom, lives in the Kingdom, and represents the Kingdom of God, which is simply representing the King. If we are faithful to do this, we do not need to fear any of the difficulties that are coming upon the earth. The Kingdom of God cannot be shaken, and if we have built our lives upon it, neither can we be shaken. Every difficulty that comes upon us now is to help us to build our lives on the Kingdom of God.

For it is time for judgment to begin with the household of God (1 Peter 4:17a).

When we hear the word *judgment,* we often equate it with the destruction caused by the Lord's ultimate wrath. If we read the Scriptures in the languages in which they were originally written, we would not feel this way. The Greek word that is translated as "judgment" in this text is *krisis,* the word from which we derive our English word crisis. A definition of crisis is "the point in a disease or trauma when it is determined if the patient will live or die." This verse could thus have been translated, "It is time for a *crisis* to begin with the household of God." The implication is that the Church will go through a crisis before the world does. God allows this so that when the world is going through a crisis, we will be on solid ground. This is why James wrote:

> *My brethren, count it all joy when you fall into various trials, knowing that the testing of your faith produces patience.*
>
> *But let patience have its perfect work, that you may be perfect and complete, lacking nothing* (James 1:2-4 NKJV).

Here we see that trials produce patience, which leads to our perfection, so that we will not lack anything. That is true biblical prosperity. This is the abundance we are called to walk in.

> *The earth is the Lord's, and all it contains, the world, and those who dwell in it* (Psalm 24:1).

Even though it is presently subject to bondage because of the Fall, the Lord is going to take this world back. We have been called to be a part of His invasion force, but we can be on only one side in this battle. We must now get free of every yoke of the enemy that causes us in any way to compromise the ways of the Kingdom of God. The trials we are now going through are all meant to help us do this.

We are on trial now for establishing our place in His invasion force and determining how much of His authority we can be trusted with. With His authority in this force there will ultimately be the management of great wealth. If there is still greed in our hearts, this will only be a stumbling block to us. Remember, we are called to be stewards, bond servants. Our faithfulness in what we have been entrusted with right now will determine whether we can be trusted with more.

If we are seated with the King of kings on His throne, what pull can any earthly position have for us? I repeat, this does not mean that we do not have a genuine care for our jobs or ministries here. We care for them because they have been entrusted to us by Him, and we engage in them as worship unto Him. If our positions here are taken from us, we are still seated with Him, and we will worship Him in whatever way He calls us to next. We are His slaves, and we must be content with whatever job He gives to us. Ultimate faith is revealed by ultimate trust.

When Christ is the life, trust, and true desire of our hearts, He can trust us with the earthly possessions and positions that we are called to rule over. But if He is not the life, trust, and desire of our hearts, our possessions and positions will inevitably rule over us. Whoever or whatever rules over us is, in fact, our lord. We are entering a time when the lordship of Jesus must be more than a doctrine—it must be a profound and continuing reality in our lives. Then we will be free indeed. When we are fully yoked to Him, having cast off all the yokes of this present evil age, He will then be free to trust us with the unlimited resources of His Kingdom.

A Vision

Does it seem that I am just saying the same things over and over, maybe just changing the wording a little bit? That is in fact my intent. In a vision I was shown a mountain that we are called to climb as well as the glory that awaits us at the top. Multitudes were climbing the mountain, but very few were making it to the top. Why?

The main reason so many were falling off of the mountain was that they were trying to go too fast, and they were failing to drive their stakes into the rock deep enough to secure them to the mountain when little slips took place. As groups of climbers were bound together by their ropes, every time one climber slipped and fell, all those who were connected together would likewise fall off of the mountain with him.

The devastation at the bottom of the mountain, the piles of dead and injured, was keeping others who wanted to climb the mountain from attempting it. Many have attempted to climb this mountain but have suffered falls that were unnecessary. Faith not combined with patience will keep us in perpetual and unnecessary danger. It is right to climb this mountain, but we must have the patience to secure every advance, drive our stakes deeply enough into the rock to ensure that they can hold us and those we are joined to if we have a slip. Those who conclude that it is not faith to be concerned about slipping are walking in presumption, not faith. Just as James wrote, "For we all stumble in many ways" (James 3:2a). This is also the message of Hebrews 6:11-12:

> And we desire that each one of you show the same diligence so as to realize the full assurance of hope until the end,
>
> so that you will not be sluggish, but imitators of those who through faith and patience inherit the promises.

There is a difference between being sluggish or slothful and being diligent. As it states here, it will take faith and patience to inherit the promises. Have you ever wondered why we have this huge faith movement but have never heard of a patience movement? It will take both. Patience can be one of the most profound demonstrations of true faith. To not combine patience with our faith will cause our faith to become presumption.

That is why I am attempting to hit certain issues repeatedly in this study. If we will allow the truth of God's Word to be driven deeply into our lives, those truths will support the weight of our life and enable us to go higher safely. We need to hit some of the truths over and over so that our faith is driven as deeply as possible into the Rock.

We must set it in our heart that we are going to climb this mountain until we get to the top. We must set our vision to walking in everything that God has called us to walk in, including all the power and all the provision. However, we also want to have the wisdom to know that the higher we go, the more dangerous it is not to secure ourselves well to our Rock. Repetition may at some times be a bit boring, but the consequences of not doing it will be far worse. Our goal must be to get there safely with all those to whom we are connected.

CHAPTER 15

RECEIVING THE WEALTH OF THE NATIONS

A law of physics states that energy is never destroyed but simply changes forms. The same is true of wealth; it is never destroyed, but it often changes hands. Even during the Great Depression wealth was not destroyed. Instead, it was transferred to those who were in a position to take advantage of the times. Those who were in this position were not in debt and had cash readily available. Businesses were bought for as little as ten percent of their value. Land was bought for less than a dollar an acre in some places. The wealth was taken from those who had overextended themselves with debt and was received by those who had the wisdom to live within their means.

It may come soon, or it may be graciously delayed even further, but the earth will experience an even greater economic upheaval than the Great Depression. Those who are not prepared for it will be devastated by it. Those who are prepared for it will experience unprecedented prosperity. They will take advantage of the times and receive authority over unprecedented wealth. We are being prepared for this by the problems God is allowing us to go through now. In Matthew 7:24-27 we are told how to be prepared:

> *Therefore everyone who hears these words of Mine and acts on them, may be compared to a wise man who built his house on the rock.*
>
> *And the rain fell, and the floods came, and the winds blew and slammed against that house; and yet it did not fall, for it had been founded on the rock.*

*Everyone who hears these words of Mine and does not
act on them, will be like a foolish man who built his
house on the sand.*

*The rain fell, and the floods came, and the winds blew
and slammed against that house; and it fell—and
great was its fall.*

We prepare by being wise enough to seek to hear the
words of the Lord and then obeying them. King David also gave
us a very wise exhortation that is related to this:

*Therefore, let everyone who is godly pray to You in a
time when You may be found; surely in a flood of great
waters they shall not reach him* (Psalm 32:6).

Now is the time for us to seek the Lord and to establish
our lives solidly on the rock of both hearing and doing His
Word. When the floods come it will be too late. That is why the
Lord is allowing the judgment that is crisis to come to His people first, before it comes upon the world. We go through troubles now that are meant to drive us to higher ground. Even if we
have been faithful in all things, sometimes the Lord still allows
us to go through troubles, just as He did Joseph, so He can trust
us with even more of His abundance.

Like Joseph, we are being prepared to properly manage
the abundance we receive so that it can save lives during the
times of famine that are coming. The Lord wants His people
prepared to use the circumstances that are coming for the sake
of His gospel, not just so we can get rich. One fundamental flaw
that will keep us bound by the spirit of poverty is selfishness.
When it comes to the Lord's trusting us with more resources,
motives are crucial.

The Lord is right now preparing His people for what is about to come. He has been warning His Church for more than 30 years to get out of debt. He has given us plenty of time to do it. However, because the expected catastrophic economic problems have taken so long to come, many have disregarded the warning. There is still time to repent and get our houses in order, but we must not delay. Those who are obedient will have nothing to fear from what is coming; instead, they can look forward to a godly prosperity in the midst of famine. Those who continue in disobedience will one day pay a terrible price for it. However, the Lord desires something much better for you.

How to Get Out of Jail

We were bought with the highest price that could be paid—the blood of the Lamb. Because "the borrower becomes the lender's slave" (Prov. 22:7), when we go into debt we sell ourselves to become the slave of another. If we belong to Christ, we are not our own to sell. When we go into debt, we are actually selling that which belongs to God.

Does this mean we should never go into debt for anything? In principle this is true. However, we must understand that we do not live under the law, and there is a difference between principles and laws. Laws cannot be broken, but there are exceptions to principles. Now, this does not mean that we can just disregard principles any time we want to. It means that we need to hear very clearly from the Lord to do so.

For example, I know some people who, more than 20 years ago, felt that they should not go into debt for a home. The mortgage would have been about the same as their rent, and the house was in an appreciating market. At the time I felt that this debt was permissible for them, but they disagreed. Now these people are still renting, with payments that are about four times higher than they were at the time they could have purchased the house. They could have owned the house outright by now, and the value of what they owned would have quadrupled instead of their rent payments.

This still does not necessarily mean they should have bought the house, especially if their consciences would not permit them to. Many believe that Romans 13:8a, "Owe no man any thing, but to love one another" (KJV), is an emphatic command that we cannot compromise. However, if it were an emphatic commandment, why did the Lord chastise the foolish servant in the parable of the talents for not at least getting interest for His money? Would the Lord encourage us to loan money at interest if it were a sin to borrow under any circumstances?

In the Old Covenant, the Israelites were commanded not to loan their money at interest to their brethren, but this had nothing to do with loaning at interest to others. This is why the Jewish people have been some of the most outstanding bankers in history. Even so, as a principle (not a law), it is better not to go into debt for any reason without a clear directive from the Lord. We must get out of debt, and stay out of debt, except when we are clearly permitted to do otherwise for a season.

Climb with Patience

If we are going to climb the mountain of God with patience, we also need to have patience in climbing over the mountain of debt that some of us now have. We will get into a few practical issues later that can help us in this, but it is important to set realistic goals. Usually, if it has taken us years to get into a mess, the Lord will not deliver us immediately because He wants us to fully understand the wrongful ways in our life that led to the mess.

For this reason it might be good to prayerfully set a goal of reducing your debt by 5 percent in one year, then by 10 percent more the next year, adding 5 percent each year. The momentum will grow so fast you will almost certainly exceed the targets quickly.

If you are living right at the edge of your income now, set a goal of reducing your expenses as well. You might want to have a five-year goal of living on just 50 percent of your income by then. Set a goal of modestly reducing your expenses the first year and increasing the amount of reduction each year afterward.

This discipline will take both faith and patience. However, I have never seen anyone who was both faithful and patient in this not get free of the terrible shackle that debt can be. Most of what we get free of is the way that our own greed, lust, and irresponsibility have been allowed into our life to cause the bondage. Again, let us keep our resolve to obey Galatians 5:1:

> *It was for freedom that Christ set us free; therefore keep standing firm and do not be subject again to a yoke of slavery.*

CHAPTER 16

CHRISTIAN ECONOMICS 101: STEWARDSHIP

It would not do us much good to tear down an evil stronghold if we are going to allow the enemy to come right back in and rebuild it. In fact, this would leave us even worse off because, as the Lord warned, when the enemy is displaced he will wander around for awhile, but then he always determines to return to his former "house." If he is able to get back in, he will bring seven more evil spirits even meaner than himself. So our goal for tearing down every evil stronghold is to rebuild a stronghold of truth in its place so that the enemy has no opportunity to return.

Christian economics is the art of good stewardship in obedience to the simple biblical procedures that the Lord has given to us. We are spending a little more time on this than you may have expected in a book about spiritual strongholds because this is one of the primary ones that we must confront and overcome as Christians, especially at the end of the age. Stewardship is the emphasis of a substantial portion of the Bible because of its importance.

As the Lord made clear in the parable of the talents (see Matthew 25:14-30), we must seek to use everything the Lord has entrusted to us in the most profitable way. Recorded in Luke 16:9-13 we have another related exhortation from the Lord:

> *And I say to you, make friends for yourselves by means of the [mammon] of unrighteousness; so that when it fails, they will receive you into the eternal dwellings.*

He who is faithful in a very little thing is faithful also in much; and he who is unrighteous in a very little thing is unrighteous also in much.

therefore if you have not been faithful in the use of unrighteous [mammon], *who will entrust the true riches to you?*

And if you have not been faithful in the use of that which is another's, who will give you that which is your own?

No servant can serve two masters; for either he will hate the one and love the other, or else he will be devoted to one and despise the other. You cannot serve God and [mammon].

The saying we "cannot serve God and mammon" means we cannot combine the motive of serving God with the motive of making money. There is abundant evidence throughout history that the love of money will quickly corrupt a ministry. But we must not exclude the first part of the Lord's exhortation in this text, that we need to "make friends for yourselves by means of the mammon of unrighteousness." In this He is not telling us to be friends with the mammon, but to use mammon to make friends.

The Yoke of the Beast

Previously we discussed why the mark of the beast is an economic mark. We also commented that the sin is not taking the mark, but worshiping the beast. The mark is just the evidence that this is what we have been doing. Some have proposed that debt is the mark of the beast. I am not convinced of that, but I could see how it could be a way that we begin to worship the beast.

As we have already addressed, debt is probably the main reason Christians today are not free to respond to the call of God in their lives. We must ask, "Does our financial condition rule us, or do we have complete authority over it?" This can be a primary indication of just how much we have built our lives upon the foundations of this present age rather than upon hearing and obeying the Word of the Lord.

Regardless of how bad your situation is, remember that faith can move mountains, even mountains of debt. However, the word that is often translated as "faith" in the New Testament also could have been translated "faithfulness." The two are really the same. Our situations can change, but they must change in obedience to the Lord and His Word. We also must remember that faith and patience go together, and some mountains are removed one shovelful at a time!

Even so, the Lord will provide a way of escape for those who will be obedient. Regardless of how disobedient or how foolish we have been, or how bad our situations are now, if we repent the Lord will deliver us. Our God really is all-powerful. When He helps there is no limit to what can be done. When His people are trapped with the hordes of the enemy bearing down on them, He delights in doing some of His greatest miracles.

If we call upon the Lord in faith, which is also faithfulness, He will part an ocean to get us free if He has to. However, true faith begins with true repentance for whatever we have been doing that is wrong. Remember, repentance does not mean just that we are sorry, but also that we turn away from our wicked ways. The Lord does not want to deliver us just to have us slip right back into bondage because we did not change our ways. Therefore, true repentance is evidence of the true faith that compels Him to respond.

A Sure Path to Financial Freedom

There is a clear biblical procedure for getting out of debt, for staying out of debt, and for becoming financially independent. Briefly, before we cover this, we need to address an important and related issue. The Church is still wounded in many areas that satan intended to cripple her. These are the very areas where she must have power for what is to come, so she must be healed in these areas now.

Remember that the formula for financial independence is *repentance + obedience = freedom*. This section deals with the repentance that most of us will have to do before we can even understand what we are required to obey.

It is by the Lord's stripes that we are healed. In the very place where He was wounded He received the power for healing. The same is true for us. In the very places that the enemy is allowed to strike us, once we are healed, we will receive authority for healing in those same areas. For example, a person who has suffered abuse becomes sensitive to others who have been abused, and their compassion for the abused can release the Lord's healing power through them.

True spiritual authority is founded on compassion. When the Lord saw that the people were like sheep without a shepherd, He became their Shepherd. Compassion releases the power of God. Every wound we have suffered in our lives was for the purpose of making us sensitive and compassionate toward others who have suffered in the same way, so that God can release His healing power through us.

Almost every person on the planet has been held in bondage to the financial yokes of this world, and/or has received financial wounds from all manner of theft and deceit. The Lord is going to use His Church to break the enemy's financial power over multitudes and set them free. He has allowed the enemy to wound His Church in this area in order to make her sensitive and compassionate so we can help set others free.

Again, before we can be used to heal others, we must be healed of our own wounds. One of the requirements for being a priest was that he could not have scabs (see Leviticus 21:20). A scab covers an unhealed wound. One who has scabs is so overly sensitive in that area that you cannot touch them. Likewise, our unhealed wounds keep people from getting close to us in those areas. This keeps us from being able to intercede for those who need our ministry. Spiritual scabs, therefore, can disqualify us from our most important ministries.

After a healing, scars may remain, which may continue to be a little sensitive, but not so sensitive that no one can get close to us. The sensitivity of scars is different from that of scabs. Scars keep us just sensitive enough to help us discern the wounds in others that have not yet been healed.

The Way of Escape

The first principle to getting out of our present financial bondage is not to get, but to give. If you cringed at that statement, it is evidence of a wound that must be healed. Our foe has the wisdom of thousands of years from ruling over his dark domain, and he has wisely attacked the most important issues with some of his biggest weapons. He has taken some of the most important words in Scripture, such as *holiness, submission,* and *giving,* and made them repulsive even to Christians. Yet, these truths will be recovered by those who overcome.

It is true that the Church has been raped. Rape is the ultimate violation of a person. Rape is therefore one of the most difficult traumas for a woman to recover from. The Church has been raped repeatedly by hype, manipulation, and those with a controlling spirit. If the Lord could have prevented this, why didn't He? What loving father would allow his daughter to be raped if he could prevent it? Remember, our heavenly Father allowed His Son to be crucified unjustly because He has a higher purpose. His goal is ultimately to use His Son, working through His Church, to remove all rape from the earth for all time.

We must understand that nothing bad has ever happened to us that the Lord has not allowed. He does love us, even more than we love our own children. He has not let anything happen to us that was not for our good and for the higher good of His whole creation. We must stop sulking over our wounds and understand that they were allowed so we could receive authority over the very one who wounded us and be the vessels of healing for other victims. This is why the apostle Paul wrote:

> *Now I rejoice in my sufferings for your sake, and in my flesh I do my share on behalf of His body, which is the church, in filling up that which is lacking in Christ's afflictions* (Colossians 1:24).

This verse does not imply that the work of Christ was not complete. The word translated as "lacking" here could have been translated "left behind." The implication is that He allows us to go through sufferings for the same reasons that He did— they are meant to help release redemptive authority into the world. That is why, when defending his authority, Paul pointed to his tribulations. Every suffering that a believer endures has a redemptive purpose.

Even though the Lord allowed His own Bride to be raped, He is going to do a great miracle. He is going to take the Church, which has been raped repeatedly and at other times has played the harlot, and make her into a pure, chaste virgin again. In the very place where she was the most severely abused, she will be healed and then be given the power to heal others.

The Lord also is going to raise up a last-day ministry that will never again rape His Bride. They will be spiritual eunuchs for the sake of the Kingdom. A eunuch cannot even have a desire for the bride. His whole purpose is to prepare the bride for the king, and his satisfaction comes from seeing the king's satisfaction. That will be the nature of the ministry that is coming. These men and women will not be in ministry to take from the Church and use her for their own ambitions, but they will be utterly devoted to serving her out of love for the Bridegroom.

There will be a people raised up before the end that follow the Lord fully. However, it is to be expected that it will take the Church a long time to trust them, or anyone, after the past abuses. Many believers have responded to the financial abuses by refusing to give anymore. This is understandable, but until they are freed from this attitude they will likely stay in financial bondage. Giving is fundamental to Christianity, and giving our money is one of the primary ways we are freed from one of the ultimate powers of idolatry. Therefore, these issues must be addressed without compromise for the sake of those who have been so wounded.

We can be free today from all of our spiritual wounds— and never look back on them. They need not affect the rest of our lives. The way of escape is the cross, which is manifested by forgiveness.

The Highway to Freedom

In dreams and visions, a highway often represents God's *higher* way. That is the path to the Kingdom that we are seeking. We simply cannot live by the standards, desires, lusts, and ways of this present evil age and the Kingdom of God at the same time. This does not mean that we cannot have a house, car, or television set. It does mean that we will have only that which we have permission to have. It also means that we "do all things for the sake of the gospel" (1 Cor. 9:23a), and that our first consideration in making any major decision will be to determine our Master's will. We also must start by doing now what is clearly written in His Word.

One of the biggest open doors that the spirit of poverty has into our lives is through our own unrighteous judgments. This is the spirit of criticism.

I once visited a state that was under one of the most powerful spirits of poverty that I have witnessed in this country. It was remarkable because it is a state of great beauty and natural resources. It had talented and resourceful people, but a spirit of poverty was on almost everyone. Another characteristic that stood out was that almost everyone I met there seemed to uncontrollably scorn and criticize anyone who was prosperous or powerful.

With every pastor of a small church whom I met (and almost all of the churches in this state were very small), the conversation would inevitably turn to criticizing "mega-churches" and "mega-ministries," which these people obviously thought were the reason for many of their own problems. What made the situation even sadder was that many of these small-church pastors were called to walk in much more authority than the leaders of the large churches or ministries that they criticized. When I prayed for them, the Lord showed me that their judgments and criticisms of others were the reason for their own poverty.

Many pastors yoke themselves and their congregations to financial poverty by criticizing how other churches or ministries take up offerings or solicit donations. Because of their judgment of others, they then cannot even take up a biblical offering without feeling guilty. They have yoked themselves by their unrighteous judgment.

Of the many people I have met with exceptional spiritual gifting, but lack of spiritual fruit, this always has been a prevailing characteristic in their lives—a critical spirit. They had judged and criticized the ministries of others who were gaining influence and had thereby disqualified themselves from being able to receive more. Our criticisms will bring us to poverty.

"Death and life are in the power of the tongue, and those who love it will eat its fruit" (Prov. 18:21).

As Solomon observed,

But the path of the just is like the shining sun, that shines ever brighter unto the perfect day.

The way of the wicked is like darkness; they do not know what makes them stumble (Proverbs 4:18-19 NKJV).

If we are walking in righteousness, we will be walking in increasing light. Those who stumble around in the dark seldom know the reason for that darkness, or they would not be in it. However, the critical person is a prideful person, who therefore will be critical of everyone but himself. As a result, he cannot see his own sin. As the Lord stated, he is so busy looking for specks in the eyes of his brothers that he cannot see the big log in his own eye.

We all are saved by grace, and we will need all the grace that we can get in order to make it through this life. If we want to receive grace, we had better learn to give grace because we are going to reap what we sow. If we expect to receive mercy, we must start sowing mercy, and most of us are going to need all the mercy we can get. As the Lord sternly warned,

You have heard that it was said to those of old, "You shall not murder, and whoever murders will be in danger of the judgment."

But I say to you that whoever is angry with his brother without a cause shall be in danger of the judgment. And whoever says to his brother, "Raca!" [empty head] shall be in danger of the council. But whoever says, "You fool!" shall be in danger of hell fire.

Therefore if you bring your gift to the altar, and there remember that your brother has something against you, leave your gift there before the altar, and go your way.

First be reconciled to your brother, and then come and offer your gift.

Agree with your adversary quickly, while you are on the way with him, lest your adversary deliver you to the judge, the judge hand you over to the officer, and you be thrown into prison [bondage].

Assuredly, I say to you, you will by no means get out of there till you have paid the last penny (Matthew 5:21-26 NKJV).

It is clear by this warning that if we have been guilty of slandering a brother, we should not try to make offerings to the Lord until we have been reconciled to our brother. The Lord links these together because we often think that our sacrifices and offerings can compensate for such sins, but they never will.

As we mentioned earlier, we must be generous and learn to give in order to receive. However, we can be the most generous people and still stay in bondage if we are allowing the spirit of poverty access to our life through our own criticism and unrighteous judgment. We will stay in the prisons we make for ourselves with our judgments until we have paid the last cent, or until we are reconciled to the brother we slandered.

Drive a Stake in Here

For this reason, I encourage you to stop here for a bit to pray. Ask the Lord to reveal to you the way that this critical spirit may have attached itself to you as well as any unrighteous judgments that you may have made of others by which you have yoked yourself. Repent of them, and be willing to go to the ones whom you have offended and humble yourself. Remember, God gives His grace to the humble, and none of us are going to make it without His grace. This is an opportunity for you to grow in His grace and begin the release from the yoke of the spirit of poverty in your life. If judgment is a reason for your troubles, you will be amazed at how this humility in repentance can start to turn things around.

CHAPTER 17

TITHING IN THE KINGDOM

The first principle in stewardship in the Kingdom is obedience to the King. Two more important biblical texts for the Church today are found in Haggai chapter 1 and Malachi chapter 3.

Thus says the Lord of hosts, "This people says, 'The time has not come, even the time for the house of the Lord to be rebuilt.' "

Then the word of the Lord came by Haggai the prophet saying,

"Is it time for you yourselves to dwell in your paneled houses while this house lies desolate?"

Now therefore, thus says the Lord of hosts, "Consider your ways!

"You have sown much, but harvest little; you eat, but there is not enough to be satisfied; you drink, but there is not enough to become drunk; you put on clothing, but no one is warm enough; and he who earns, earns wages to put into a purse with holes."

Thus says the Lord of hosts, "Consider your ways!

"Go up to the mountains, bring wood and rebuild the temple, that I may be pleased with it and be glorified," says the Lord.

"You look for much, but behold, it comes to little; when you bring it home, I blow it away. Why?" declares the Lord of hosts, "Because of My house which lies desolate, while each of you runs to his own house.

"Therefore, because of you the sky has withheld its dew, and the earth has withheld its produce.

"I called for a drought on the land, on the mountains, on the grain, on the new wine, on the oil, on what the ground produces, on men, on cattle, and on all the labor of your hands" (Haggai 1:2-11).

"Will a man rob God? Yet you are robbing Me! But you say, 'How have we robbed You?' In tithes and offerings.

"You are cursed with a curse, for you are robbing Me, the whole nation of you!

"Bring the whole tithe into the storehouse, so that there may be food in My house, and test Me now in this," says the Lord of hosts, "if I will not open for you the windows of heaven and pour out for you a blessing until it overflows.

"Then I will rebuke the devourer for you, so that it will not destroy the fruits of the ground; nor will your vine in the field cast its grapes," says the Lord of hosts.

"All the nations will call you blessed, for you shall be a delightful land," says the Lord of hosts (Malachi 3:8-12).

Another one of the words that the enemy has done his best to corrupt so that we cannot use it is *tithing*. Like the other words he has directed his greatest powers of corruption toward, this word represents a truth that he knows will set us free from his yokes of bondage. I therefore will use that word as much as I can without apology.

Tithing is the biblical term for giving the firstfruits of our labors to the Lord. It was specifically directed to be ten percent. It was practiced by the patriarchs before the Law of Moses was given. Abraham gave Melchizedek a tenth of the spoil he won in his battle with the kings, and Jacob also promised to give the Lord a tenth of all that the Lord gave to him. (See Genesis 14:20 and Genesis 28:22). Because we in the New Testament are called to the Melchizedek priesthood, tithing is especially important to us under the New Covenant. There were other offerings that one could make to the Lord, but this one was required.

Like most Christians, I have heard considerable teachings about tithing, both for and against. There are good arguments for and against it being a part of our New Covenant disciplines. Make no mistake about it, however; this is a crucial truth for our times. God still honors it just as He promised in Malachi.

Tithing is not necessarily trying to live by the law, and it is not legalism, though it can be. There are people who pray legalistically, but does that mean that we should stop praying? I know people who witness, read their Bibles, and even worship under the compulsion of a religious spirit, but does that mean we should quit doing those things? Of course not. We may examine ourselves to be sure that we are doing them in the right spirit, but we must continue doing the fundamental disciplines of the faith. Giving the firstfruits to the Lord is one of those disciplines.

Giving the firstfruits of our income to the Lord in the right spirit is an act of faith. "And without faith it is impossible to please Him, for he who comes to God must believe that He is, and that He is a rewarder of those who seek Him" (Heb. 11:6). The Lord requires faith before He will release His power toward us, and giving our firstfruits to Him is an act of faith by which we are declaring that we trust Him as the Source of our provision.

The word of our testimony is one of the factors by which we overcome the world (see Rev. 12:11). I have the testimony that the only times I have suffered financially since becoming a Christian were when I neglected to tithe. This was usually done out of carelessness because I have always believed in tithing. Every time I have suffered financial trouble and gone back to check my records, I found that my troubles began when I became careless in this one thing. When I repented of my carelessness and started giving the firstfruits of my income to the Lord again, the windows of Heaven always quickly opened, just as He promised.

When I became a successful businessman, I was giving large donations to churches and ministries. I was giving so much that I started to assume that I was giving at least ten percent and quit keeping up with it. At the very peak of my success, my business went into a tailspin and collapsed. Later, I felt compelled to go back and check my tithing record, and I found that my troubles began almost immediately when I started falling short in giving the first ten percent to the Lord.

We tithe in the ministry. MorningStar Publications does not take tithes and offerings from our churches, but rather gives a tithe to the Church. Our churches tithe to ministries. Just as in my personal life, we have learned to examine our records whenever we start to have financial problems, and usually we have found that we had been careless in tithing in at least one area of the ministry.

Over the years, I have heard innumerable testimonies of dramatic turnarounds for people who committed themselves to tithing. When I taught this in our local church, I almost immediately started hearing testimonies of how financial difficulties quickly began to change for people after they became obedient in this area. Without exception, the ones I have met who have chronic financial problems are also the ones who do not give their firstfruits faithfully to the Lord.

This does not mean that if you tithe this week, all your problems will be over next week. However, most people do almost immediately see the Lord begin to intervene and turn things around for them. I have witnessed many financial miracles, but sometimes the Lord intervenes by revealing other related strongholds that are hindering us. Regardless of how He does it, the end result of good biblical stewardship will be financial independence.

Good Intentions Are Not Obedience

I have watched quite a few people sink financially who did believe in tithing. Like I once foolishly did, they often said they were going to set aside their tithes until the Lord directed where to give them. This may sound noble, but if the money is still in our account, we have not given it. The Lord has already told us in His Word where to put it—in His storehouse, which is the Church. Even if you do not agree with where your church leaders spend it, if you are a part of a local body, then that is where your tithe should go.

I have heard others say that they do not tithe because everything they have is the Lord's. This is another tragic delusion. If everything they had was truly the Lord's, they certainly would be obeying His command to give the firstfruits. God does not need our money. The whole world is His. This is for us, not Him. Our excuses are only hurting us.

Since the Church is the storehouse of God, does that mean our congregations should tithe? Yes. First, it is a privilege, not a punishment. The Lord wants all of His people to be vessels through which His provision can flow to meet the needs He wants to meet. If we do not give, we cut off this flow. If you want proof that God honors the tithing principle with churches and ministries as well as with individuals, check the ones that are always struggling and those that always seem to have an abundance.

When it was prophesied in the Book of Acts that a famine was going to come upon the whole earth, the churches did not begin to hoard; they took up an offering and gave! (See Acts 11:28-30.) When we give, we are putting our treasures in Heaven and our trust in God. If you believe that economic catastrophe is coming, the only wise place for you to invest is in the Kingdom that cannot be shaken. You may think that you cannot afford to tithe, but you cannot afford not to. Most of us do not really need more income; we just need to have the devourer rebuked. But the Lord promises to do more than that; He promises that we will be so blessed that we will not have room enough to hold it all. That is the "abundance for every good deed" that we all are supposed to be walking in (2 Cor. 9:8c).

Are you that blessed? If not, then bring the "whole tithe" into the storehouse. That means the before-taxes tithe. If we really believe the Word of God, why would we not want to bring the whole tithe, and even much more? He promises a blessing that is so great that we cannot even contain it anyway.

In ancient Israel the tithe was actually the way that a family boasted in the Lord. When they brought their tithe to the storehouse, they were saying with it, "Look how much the Lord blessed me this year!" It is an act of faith and a way that we honor the goodness of the Lord in our life.

The following are a few other biblical promises that the Lord has given in relation to this discipline. Knowing these, and living by them, can turn your whole financial life around. They are God's Word, and He cannot lie.

Give, and it will be given to you. They will pour into your lap a measure—pressed down, shaken together, and running over. For by your standard of measure it will be measured to you in return (Luke 6:38).

He who gives to the poor will never want, but he who shuts his eyes will have many curses (Proverbs 28:27).

There is one who scatters, and yet increases all the more, and there is one who withholds what is justly due, and yet it results only in want.

The generous man will be prosperous, and he who waters will himself be watered (Proverbs 11:24-25).

Now this I say, he who sows sparingly will also reap sparingly, and he who sows bountifully will also reap bountifully. Each one must do just as he has purposed in his heart, not grudgingly or under compulsion, for God loves a cheerful giver.

And God is able to make all grace abound to you, so that always having all sufficiency in everything, you may have an abundance for every good deed (2 Corinthians 9:6-8).

PART IV

SPIRITUAL AUTHORITY

CHAPTER 18

TRUTH OR CONSEQUENCES

As already discussed, the Lord is going to judge the earth, and He is going to start with His own house. Judgments are not always condemnation, but they are the last call to repentance before the condemnation comes. It does not matter how much we attend church or how much truth we know. We will be judged by our deeds and by how we have lived. According to the Scriptures, to know the truth and not live it will only bring a more severe judgment.

Paul warned us to "behold then the kindness and severity of God" (Rom. 11:22a). Many are deceived because they only see the kindness of God without also seeing His severity. Others are deceived because they only behold His severity but do not understand His kindness. To know the truth, we must see both His kindness and His severity together.

Many presume that because we are now in the age of grace we can go on willfully sinning and God will overlook it. That is a most tragic delusion. We are in the age of grace *and truth* (see John 1:17). Our God is a God of His Word. Our salvation depends on the fact that He keeps His Word. His people, who are called to be like Him, also will be a people who keep their word. Our yes is supposed to mean yes, and our no is supposed to mean no, without compromise.

To break our word to man is bad, but to break it with God could be the greatest human folly. Ananias and Sapphira bore the consequences of this, which Peter called lying to the Holy Spirit. They wanted to be identified with the people who were giving everything, while they "kept back some of the price"

(Acts 5:2a). We would be much better off to never commit ourselves to being a bond servant of Christ than to have made such a commitment and hold back part of the price.

It is fundamental to the purpose of the Church that we become a people of our word. As we addressed before, the bridge that every relationship is built upon is trust. Without trust you can have forgiveness, and even love, but there can be no genuine relationship. The strength of the trust will determine the strength of every relationship. For the Church to be the bridge-builder that helps restore the relationship between God and man, we must be trustworthy.

The spirit of poverty gained major inroads into the Church when some public ministries were caught in lies, unfaithfulness, or misuse of the donations that were being given to them. Overreacting to this, many people stopped giving, which has caused serious repercussions in their lives. Many began to break their pledges to churches or ministries. Even ministries that were functioning by the highest standards of integrity were hurt. But the people who broke their pledges were hurt even more. To break a pledge is a serious matter, and the Scriptures make it clear that there are repercussions to doing so. Many are now suffering them.

Authority and Responsibility

Because it is obvious that economics will be one of the major tests that all will be facing at the end of the age, it is imperative that if we are going to be a light in the darkness, we must live by much higher standards of integrity in financial matters.

The Scriptures exhort us, "If we judged ourselves rightly, we should not be judged" (1 Cor. 11:31). If we will examine ourselves, praying for the Lord to send His Holy Spirit to convict us of any evil way and embracing correction as a sign of God's favor, we will not have to endure the worse judgment when it comes.

To serve the Lord's own household and to be stewards of His resources is a most serious matter. If we are called to do this, we must live by the very highest standards of integrity. We must understand the great responsibility we have been given and treat it with the seriousness that it deserves. It is not just the money that makes it serious; it is the integrity of His household.

Before the end, when nothing else on this earth is stable or trustworthy, the world will look at the Church and see a people who can be utterly trusted, whose word is their bond. They will start to trust God when they see that His people are trustworthy. The strength of our witness will be determined first by how much we trust God's Word and then by how much our word can be trusted. If we really believe God's Word, we will become like Him, and *our* words will be true as well.

We must address these serious issues because we are coming to the most serious of times. There has never been a more serious business than our relationship with God. The judgment that will ultimately come upon the whole world is basically the result of the world's treating Him so frivolously. Can we, who should know better than anyone, do that and expect to get away with it?

The God who loved us so much that He gave His only Son is not so harsh as to condemn us for petty mistakes. He knows the difficulties and pressures that we are subject to in this world. But although He knows that we will all stumble at times, the Scriptures are clear that presuming upon His grace and holding back when we have committed to give all will ultimately result in tragedy. It is not enough to know His Word—we also must keep it.

When Fear Is Freedom

When the storms come, it will be too late to try to build your house on the Rock. Let us now take heed to the Word of God that exhorts us to obedience:

Behold, the eye of the Lord is on those who fear Him,
on those who hope for His lovingkindness, To deliver
their soul from death and to keep them alive in famine
(Psalm 33:18-19).

This poor man cried, and the Lord heard him and
saved him out of all his troubles. The angel of the Lord
encamps around those who fear Him, and rescues them.
O taste and see that the Lord is good; how blessed is the
man who takes refuge in Him! O fear the Lord, you
His saints; for to those who fear Him there is no want.
The young lions do lack and suffer hunger; but they
who seek the Lord shall not be in want of any good
thing (Psalm 34:6-10).

The greatest promises in the Scriptures are to those who fear the Lord. Those who properly fear the Lord do not have to fear anything else on this earth. Those who know Him, but who do not properly fear Him, have fallen to some of the greatest human tragedies. John was intimate with the Lord, while Judas was merely familiar with Him. There can be a great difference. A familiarity with God that breeds presumption is possibly the most terrible delusion. However, familiarity that breeds an increasing revelation of just how awesome He is will foster obedience.

To make a commitment to be a bond servant of Christ and then go on living for ourselves would be a tragic folly. To know the truth and commit ourselves to live by it, and then not do it, is the very definition of a hypocrite—a person for whom the Lord reserved His most vehement condemnation.

Even though we were bought with a price by the blood of the Lamb, He will not force us to serve Him. Obedience is required, but we must choose to obey because there is liberty not to obey. We may go years without suffering the consequences of our sins, but we will eventually reap what we sow. As King Solomon stated in Ecclesiastes 8:11, "Because the sentence against an evil deed is not executed quickly, therefore the hearts of the sons of men among them are given fully to do evil."

That God does not swiftly judge our sin is often interpreted to mean that it does not matter to Him, but this is the delusion of a darkened heart. That He does not quickly discipline us is in itself a judgment that leads to further hardening.

We may think then, that if the Lord would just execute His judgments quicker, we would not be prone to be so evil. That is true, but that also would inhibit the freedom that He gives us so that we can prove our devotion to Him. Who would ever disobey if they knew that swift judgment was coming? The same freedom that He gives us to disobey is the freedom that He gives us to obey and therefore prove our devotion. So those who love the truth will live by the truth—even when it is not convenient or seemingly expedient.

CHAPTER 19

SPIRITUAL AUTHORITY

We have covered how the Lord gave two different mandates of authority on the earth—the authority for civil government and the spiritual authority of the Church—and how an important difference in these authorities is the weaponry that they have been given to accomplish their mandates. This is important because the Church is going to move into the realm of authority that displaces principalities and powers over entire regions and nations. We must understand this issue in order for us to grow in and exercise the spiritual authority we have been given and to avoid some devastating traps that the enemy will try to push us into.

The mandate to the civil governments to keep order on this earth requires "carnal," or physical, weapons. The spiritual authority given to the Church is exercised by spiritual weapons—truth, love, peace, patience, etc. We also have been given spiritual authority to deal with spiritual problems, such as casting out demons, healing the sick, and doing miracles that are not subject to natural laws. If the Church falls to trying to use carnal or civil authority to accomplish our mandate, we forfeit the more powerful spiritual authority. That is why we must learn to distinguish between the two and keep them separate.

Nature of the Two Authorities

Even though the civil authority is given by God, no human authority is going to be perfect, and in some cases it even may be evil. All authority in both Heaven and earth have been given to Christ, but He has not yet *directly* taken His authority over the earth, nor given it to His people. This is because He has not yet set up His Kingdom on the earth. However, He has *indirectly* taken His authority over the earth because there is no earthly ruler, or spiritual principality, that gains dominion without His permission—even the most wicked.

The Lord sometimes allows the wicked to rule as judgment over regions and nations. We must remember that when Paul wrote Romans chapter 13 concerning our need to submit to civil governments, he wrote it during the reign of Nero, one of the most wicked of the Caesars, the one who instituted persecution against Christians, and even the one who was to take Paul's own life.

At the time Paul wrote this chapter, there was no civil government on the earth that was favorable to the Church. The opposition of civil governments to the Church also was a part of God's plan to keep these two separate. Even so, the Christians were not to rebel against civil authority; rather, they were commanded to give those authorities due respect.

One reason the Lord wanted to keep the Church and the civil governments apart was because the authority given to the Church is *much greater* than that entrusted to civil authorities. Civil authority is temporary—ours is eternal. Civil authority can change laws, but they cannot change men. The Lord does not want His Church to seek influence by carnal means, but by the power of the truth and the anointing of the Holy Spirit, which are much more powerful.

This does not mean that Christians should not try to influence laws and the seating of righteous men and women in positions of civil authority. However, we must do this as citizens of our nations, not as representing the Church.

To model our relationship to the civil government after biblical Israel is not appropriate because, besides the general mandate that God gave to civil authority, He has not made a covenant to any other nation like He did with Israel. Biblical

Israel was intended to be a type of God's relationship to His Church, not the nations. However, even in biblical Israel the realms of priestly and civil authority were distinct and separate.

The wisdom of the American founding fathers to keep civil authority and the Church separate was certainly wisdom from above. It is also true that this was not done to keep the Church from influencing government as many secularists today assert. It was done more to keep the government out of the Church's business. Even so, America is not the Kingdom of God. This nation and many others have certainly enjoyed the blessings and favor of God in many ways. Many righteous men may have dedicated our land to the Lord, but every covenant that God honors is one that He initiates, and there is no evidence that God has made any kind of special covenant with any nation in history except Israel. His special covenant during this age is with His holy nation, the Church.

This still may not be clear to some, so we will look at it a little deeper. It is important for us to understand this matter if we are going to walk in the authority that we have been given as the Church and prepare the way for the coming of the Kingdom by preaching it. It is the "Gospel of the Kingdom" that must be preached in all nations before the end comes, and to date this has hardly been preached at all because of this and a few other points of confusion.

A Law in Our Heart

Margaret Thatcher, the former Prime Minister of Great Britain, once observed, "The veneer of civilization is very thin." She made this remark after watching men behave like animals when the power went out in New York City. When the lights and alarms go off and the police are not immediately present, the true nature of men is often revealed. This "thin veneer" is the realm of civil authority. We need the lights, the alarms, and the police, and we should thank God for the civil authorities that provide them, limited as they are.

Spiritual authority is not found in the streetlights that keep men in check. Spiritual authority is the light in men's hearts that compels them to do right even when the lights go off and the police are not around. It is this light that keeps young men or women morally pure or, after they have made a mistake, shows them such love and respect for life that they would not even consider an abortion.

Prepared to Rule

Even though in this age there must be a separation between spiritual and civil authority, the Church is being prepared to rule with all authority in the age to come. King David is one of the great biblical examples of a man who walked in true spiritual authority while being a civil authority. He was a prophet. He led worship, and he was the king. He is also one of the great types of Christ, who will one day exercise both spiritual and civil authority over the earth with His Church.

One of the great trials that David had to pass, and one that in some ways was the greatest demonstration of his character, was when he was unjustly persecuted by the civil authority of his nation. Even after he had been already anointed to take Saul's place, David would not lift his own hand "against the Lord's anointed" (see First Samuel chapters 24 and 26). His heart was smitten for even cutting off the edge of Saul's robe. That revealed the deep respect that he had for all authority, and it was a primary reason he was trusted with unprecedented authority in his time. This is also the test that those who are going to reign with Christ must pass. This is also one reason why churches that are persecuted by civil governments tend to thrive spiritually.

When David was persecuted by Saul, he was cast upon the Lord with even greater dependence. The limit of the authority that we can be trusted with is basically dependent on the level of our dependence on the Lord. The great respect for every authority that David demonstrated was rooted in his trust in the Lord as the ultimate authority. This respect for authority enabled David to build a house and a throne that would last forever—as Jesus Himself is "seated upon the throne of David" (see Isa. 9:7). One who walks in true spiritual authority will not undermine any authority that has been established by God, and he would never take a position by his own hand. The sons of God are those who are led by the Spirit of God, and they will patiently wait for the Spirit to make the way for them. If we aspire to sit with Jesus on His throne, it can be accomplished only in this way.

The Lord is presently allowing His Church, which is called to rule with Him, to be subject to all the trials that David went through to prepare him for the throne because we too are being prepared for authority. As we also discussed, satan tempted Jesus to take His authority over the world prematurely, before going to the cross, which was to die at the hands of the civil authority. This is also satan's primary temptation for the Church. He knows that if he can get the Church to try to seize temporal authority before we have been through the trials that are meant to prepare us for this rule, we will end up ruling according to the ways of this present evil age, and by that actually do the devil's bidding.

Thus far the devil has been quite successful with this temptation. We can follow a trail of spiritual tragedies throughout history that are the result of the Church trying to accomplish her goals by using civil authority, or carnal weapons.

The Intercessor

There have been a number of Christians in history who were called to take a position in the realm of civil authority, and they accomplished great things by this. William Wilberforce, a politician in the House of Commons of Great Britain who succeeded in abolishing slavery in the British Empire, was one. But even this great accomplishment was still just a superficial victory in the realm of the "thin veneer," as exploitation through colonialism would continue for centuries, and economic oppression in many forms continues today. Even so, in the realm of human history, this was a huge step in the right direction for humankind.

Even though this entire age is mostly for the preparation of those who are called to be joint heirs with Christ and therefore to rule with Him, the Lord obviously cares that conditions on this earth be as good for people as possible. He loves all people, and He often intervenes to make conditions better for them—even those who do not know Him. However, He will not intervene without an intercessor. This is because, as we read in Psalm 115:16, "The heavens are the heavens of the Lord, but the earth He has given to the sons of men." The Lord delegated authority over the earth to men, and He will not intervene until we ask Him to.

This is why we must pray even though He already knows our needs. This is also why one intercessor can accomplish more than any congress. An intercessor can move the hand of God. Many who have the greatest authority in Heaven have little or no authority on the earth. Likewise, many who have great authority on earth may have little or no authority in Heaven. Which would you rather have?

The Stumbling Block

There is considerable confusion over this issue of how much temporal authority the Church should be exercising when we fail to distinguish the Scriptures that are for the age to come and try to apply them in this age. In this age, whenever the Church has left her true realm of authority to impose her will in the realm of civil authority, she has fallen to tragic, and often even diabolical, excesses. The key here is that these mistakes have taken place *whenever she has left her realm of authority to take temporal authority*. The Church has been called to be the "light of the world" (Matt. 5:14), to be a force for good, upholding God's standard of righteousness. The Church should be a conscience to the civil governments. The trap she often has fallen into has been to try and accomplish this through the civil authority not within her realm.

The Church will never be the light because she excels at the ballot box. When the people came to make Jesus king, He fled to the mountains. If the people make you king, who is going to rule? The fact that the people wanted to make Jesus king seems very noble, but it was actually one of the most presumptuous acts in Scripture. The people thought they could make God King! He was *born* King! The source of His authority never came from the people but from the Father above. Likewise, the Church's authority also comes from above. Every time she has sought authority from any other source, the consequences have been devastating.

Our Sphere of Authority

Paul explained to the Corinthians that he had been given a sphere of authority that he would not presume to go beyond. (See Second Corinthians 10:13-14). Those who understand spiritual authority will be very conscious of the sphere that has been appointed to them, for to go beyond it invites disaster. Just as a police officer from Atlanta has no authority in Mexico City—and would probably get hurt if he tried to use it—we do not have spiritual authority beyond the realm God has given to us.

The sphere of authority given to civil governments is different from that which is given to the Church. Whenever the Church has tried to accomplish her means by using the sphere appointed to the civil authorities, or whenever the civil authorities have tried to accomplish their ends by using the Church, there have been tyranny and oppression. The sphere of authority for civil governments is the realm of law, and the sphere of authority appointed to the Church is the realm of the spirit. The boundaries of our sphere of authority can be easily recognized as the "fruit of the Spirit."

As Jesus said, "But if I cast out demons by the Spirit of God, then the kingdom of God has come upon you" (Matt. 12:28). If we try to cast out these demons by any other spirit, we can be sure that the kingdom of darkness will come upon us and that we will be left wounded and naked, at best. The Lord Jesus never once tried to use the civil authorities to accomplish the Father's purposes—neither did the apostles or other leaders of the early Church. They understood that to do so would have been to come down from the high position that they were given. They let Caesar have that which was his, and they gave themselves to the things that were God's.

Prophetic Authority

The Church is called to speak prophetically to governments. It is that prophetic anointing that is a foundation of our mandated influence with governments. Prophetic authority is the moral authority and power to speak the truth, clearly articulated and established by a righteous and just life. Moral authority is built on the foundation of morality. Spiritual authority is built on the foundation of influence with God that is based on us abiding in His King, Jesus.

The Church must not continue to expect the government to do our job. Not only abortion, but also infanticide was a major problem in the first century Roman Empire, but writers of the New Testament did not even mention these issues. Their silence was not because they were ignorant of the problem, and it was certainly not because they thought such practices were acceptable. They were not going to waste their time flailing at the branches. They chose instead to put their ax to the root of the tree—sin and estrangement from God. When men are reconciled to God, abortion and every other evil will be dealt with.

Jonathan Edwards, who was used to ignite the first Great Awakening, preached one anointed sermon, *Sinners in the Hands of an Angry God*, that accomplished far more for the morality of this country than all the laws that were on the books at that time, and maybe since. All of the morality laws combined could not accomplish what the Great Awakenings did. Protests and demonstrations can have a place in a democratic society, but the Church has a much higher calling. The Church's authority is not found in the power to demonstrate, but in demonstrations of power.

Leo Tolstoy, possibly the greatest novelist who ever lived, once said, "Prophecy is like a spark lit in a dry wood. Once it ignites, it will burn and burn until all of the wood, hay, and stubble has been consumed." The history of slavery was given to us as an example. This had been an accepted institution until it was clearly articulated under the anointing that it was wrong. The truth spread like a fire lit in dry wood. Within just a few years the world was aflame with this truth, and slavery, at least in its most blatant forms, was quickly abolished throughout the earth.

One of the great sparks thrown on the dry wood of slavery was Harriet Beecher Stowe's novel, *Uncle Tom's Cabin*. This novel so clearly revealed the evils of slavery that it became impossible for that evil to abide any longer in the civilized world. When Abraham Lincoln met Mrs. Stowe during the middle of the Civil War, he exclaimed, "So you're the little lady that started this great war!" She was.

One of the greatest demonstrations of prophetic power in the Church Age came through Martin Luther. Luther was just a monk, but when he nailed his *Ninety-Five Theses* to the door of a tiny church in the obscure little town of Wittenburg, Germany, the whole world changed! Not only did he change the world in his own generation, but he also set in motion changes that have profoundly impacted every generation since. There has never been an emperor, king, or even a dynasty that has so influenced the world as this one monk.

Martin Luther is a profound testimony that even the most humble man armed with God's truth, refusing to compromise his convictions, is more powerful than armies. The power of Luther's prophetic stand is unequaled since the first century when Paul and Silas caused the most powerful rulers of the most powerful empire to tremble in fear, declaring in dismay, "These who have turned the world upside down have come here too" (Acts 17:6c NKJV).

Later in Martin Luther's life, he drifted more and more toward trying to accomplish spiritual goals through the civil authorities. It was during this time that some very diabolical teachings came from him, which some consider to be the seeds that became the Holocaust.

It is my opinion that Martin Luther King, Jr. would have accomplished even more had he not started to rely so much on civil government and civil authority to accomplish his vision of a just America that was free of bigotry. I concur that the laws he sought to have passed needed to be passed, but at the time when his moral authority was at its zenith, it seemed to get diluted by an over-attention to what the civil authorities were doing. Even so, Martin Luther King, Jr. is one of the great prophetic voices yet produced by this nation in the realm of moral authority. The tragedy is that the Church did not arise with this message two centuries before.

Mahatma Gandhi was said to have had a genuine conversion experience. However, he refused to be baptized when he saw how the event was being made a spectacle for the self-promotion of the evangelist. Nevertheless, he clung to many of the teachings of Jesus. He was especially captured by the Lord's admonition to overcome evil with good and to turn the other cheek when assaulted. He determined to live by this code. By focusing on just this one small part of the Lord's message, Gandhi was able to bring the most powerful empire of his day to its knees, and it gave birth to a nation.

Gandhi refused to accept a political office, even though he easily could have been India's first prime minister. He simply stated that he had found a power greater than any power that a political office could ever give to him. He was right. This is also true of the Church. However, we do need to discern and proclaim the crucial issues of the times and be the moral and spiritual authority that we have been called to be.

If Gandhi could so change his world by living such a small fraction of the gospel, what kind of power would the Church have if we all started to live by the whole gospel? If we really understood the power we have been entrusted with, no pastor of a flock would ever care to stoop so low as to just become a president, much less a senator or congressman, unless it was a yoke placed upon him by the Lord. This is not intended to demean any public servants, but what we have been called to is so much higher.

When the government undertakes the great moral issues and dictates laws to address them, this is better than nothing. Those who champion such legislation are doing the best they can, but they should not have to do these things. It is because the Church has been the silent prophet, like Jonah running from our calling and sleeping through the great storms of our times so that the heathen have to wake us up!

The Deadly Trap

Even so, one of the greatest traps that is set for one with spiritual authority is the temptation to use his influence in the realm of secular, civil authority. It is possible to use our influence to do good there, but good can be the worst enemy of best. This is the same seduction that began in the Garden—the appeal to the positive aspects of the Tree of the Knowledge of Good and Evil. If we eat from that tree, we may be able to do a lot of "good," but in the end we, and the good that we have done, will perish.

Some have been called to serve in political positions, but this is not the "high calling." It is in fact a low calling as compared to a position of spiritual authority. When we have truly come to see who Jesus is and who He has called us to be, we will have the constitution of Elijah, who could stand before the king and declare, "As the Lord, the God of Israel lives, *before whom I stand*" (1 Kings 17:1b). By this Elijah was saying to Ahab, "I am not standing here before you. You're just a king, a mere man. I don't live my life before men; I live my life before the living God." When the Church likewise learns to live before God rather than men, she will be entrusted with similar power.

Why should we even want to see a king, or president, or any other man unless we have a divine mandate? We can go directly to the King of the universe anytime we choose. Why should we want to waste time trying to get legislation passed through the bizarre chaos of our legislatures? If we have seen the King in His glory, how can we even be impressed with presidents or kings from this earthly realm?

Discerning Authority

A main source of confusion comes from our not understanding our purpose and how we relate to others to accomplish it. This confusion is a basic reason for the discord and lack of peace in the world. One of the ways that we can come to understand who we are and how we relate to others is by understanding the existing authority and our place in relation to it. This begins with our understanding the two main general mandates of authority given by God on the earth and where we fit in relation to them.

There are ways that Christians can function under both mandates of authority. For example, a Christian who is in the military, or who is a police officer, must function under the mandate of civil authority while on duty. When on duty as a soldier, or in law enforcement, the Christians must use the sword, or weapons they have been given, to do their job. However, when doing their duty as a Christian, these weapons have no place; rather truth, love, peace, etc. are their weapons for establishing or maintaining the authority of the Kingdom.

Summary

To address this subject adequately would require a book in itself, and we are dealing with it only superficially here because it is essential if we are going to understand how to be free of the illegal strongholds of the enemy and how to establish realms of authority in which the Kingdom is established.

God is the ultimate authority. His mandates are supreme. If a government, spiritual or civil, exceeds its mandate, it is His place to correct it. He may choose to do this through another government as He used the nations around Israel to discipline Israel when she fell into apostasy. As King David rightly discerned when asked to choose his discipline, it is much better to suffer natural disasters, or even famines and plagues, than to fall into the hands of other men. War is the worst judgment of all on a nation. There is nothing more devastating than having an army sweep through a nation. In modern times the devastation from armies has grown exponentially, probably coinciding with the degree of rebellion against God that has come on the earth.

As the Lord and the prophets and apostles all warned, lawlessness is one of the ultimate evils at the end of the age. Lawlessness is basically a disregard for authority. This begins with a disregard for God's authority. Without God as the moral force behind an authority, no one can rule without increasing the shackles of fear and control. Freedom and democracy cannot last without the fear of God as the moral force underpinning it. As the lawlessness of godlessness increases in the world, places where realms of Kingdom authority are established will become the only areas where true peace can be found.

It is also a major purpose of the Church to underpin civil authorities with our moral authority. This can be done only by the power of truth—that because of our respect for the Lord and His authority, we show and impart a respect for all legitimate authority. Whether it is for a teacher, a manager at work, a police officer, mayor, or the president, we always should give authority the dignity and respect they deserve being "servants of God." Doing this is a primary way that we find peace ourselves and are delivered from fear.

CHAPTER 20

THE BATTLE FOR LIFE

Now that we have at least superficially covered the two mandates of authority, let's look at how they apply to one of the great spiritual battles being waged on the earth today—the battle over abortion. The side that wins this conflict will have taken one of the truly important battles of our time, and it is right for the Church to be fully engaged in this battle. We cannot rightly address spiritual warfare without dealing with this issue. However, if we "win" in the wrong spirit, or by going beyond our realm of authority, the consequences can be a major defeat for the cause of the gospel as well as for the cause of life.

If there is a greater demonstration of the depravity of humanity than that revealed through the institution of slavery, it is abortion. Regardless of how many laws are passed legalizing this great evil, the laws of nature already have been passed. Nature itself reveals that abortion is probably the lowest level to which depraved humanity has yet fallen. Even the beasts will instinctively sacrifice their own lives to protect their young, but we have proven willing to sacrifice our children for the most petty reasons of convenience and selfishness. While we bemoan the whales and spotted owls, we massacre our own young, helpless and innocent, by the most cruel, torturous means. This is a tragedy of epic proportions. How the Church confronts this great evil can potentially result in one of her greatest victories, or greatest defeats, with even more lives being lost for eternity.

Revival is usually God's final attempt to show mercy instead of judgment. The first Great Awakening came before the Revolutionary War. It was an opportunity to avoid this war, which was far more devastating to both nations than mere history books can convey. The last Great Awakening this country experienced came just before the Civil War. That awakening was given by the Lord as a way to prevent the Civil War. Had that revival continued on track, it would almost certainly have abolished slavery without the worst bloodshed this nation has ever experienced. When the revival was turned from its course by the political zealots of that time, the abolitionists, the fate of the nation was sealed and bloodshed was inevitable.

The abolitionists were some of the most courageous, truth-loving, and self-sacrificing people in the country. Most were Christians, and they were true patriots. However, they also were driven to extremes and blown about by the winds of impatience. There is no question that their goals were noble, but their means were the way of destruction. They did not comprehend the nature of the wisdom from above as described by James:

> *Who among you is wise and understanding? Let him show by his good behavior his deeds in the **gentleness of wisdom** (James 3:13).*

> *But the wisdom from above is first pure, then peaceable, gentle, reasonable, full of mercy and good fruits, unwavering, without hypocrisy.*

> *And the seed whose fruit is righteousness is sown in peace by those who make peace (James 3:17-18).*

The abolitionists had the right moral goals, but they tried to achieve them by the wrong means. Whenever we do this, we will depart from the wisdom that is from above and then display a nature that is quite the opposite of the Savior's. Zealotry is the wisdom of Judas Iscariot who thought he could force the Lord to take His authority and declare His Kingdom. Such political manipulation comes from the spirit of the evil one, regardless of the motives of those who use it. The Kingdom of God will not come that way.

One of the ultimate choices now facing the Church is to decide whether we want our political goals to be accomplished or the Kingdom of God to come. John Brown (of the famous "John Brown's Raid") was considered by many, including himself, to be a prophet. There are many with his same spirit moving throughout the Church today. They pressure others to act prematurely and to use carnal weapons to assault spiritual fortresses. They exert this pressure with the argument that so many babies are being lost each day because of abortion. This is a truth that should weigh on us, but these means will not result in any less being aborted, and these ways ultimately can lead to more bloodshed than we can now comprehend.

Whenever spiritual men have tried to establish authority or influence in the civil realm, without being called to such a position, they almost always have become extremists who inevitably damage their own cause. Those who fall into this trap are usually the most zealous for the Lord and His purposes, but zeal without humble submission to the Holy Spirit will become a most useful tool of the enemy. If he finds someone he cannot stop, he will then try to push them too far. Unfortunately, this is often very easy with the zealot. As soon as the enemy is able to push people into a realm they have not been called to, beyond the grace that they have been given, he can use them as effective weapons in his hand.

We must stop expecting the government to do our job. The Lord hears prayer, and He has more power than the President, Congress, and Supreme Court combined! The issue of abortion still has the power to divide this country like it has not been divided since the Civil War. Prayer can bring a revival that can prevent this. The revival, if it is not sidetracked by zealots, will have the power to abolish abortion and replace it with the greatest esteem for life that civilization has yet realized.

God's History Book

The Book of Life is God's history book. It is very different from human histories. In God's history, many of the great heroes are men and women whom the world has not known. These praying saints had authority with God and accomplished much more for the human race and the human condition than any president, prime minister, or king ever did. Praying saints have freed many more slaves than Wilberforce and Lincoln combined—and they brought about a freedom that was much greater! This is why the Lord said in Luke 10:18-20,

> *...I was watching satan fall from heaven like lightning.*
>
> *Behold, I have given you authority to tread on serpents and scorpions, and over all the power of the enemy, and nothing will injure you.*
>
> *Nevertheless do not rejoice in this, that the spirits are subject to you, but rejoice that your names are recorded in heaven.*

It is a wonderful thing to have been given authority over all of the power of the enemy, but it is an even greater thing to be found in God's history book—the Book of Life. The way that we make His history book is to live by the authority of His Book, without succumbing to the temptation to live by human authority. What good will it do us to be known by all men, but not be known by God? It is much better to have influence with God than to have influence with all men. Jesus warned us,

> *Not every one who says to Me, "Lord, Lord," will enter the kingdom of heaven; but he who does the will of My Father who is in heaven will enter.*
>
> *Many will say to Me on that day, "Lord, Lord, did we not prophesy in Your name, and in Your name cast out demons, and in Your name perform many miracles?"*
>
> *And then I will declare to them, "I never knew you; depart from Me, you who practice lawlessness"* (Matthew 7:21-23).

In nature the preservation of life is the most basic and powerful motivation. Because of this, except for only a few of the most base species, *family* is a primary drive of life. It was no accident that the very first test of Solomon's wisdom was concerning the issue of a mother's sanctity for life. The very first test of wisdom for any government is its commitment to the sanctity of life.

Just because something is legal does not make it right. As stated, there are fundamental laws that prevail in nature that reveal a great deal more wisdom than politicians have been able to display. True morality is not measured simply by legal compliance; true morality is doing what is right. Yes, a civilization that is not based on law will be open to despotism and tyranny. Yet a civilization that cannot rise above the law to live not just by what is legal, but also by what is moral, has lost its humanity and its potential for true greatness. Lawlessness always results in tyranny. The inability to rise above law also results in tyranny. The preservation of life is fundamental to both nature and morality.

Parents who sacrifice their offspring would have difficulty finding acceptance even in the animal kingdom. There will be no peace of mind or peace on earth until life is esteemed above selfish ambition or convenience. It is not only unnatural for a mother to destroy her child, born or unborn, but it also reveals a fundamental departure from civilization to embrace barbarism in its most base and inhuman form. Resolution of the abortion issue gives us the opportunity to provide the world with leadership in finding higher standards of morality, justice, and esteem for life. Failure to resolve it with courage and honor, not just with law, will certainly leave a major crack in our foundation, which ultimately leads to tyranny of the most frightening kind. To deprive one of his or her life is the ultimate offense against that person, and the battle over abortion may be the ultimate moral battle of our time.

As stated, there is no question that the Church should be involved in the battle for life, whether it deals with abortion, euthanasia, or other issues, such as those being raised in the field of biochemistry. The questions are, "Under what sphere of authority will we address them?" and "Will we compromise our given authority by trying to do the right thing in the wrong realm?"

The Foundation for Authority

Spiritual authority comes from the Holy Spirit, and He is the Spirit of Truth. He will endorse with His authority only those who are true, who live what they preach. Can we cast stones at the mother who aborts her child if we are sacrificing our living children at the altars of the petty gods of selfish ambition and personal success? Could even the greatest success of our enterprises be interpreted as anything but a terrible human failure if we lose the souls of our own children in the process?

Who can count the "successful" Christian business people, athletes, coaches, and even church leaders who have accomplished their goals, only to say that they would trade everything just to have their families back? The first condition that God said was not good was for man to be alone—and it is not good. Yet that is exactly where we will end up if we do not give our families the priority they deserve.

Spiritual Abortion

In 1989, I had an experience in which the presence of the Lord filled my hotel room. In this experience I was a witness to the anger of the Lord over abortion. To my surprise, His anger was directed at the Church and not at the heathen. He declared that if the Church had not aborted the *spiritual* seeds that He had planted in her—for missions, outreaches, and even the simple witness to our neighbors—then the heathen would not be living in such darkness and would not be aborting their *natural* seed. He said that the Church was aborting His spiritual seed for all the same reasons that the heathen were aborting their unborn—because of our selfishness. These "children" were expensive, and we did not think we could afford them or give them our time. He affirmed that judgment would come upon our country because of the evil of abortion, but that He was going to start with His own household first!

How many of those young women would not be needing abortions now if we had responded to the Holy Spirit when He impressed us to witness to them? It is time for us to quit flailing at the branches and put the ax to the root of the tree! Abortion is a great evil, but it is just one of the symptoms of the terrible disease of humanity, which is sin.

Abortion must be stopped, but it is now far beyond the government's ability to stop it. This does not excuse the government for not trying, but the only thing that can stop abortion in this country now is a revival on the level of another Great Awakening. As a believer I will give the majority of my attention to obedience, prayer, and seeking revival. In a revival atmosphere effective laws can be passed that will help fight against this evil, just as Finney's revivals helped to spark our government's actions against slavery. Without revival the same laws would be useless—the people would simply break the law on a scale that the government could do little about.

It is fundamental at this time for the Church to repent of her own sins, then realize the Source of her power if she is going to accomplish anything of significance regarding abortion or any other issue...

> *for the weapons of our warfare are not of the flesh, but divinely powerful for the destruction of fortresses.*
>
> *We are destroying speculations and every lofty thing raised up against the knowledge of God, and we are taking every thought captive to the obedience of Christ,*
>
> **and we are ready to punish all disobedience, whenever your obedience is complete** (2 Corinthians 10:4-6).

When our obedience is complete, we will have the authority to deal with "all disobedience"—not just with demonstrations, but with demonstrations of power that can accomplish far more.

Summary

Why have I belabored this issue so much concerning the differences between spiritual and civil authority? It is because the Church cannot accomplish her last-day mandate until this issue is clear. Otherwise she will be continually distracted from her ultimate calling by a multitude of lesser purposes. This is not to belittle the importance of any cause; it is to emphasize the only way that the Church can effectively confront them. If we spent the time, money, and other resources seeking the anointing that we spend seeking influence on the human level, the world would be a radically different and better place already. When we recognize the difference between authorities, there is no limit to the amount of light that would be shining into these times and the number of souls that can yet be saved.

CHAPTER 21

THE BATTLE FOR
MORAL AUTHORITY

If we believe the Bible is God's Word, we must understand that homosexuality is sin. So we must ask the question, "Should the Church tolerate sin?" Now that gets a little sticky. Most of us are still struggling with some problems that would have to fall under the sin category. "Outbursts of anger" and "strife" are listed right along with immorality, idolatry, and sorcery as works of the flesh in Galatians 5:19-21. If we tried to remove everyone from the Church who had a problem with anger, there would not be many people left.

However, the Lord did not call every sin in the Bible an "abomination" and "perversion" like He did homosexuality. The Lord named abominations only those sins that were especially corrupting and destructive. Homosexuality falls into that category. The Lord destroyed Sodom for this sin, and there is a point at which the Lord will judge a nation for the spread of this sin because of its corrupting influence.

Paul called homosexuality a sin "against nature" in Romans 1:26 (KJV), and he promised that those who practiced it would receive "in their own persons the due penalty of their error" (Rom. 1:27). AIDS is an obvious example of this penalty. Biblically we can see that most plagues have their origin in the spiritual realm, as the result of widespread sin. The characteristics of the plague usually reflect the sin that has released it. AIDS is a virus that causes the destruction of the immune system, or the body's defenses. Homosexuality and other forms of perversion are the cause of the release of AIDS, and those sins do destroy a society's defenses against evil in all forms.

God Loves Gays

So how should the Church respond to homosexuals? Love them! Love them because God does. He "desires all men to be saved and to come to the knowledge of the truth" (1 Tim. 2:4). God is love, and even His judgment is a result of His love—it is His last call to repentance that they might be saved. The Church will not have any true authority over this problem until she loves those with the problem.

Does this mean we should just open our churches, our schools, and our families to the influence of homosexuals? No. Homosexuality is a genuine threat to the very foundation of our social order. It also will become an increasingly blatant threat to our religious liberty, which is the greatest threat to their particular sin. Even so, we must remember that satan will not cast out satan. If our confrontation with this sin is not in the right spirit, then we are multiplying the power of the evil we are seeking to cast out. This may come as a shock, but the Church also must repent of her part in being a major cause of the release of homosexuality in society.

Homosexuality and Worship

The growing release of homosexuality in society is the result of an increasing departure from true worship in the Church. How could this be? Fundamentally, humankind was created to worship. If people are not devoted to the proper worship of the Creator, they will fall to worshiping the creation. As Paul explained in the first chapter of Romans, this is a primary cause of homosexuality.

Music and other forms of art were talents given to man so we could express our adoration for God. Using our spiritual gifts or natural talents in adoration for God is the highest form of fulfillment we can know on this earth. However, many of the most gifted and talented artists in history were homosexuals. Many of these fell to homosexuality because there was no outlet in the Church for their worship through the arts. Therefore, they would turn to worshiping the creation instead of the Creator. Homosexuals who are delivered from their sin and given a proper outlet for the gifts God has given them, will become some of the most pure worshipers of the Lord, and they will help to release true worship in the Church.

This is not to imply that the entire problem of homosexuality is the result of the Church being closed to certain forms of worship through the arts. The bulk of the depravity is the choice of men to worship the creature rather than the Creator. However, the Church is called to be the light of the world. If the world is falling into increasing darkness, we should not blame that fact on the government, or even society, but on the Church. The answers to all society's problems are spiritual, not political. When we seek to combat social and moral problems, we must share the truth that will set people free, not just condemn and alienate them.

Homo-sect-uality

There is a "spiritual homosexuality" that the Church must be delivered from if we are going to have spiritual authority over this sin. Spiritual homosexuality is having relations only with your own kind, which is sectarianism.

A root of homosexuality is the fear of rejection, which pushes one toward isolation and the compulsion to stay away from those who are different. Men and women represent the ultimate human differences, and almost everyone has to overcome the fear of rejection in order to cross the bridge to a relationship with the other sex. The same is true in the Church—it is the insecurity of much of the leadership that causes them to refrain from any kind of relationship with those who are different. This results in sectarianism, which is a subtle form of spiritual homosexuality.

An important key to the deliverance of those who are in the bondage of homosexuality is not to reject them, but to love and accept them—not their sin, but them. "Perfect love casts out fear" (1 John 4:18b), and it is fear that holds them in bondage.

One of the remarkable characteristics of the Lord's own ministry, which is to be the model for all true ministry, is that He was the friend of sinners. Not only did He feel comfortable around them, but even more amazingly they also felt comfortable around Him. Jesus did not condemn sinners, He changed them by loving them. This is not to imply that He did not challenge their sin; He did, but He did it with genuine love. This enabled Him to share the truth that would set them free, not just heap more burdens on them.

We must learn to treat sinners the way Jesus did, with open arms and the answers to their problems. The answer is not to alienate them further, but to reach out to them with genuine love and help. We must always remember that the majority of them are not like the extreme caricatures we have often made them into, just as most Christians are not the caricatures that unbelievers tend to see us as.

Can a Christian Be a Liberal?

For some, this is an even more sticky question than the issue of homosexuality. Can one be a Christian and be a political liberal? Many sincere Christians would be more prone to ask if one can be a true Christian and be a political conservative. There are many sincere Christians who are political liberals. Unfortunately, this is usually because they see more genuine caring for the poor and the oppressed among liberals than they do among conservative Christians. I heard one politician remark that when he sees Christians caring more for the needy than the liberals do, they will start listening to the Church more than the liberals. This is the mind-set of many people.

Winston Churchill once said, "If a man is not a liberal when he is twenty he has no heart. If he is not a conservative when he is forty he has no mind." Most Christians agree with liberals that we must take care of the needy and the oppressed, but they disagree with the premise that the government should, or even can, do it. Liberals would argue that this is true, but if it were left to Christians, even less would get done. They too have a case. Of course, there are many churches and ministries that are doing a great deal for the poor and the oppressed, but the majority of Christians do little or nothing.

There are some people who really do need charity and will need it their entire lives. As the Lord said, "You always have the poor with you" (Matt. 26:11a). It is not realistic that poverty will be eradicated before the Kingdom comes. We also must recognize that the poor are an opportunity for us to love and help others, and it is a great privilege to be able to do it. But when we try to do this through the government it becomes depersonalized and institutionalized, not to mention the fact that it gets so bogged down in waste and inefficiency that only a fraction of the resources will actually reach the needs of the people.

This is a general problem with the government. When any charity becomes institutionalized, it has a way of dehumanizing the people and perpetuating a dependency on the institution. Many times the government and charities' cure for society's ills has proven worse than the disease. Even so, they would not even be attempting these things, or feel the need to do so, if the Church was doing her job.

The Church and the needy have greatly suffered from the recent tendency to expect the government to do the Church's job serving the poor and needy. Those who are doing this will carry the moral authority with the multitudes to establish and uphold moral standards. We can also point to the tendency of the government to attempt to be the answer to all of our problems because of the failure of the Church to live up to her mandate. The government is likely to continue degenerating into socialistic delusions until the Church stands up to do her job. The answer to every human problem is found at the cross. The answer to every human need is found in Christ. Until the Church lifts Him up, the world will continue to live in darkness and delusion.

Our Ultimate Calling

The Church has had a long history of trying to bring the Kingdom of God to earth by might and power, without the Spirit. But the Lord stated, "That which is born of the flesh is flesh; and that which is born of the Spirit is spirit" (John 3:6). Even if we are trying to attain the right goal, if it is not done by the Holy Spirit, we will end up wounding instead of healing and bringing further division instead of reconciliation.

The historic Church, called to carry the gospel of salvation to the world, has been responsible for some of the deepest wounds that humankind has suffered. Inevitably the roots of these tragic mistakes can be traced to the same problem: well-intentioned men trying to use the civil realm of authority to accomplish spiritual goals. Whenever men have tried to bring down spiritual strongholds with carnal weapons, it has resulted in a terrible defeat for the gospel. Such will always fall to using another spirit to accomplish the purposes of God, and as a result the spiritual strongholds of the enemy are only made stronger, regardless of the political consequences.

The whole world is very aware of this history of the Church. It seems that only the Church is ignorant of this history, so each new generation has stumbled into the same traps. Regardless of how painful it is, we must examine our history and judge the fruit of the methods and teachings that we continue to repeat.

Contrary to popular belief, time does not heal wounds; they heal only if they are dressed and closed. The terrible wounds inflicted upon Muslims and Jews by the Crusades remain open and have become increasingly infected with the passage of time. It is for this reason that the sins of the fathers are passed on to the children, generation after generation. This is not to punish the children for what their fathers have done, but until a generation arises to repent of the sins and address and bring closure to the wounds, the sins continue to be perpetuated. This is why the leaders of restoration movements in Scripture, such as Ezra and Nehemiah, gave so much attention to addressing and repenting for "the sins of our fathers."

The enemy knows the power of the Church when she devotes herself to the ministry of reconciliation. That is why he continually tries to divert her from this commission, and he has been very successful in doing so. Every new movement somehow allows the same seeds of its ultimate destruction to be sown within it. Churches, denominations, movements, and even individuals are still trying to conquer by might and power rather than by the Spirit—and every such "crusade" only results in more wounds.

It is true that there were many historic atrocities inflicted upon Christians by Muslims, and even by Jews, but that is not our problem. Regardless of what was done by others, *our* mistakes were the most tragic of all because they were done in the name of the Savior who had come to deliver men from such evil.

In order for the Church to accomplish her last-day mandate, she does not need public opinion, force of numbers, financial resources, or political power—*we need the grace and anointing of God*. Because God gives grace to the humble, we must learn to take every opportunity we get to humble ourselves. One of the primary ways for the Church to do this is by acknowledging our historic mistakes and asking forgiveness from those we have so tragically persecuted and wounded. There is an extraordinary power in such humility to tear down the barriers and walls that separate people and cultures, so that the ministry of reconciliation can be released.

This powerful weapon of humility was demonstrated by Jesus on the cross, when He suffered the worst humiliation that the ruthless powers of this world could muster against Him for the sake of the very ones who tortured Him. In His most pressing moment, He did not ask for retaliation; He asked for forgiveness on behalf of His tormentors. By the power released through His humility, He overcame the world and was exalted to a position above all powers and authorities.

The Scriptures are clear that in the final days of this age, the Church will be exalted to a position of spiritual authority like she has never experienced before. This authority is essential for her to accomplish her last-day mandate. The path to that great exaltation is humility. Only when she has been properly humbled can she be trusted with this great authority.

From the time that there were just two brothers, Cain and Abel, men have not been able to get along and murder has gripped the fallen human heart. Until true redemption prevails, war will be with us. The Lord is now looking for a generation that will live by another spirit, the Holy Spirit, those who will humble themselves and pray, seeking the Lord's face and turning from these wicked ways. Then the Lord will hear from Heaven and heal our land. When this healing has reached Jerusalem and touched the heart of the Jew with the grace and truth that is realized through Jesus Christ, it will mark the completion of the great work of this Church Age. Then we will know that the Bride has come of age, and the spots have been removed.

Summary

Authority has a foundation. Spiritual authority is built on a spiritual foundation, and moral authority is built on a moral foundation. What the Church releases in Heaven by either our obedience or our sin, gets released on the earth. I have addressed the issues of abortion, homosexuality, and other sins of our times because the Church will never be able to be the light that can overcome this darkness until we are ourselves on the strongest foundation. When the root causes of these tragic sins are removed from the Church, we will then have the spiritual and moral authority that enables us to carry a light no darkness can overcome.

CHAPTER 22

WHERE DO WE GO FROM HERE?

Even though this book is larger than I intended it to be, it is still but a superficial study of this subject and of the different strongholds that we addressed. There are many other deceptions and strongholds the enemy uses against us. I addressed those that we covered because they are primary roots of deception. If we understand these, and get free of these, we will quickly and easily discern and get free of the others.

For further study on spiritual strongholds, I would like to highly recommend Francis Frangipane's book *The Three Battlegrounds*. This is considered by many to be the best book ever written on spiritual warfare, and I concur that it is the best that I have ever read.

Throughout this work I have tried to sow an understanding of the glory of the Lord and His truth as well as illuminate the schemes of the enemy. Our primary goal must always be to know the Lord, to see His glory, and to be changed into His image. We are in a battle for the time that we are on the earth. While I have not found any instance in Scripture where we are encouraged to take off the full armor of God, we must remember to never lose sight of the fact that we are called first to be worshipers who worship God in Spirit and in truth.

We are warriors, too, but that is not our first calling. Our first calling is to love—love God and love one another. As we are told in First Corinthians 13:8, "Love never fails...." If we will walk in love, we will win every battle. Every attack of the enemy, and all of his evil strongholds, are basically meant to turn us from loving God and one another. We must never forget that love is a weapon that we must always keep and use because it cannot be defeated.

We also must continually resolve that we are going to walk in truth. We must build our lives on a commitment to God's Word. His Word is true, and just as even the Word Himself took His stand on the written word of God when tempted by the devil, we must do the same. If we are walking in truth, our own words also must be true. It is simple, really. Lies come from the devil who is the father of lies. If we do not want him to have any part in us, we must be committed to truth. If we are going to be revealed as sons and daughters of the King of kings, we must walk in a manner worthy of this high calling, which is to walk by the highest standards of integrity in all things.

Being able to discern the schemes of the enemy is the biggest part of the battle, but it is not the whole battle. We must take our stand and resist the enemy until he flees. If the attack is personal you can do this personally. If the attack is more public, such as coming against your church, you may have to take a more public stand.

Resisting Evil

A couple of years ago a prophetic friend of mine named Bob Jones called to tell me of a vision he had received that concerned me and our ministry, MorningStar. He saw our ministry as a warship and I was standing on the bridge. He saw the enemy come as a submarine and fire three torpedoes at us. In the vision, the first torpedo was named "Friendly Fire," the next one "the Media," and the last "Witchcraft." They all struck our ship and rocked it. However, none of them did any real damage but just "shined us up" by knocking the dead paint off.

In this vision Bob saw that I was so focused on looking ahead that I did not pay any attention to the attacks. This was a warning. He said that as the captain of the ship I needed to deal with these attacks. I remembered this warning, and I am very glad that I did.

Not long after Bob shared this vision with me, some people who had quickly become some of the best friends our ministry had ever had just as quickly turned against us. They made a number of wild and blatantly false accusations against us, saying that they were told these things by a man whom we consider to be one of our spiritual fathers. I went to this man to confirm what I already knew, that he had not, nor would he have ever, said such things about us. Our friends, who were now acting like enemies, were undeterred, so I took the issue before our local congregation, which was being affected. I tried to do it with as much grace as possible, but I did address the issues and the false accusations directly. They stopped immediately, and what had been a big discouragement became a source of peace and confidence in our people.

Then the second torpedo hit. It was an article written in a Christian magazine about myself and the ministry. After attempts to get the owner of this magazine to correct the inaccuracies and false statements about us, I then publicly answered it. Again, what was a devastating attack turned into a positive.

The last attack, from witchcraft, rose up in the most blatant form I had ever experienced in a local church setting. We actually had people moving to our community with the express purpose of "bringing MorningStar down." A large, international New Age community started putting the word out that they were going to drive us away. The most bizarre manifestations of all were from individuals in our congregation who had a history of problems with witchcraft. A pall of depression seemed to settle over the entire ministry that was so thick even our best people started feeling like quitting. It even got to the point where I started thinking about how much easier my life would be without these churches, and even the ministry, as I can easily make a good living just writing books. Again, I took a public stand, and it broke almost immediately.

First, I went to individuals in the congregations who were involved, warning them that if they did not publicly repent of the things they were doing I would publicly address them. They would not repent, so I did it the next Sunday morning, with those involved sitting right up front. It was like lifting a dark, wet blanket off of the congregation. Spiritual gifts started functioning again; vision, purpose, and zeal for the Lord and His purposes quickly returned.

My point is that I had to resist these attacks by confronting them. My tendency is to pay little attention to things like this because they don't bother me much personally, but I know now that if I had not heeded the warning from Bob's vision, there would have been many needless casualties.

There is a time to turn the other cheek to one who strikes us, and there is a time to stand up and defend ourselves. The apostle Paul had the wisdom to defend himself against his accusers and critics so that the churches could be spared the diversion that the enemy was leading them into by attacking Paul and his message.

Paul was not responding just out of a personal rejection, but for the sake of the churches. If I had taken these attacks too personally, I do not think that I could have responded rightly, and I even could have aggravated the attacks. That is one way that I have learned to distinguish the attacks that are coming as discipline from the Lord, and that I simply need to cover with love, from those that I need to respond to for the sake of those who have been entrusted to my oversight.

As Jesus said in Matthew 12:28, "But if I cast out demons by the Spirit of God, then the kingdom of God has come upon you."

We always must keep in mind that our position in the Kingdom of God is defined by the fruit of the Spirit. If I react to an attack in the wrong spirit, I am only multiplying the evil that we are trying to cast out. I had to stop and check my motives for confronting the attacks on us. It was when I knew that I still had a deep affection for those attacking us and wanted their freedom from the enemy as well as our own, that I went forward. I also tried to do the public correcting in the most generous and conciliatory way possible for the people, because we are not warring against flesh and blood, but against spiritual forces that at times have been able to use all of us.

Again, this brings us back to love being the foundation of what we do. If we keep it as our base, we can be sure that "love never fails" and that we always will experience the victory. We always must keep in mind that "the goal of our instruction is love from a pure heart and a good conscience and a sincere faith" (1 Tim. 1:5).

HOW TO USE THE STUDY GUIDE

SPECIAL FORCES TRAINING

This Study Guide has been designed to help you better understand and apply the principles discussed in *Breaking the Power of Evil*. Whether you use this guide for individual or group study, the following approach will help you get the most out of each chapter. The four sections of the studies will help you balance your "Special Forces" training. We have outlined some of the benefits of each section below.

SECTION 1: Put On Your Armor

Take time to pray before you read each chapter and ask the Holy Spirit to enlighten your understanding as to how you need to adjust your thinking in the battle for your mind. Jot down anything that the Lord tells you. This section puts you in an attitude of submissive instruction. Open your heart beyond the written page to accept direct interaction with the Commander in Chief, Jesus Christ.

SECTION 2: Work Your Battle Strategy

Read the chapter and highlight anything that stands out to you. Read as if you will be tested on the information by your commander. As you read, ask yourself: "What...? Why...? When... Who...? Where...? and How...?" Work your head and your heart at the same time. After you have finished reading, review the items you highlighted before going to the Training Drill questions.

SECTION 3: Participate in Training Drills

Answer the questions, being open to the Holy Spirit's interaction with your mind and heart. If you become aware of Him speaking...STOP! Jot down what you hear in the margins. This

section is designed to develop your spiritual muscles. Try to recall the answers from memory, if possible. The questions are to help you remember what you read and recognize how to apply the principles to your life. Look for the answers to the Study Guide questions.

SECTION 4: Covert Operations Yield Victory

Review what you prayed in the beginning of the chapter, the highlighted items in the book, and notes you made during the Training Drills section. Now spend time asking the Lord for specific ways in which you need to change your thought processes, alter your daily life, and/or make adjustments to relationships you have. This section is to prepare you for battle that will probably take place immediately! Write your action plan for battle and follow through with its pursuit.

PART I

THE BATTLE FOR THE SOUL

CHAPTER 1
THE FREEDOM FIGHTERS

Put On Your Armor

Take time to pray before you read Chapter One to ask the Holy Spirit to enlighten your understanding as to how you need to adjust your thinking in the battle for your mind. Jot down anything that the Lord tells you.

Work Your Battle Strategy

Read Chapter One and highlight anything that stands out to you. Read as if you will be tested on the information by your commander. After you are done reading, review the items you highlighted before going to the Training Drill questions.

Participate in Training Drills

Answer these questions, being open to the Spirit's interaction with your mind and heart. If you become aware of Him speaking…STOP! Jot down what you hear in the margins.

1. The battle that is raging for our souls is a battle between _____*life*_____ and _*death*_____

2. Every day we live, we are doing one of two things. What are they? _*Taking ground or losing it*_

3. The only reasonable course that we have is to do three things. They are:

   a. _*understand the battle*_
   b. _*fight the battle*_
   c. _*win the battle*_

4. Choose the statements that are true about this battle:

   a. There is a question as to whether God or satan is more powerful.

   b. We have stepped into the demilitarized zone between Heaven and hell.

   c. God could end the battle at any time.

   d. Our souls are the territory that is being fought over.

5. Why has God decided not to end the battle and dispense with satan? _*His commitment to freedom for His creation*_

6. When we have understood God's commitment to our freedom, we can understand the following things:
   *Conflict in the world, soul, the nature of God*

7. Why has God created man to be free? _We cannot be_ _who we were created to be without freedom_

8. Write Second Corinthians 3:17 in your own words and describe how this verse reflects one of the most basic differences between the kingdom of darkness and the Kingdom of God. _There is freedom wherever the Holy Spirit is_

9. Contrast the difference between the Tree of the Knowledge of Good and Evil and the Tree of Life. Tell which tree the statements below describe.

Good & Evil Life

a. Fruit releases man into his ultimate potential and purpose _Tree of life_

b. Placed in Eden to prove Adam and Eve's obedience _Knowledge of good & evil_

c. The knowledge of simply knowing God _Tree of Life_

d. Promotes the pursuit of wisdom and truth _Tree of life_

e. Given so that man had the freedom to disobey _Knowledge of good & evil_

10. TRUE or FALSE:

a. Man's free moral agency infringes on the sovereignty of God. _F_

b. Our main goal must be to obey God because we love Him, not because we are afraid of punishment. _T_

c. Freedom involves choices, consequences, and responsibility. _T_

d. God has not called man to rule with Him. _F_

e. Authority can be given without attaching responsibility to it. _F_

f. The greater the authority, the greater the potential for good or bad. _T_

11. To the degree that we are given authority, we can also release _good_ or _evil_ into that domain.

12. What happens when the chains of bondage that yoke our souls are illuminated? _We can better defeat Satan_

13. What does Second Corinthians 2:11 teach us about how we leave room for satanic activity in our lives? _we cannot open the door to Satan thru sin_

14. MATCHING: Draw a line to and from the beginnings of statements on the left side to their endings on the right side.

   a. Satan takes advantage of the Church because

   b. When we become knowledgeable of the devil's schemes

   c. We must place true watchmen on the walls

   d. Our main purpose must always be to

   e. We will fail if we do not discern the devil's constant attempts

   i. who have knowledge and discernment of the devil's schemes.

   ii. partake of the fruit of the Tree of Life.

   iii. to lure us to the evil tree.

   iv. of our neglect to understand satan's schemes.

   v. he can no longer take advantage of us.

15. Write Second Corinthians 10:3-6 in your own words and underline words that help you understand the meaning of this passage. _Our war is not with people and we don't use traditional weapons. Our powerful weapons destroy strongholds_

16. Why is it true that the Church is here not just to defend against the attacks of the devil? What other things are we to do? _We must tear down strongholds to release as many souls as possible from bondage._

17. How do we know every Christian is called to be a freedom fighter? What scriptures support this? What is a freedom fighter supposed to do? _John 17:18 - Jesus sent us out into the world._

Covert Operations Yield Victory

Review what you prayed in the beginning of the chapter, the highlighted items in the book, and notes you made during the Training Drills section. Now, spend time asking the Lord for specific ways in which you need to change your thought processes, alter your daily life, and/or make adjustments to relationships you have. Write your action plan for battle and follow through with its pursuit.

CHAPTER 2
THE REASON FOR THE BATTLE

Put On Your Armor

Take time to pray before you read Chapter 2 to ask the Holy Spirit to enlighten your understanding as to how you need to adjust your thinking in the battle for your mind. Jot down anything that the Lord tells you.

Work Your Battle Strategy

Read Chapter 2 and highlight anything that stands out to you. Read as if you will be tested on the information from your Commander. After you are done reading, review the items you highlighted before going to the Training Drill questions.

Participate in Training Drills

Answer these questions, being open to the Spirit's interaction with your mind and heart. If you become aware of Him speaking... STOP! Jot down what you hear in the margins.

1. In Matthew 13:39b, Jesus said, "The harvest is _the end of this world (age) and the reapers are the angels_ ."

2. When the Church emerges from the wilderness in this age, she will be the glorious, beautiful _banner_ that Solomon describes, and she also will be a mighty _army_ We are called to be not only passionate _worshippers_ of God, but also _warriors_ .

3. The most common title given to God in Scripture is _LORD of Hosts_ which literally means _the Lord of armies_ .

4. TRUE OR FALSE:

   a. David was a great warrior, but he was not as great in the worship area. _F_

   b. If we are following the Lord, we are in an army. _T_

   c. If we do not see the battle that is raging around, we are experiencing a delusion. _T_

   d. The ultimate outcome of the battle has yet to be determined. _F_

   e. The Church Age is our training for reigning. _T_

   f. We are called to be joint heirs with Christ. _T_

5. Nothing reveals the true character of a person like _____ _of_ *Conflict* .

6. Many of the conflicts that Christians experience are because *of what they are doing right, not what they are doing wrong.*

7. MULTIPLE CHOICE: *wrong*

  A. The Lord wants His joint heirs to have:

    1. an easy life.

    (2.) the best training.

    3. conflict for conflict sake.

  B. The trials and battles of this age are the forge by which the Lord is raising His sons and daughters to be:

    (1.) worthy heirs, whom even the angels will acknowledge.

    2. door mats for the world to step on.

    3. unchanged by the battle or trial.

  C. The whole creation will consider the Lord's Bride to rule with Him because:

    1. she will have conquered the enemy without having to depend on God's help.

    2. she will have lived a perfect and holy life.

    (3.) she proved her devotion to Him and His truth.

  D. We are not here on earth to enjoy ourselves but we are here to:

    (1.) stand for truth and proclaim the gospel

    2. wait patiently in seclusion for the second coming of Christ.

    3. be restful but not in slumber.

8. What is the inevitable result of those who refuse to acknowledge the reality of the spiritual warfare in which we are engaged? *They are inevitably overcome by it.*

9. Why don't we need to fear the war around us? (Give a Scripture to answer this.) *because God is greater and He lives in us. James 1 John 4:4*

10. How are we to maintain our position in Christ? *take on the full armour of God and remain vigilant*

11. Explain why the enemy is successful in using the same traps in successive generations. *We've never learned to recognize them*

12. It is the Lord's purpose for our life that we be ___free___ _____ from every ___yoke___ but one— His ___yoke___ He then wants to ___use___ us to ___set___ others ___free___.

13. What are the two things we are called to walk in so that evil flees from us wherever we go? _light and truth > authority &_

14. Using Daniel 11:31-32, fill out the following chart: _dominion_

What The Enemy Will Do	Our Response
Raise up evil forces	Display strength and take action
Desecrate the sanctuary fortress	

Where will our strength and action come from? _Knowing our God_

15. Jesus was not just the Son of David by lineage, but also because He was here to _do the deeds of David_.

16. MATCHING:

   a. Moses   i. The promised land was confirmed through him.

   b. Jesus   ii. The first to conquer and possess the Promised Land

   c. Abraham   iii. Came to fully possess the Kingdom

   d. David   iv. Canaan promised through him.

17. Our first calling is to ___worship___ but we must do so with a ___sword in our hands___.

18. What does First Timothy 1:5 tell us about the goal of our instruction? _love from a pure heart and good conscience and sincere faith_

19. What two divinely powerful weapons do we have at our disposal? _love and truth_

20. True worship does not come in order to _see the Lord_ it comes from _seeing the Lord._

21. To the degree that we see Him with the _eyes of our heart_ we will _worship Him._ We need many times as much _worship_ as warfare.

22. Using Colossians 3:1-2, describe the primary way that we will win our battles. _by setting our minds on things above not on things on the earth_

Covert Operations Yield Victory

Review what you prayed in the beginning of the chapter, the high-lighted items in the book, and notes you made during the Training Drills section. Now, spend time asking the Lord for specific ways in which you need to change your thought processes, alter your daily life, and/or make adjustments to relationships you have. Write your action plan for battle and follow through with its pursuit.

CHAPTER 3
FIGHTING THE RIGHT WAR

Put On Your Armor

Take time to pray before you read Chapter 3 to ask the Holy Spirit to enlighten your understanding as to how you need to adjust your thinking in the battle for your mind. Jot down anything that the Lord tells you.

Work Your Battle Strategy

Read Chapter 3 and highlight anything that stands out to you. Read as if you will be tested on the information from your Commander. After you are done reading, review the items you highlighted before going to the Training Drill questions.

Participate in Training Drills

Answer these questions, being open to the Spirit's interaction with your mind and heart. If you become aware of Him speaking...STOP! Jot down what you hear in the margins.

1. What are some of the composite factors that make up what individuals are? *basic gifts, talents, knowledge, experience, fears and social wounds* This composite of an individual for the purposes of this study is called the _*Soul*_.

2. Describe the composite of a group. What types of groups have a composite soul? *Churches, businesses, sports teams & clubs.*

3. The Great Commission was to disciple all _*nations*_ not just _*individuals*_ So it is important that we discern the _*nations*_ that we are called to _*minister*_ to.

4. MATCHING:

a. Those who do not understand this conflict   i. to keep men in bondage to do his will.

b. The devil uses fear   ii. to set men free to serve Him.

c. We must recognize and understand the basic power that satan uses   iii. will be defeated by it.

d. The Lord uses faith   iv. to keep the world under his power.

211

5. Why do you think that the devil is so successful in using fear as his basic power over humankind? _Because we are_ _ignorant of his schemes_

6. What two choices are there that will dictate the course of our lives? _living in fear or faith_

7. What is one basic definition of faith that this chapter uses? _to fight fear_

8. TRUE OR FALSE:

   a. We are under the control of evil to the degree that fear is allowed to control our life. _T_

   b. If fear controls us, then fear is under our feet. _F_

   c. To walk in obedience to the Lord requires us to walk in ~~obe-~~ _Faith_dience. _T_

   d. If anyone draws back, God will still find delight in him. _F_

   e. It should be a basic goal in our life to grow ourselves through each gift God gives us. _F_

   f. We are required to renew our minds, by changing the very thinking by which we perceive ourselves and the world around us. _T_

9. Faith in God is _always singular_ but there are a _multitude_ of fears that seek dominion over us.

10. The faith walk is one of _liberation_ while fear is much more _complicated_ .

11. Name some of the multitude of fears that come under the broader category of the fear of man. _rejection, failure_ _embarrasment, humiliation_

12. What are the three wonderful results that come as we grow more in our faith in God? _peace, rest and fulfilment_

13. Fear causes us to do things that we would not have done if we were _living by faith in that area._ .

14. Fear actually causes the _release_ of the things we fear.

15. ELIMINATE THE ONE CHOICE THAT IS INCORRECT:

    A. There will be a continual battle to maintain position by

       1. suppressing the ambitious ones below us.

       (2.) bringing new issues to light as we see them.

3. nosing out those above us.

B. The tendency to establish position within a group is the result of

1. missing our calling due to our blindness.

2. the perversion of the purpose of humankind.

3. the purpose of humankind to rule over the earth.

4. using our rule for selfish reasons instead of for serving others.

C. Those who have true spiritual authority will tend to have

1. a reaction to other influential Christians in the room.

2. time to get to know others rather than trying to establish their own greatness.

3. an interest in asking what others are doing.

4. a very distinguishable peace about them.

16. What is the main reason for the continual, basic human conflicts? _trying to establish the pecking order_

17. Fear arouses demonic forces to swarm to the _vulnerable_ _____. Likewise faith _repels_ them.

18. The basic purpose of every Christian is to walk in the _____ _faith_ that _resists_ the enemy's attempt to _dominate_ us. We must grow in our _dominion_ and _faith_ for the purpose of _serving_ others, setting them _free_ and not _____ _dominating_ them.

19. Describe the issues that the author has experienced in terms of the "pecking order in the church." Which of these have you experienced? _Sports /business_

20. How does our competition within the church resemble the way the people built the tower of Babel? _it needs to be redeemed and focused rightly to not become Babel_

21. Outline the principles that you see in Second Corinthians 10: 8-12 that speak to the characteristics of true spiritual authority.
It encourages
It is not shameful
It is consistent
It is confident

22. MULTIPLE CHOICE:

A. Those who have a true understanding of the Kingdom rejoice

     1. when they are given praise for what God has done through them.

     2. when they know people see them as role models.

     ③. in the promotion of the Kingdom whomever it comes through.

  B. Don't waste yourself

     1. on small things that might not amount to much.

     ②. building the wrong kingdom.

     3. on those who will not appreciate your efforts.

  C. If we are going to be freedom fighters, then we must

     ①. fight in the right army and by the right Spirit.

     2. train, retrain, and retrain, again.

     3. approach the enemy with a full body press.

  D. We should start measuring our success by

     1. the number of spiritual gifts we have.

     2. the number of scriptures we have memorized.

     ③. how others who we helped succeeded.

  E. There is a competition on the earth right now for

     ①. where we are going to be positionally for eternity.

     2. whether we can sit at Jesus' right hand or not.

     3. how well we will stand in the face of ridicule.

Covert Operations Yield Victory

Review what you prayed in the beginning of the chapter, the high-lighted items in the book, and notes you made during the Training Drills section. Now, spend time asking the Lord for specific ways in which you need to change your thought processes, alter your daily life, and/or make adjustments to relationships you have. Write your action plan for battle and follow through with its pursuit.

CHAPTER 4
FROM DEMONS TO WORLD RULERS

Put On Your Armor

Take time to pray before you read Chapter 4 to ask the Holy Spirit to enlighten your understanding as to how you need to adjust your thinking in the battle for your mind. Jot down anything that the Lord tells you.

Work Your Battle Strategy

Read Chapter 4 and highlight anything that stands out to you. Read as if you will be tested on the information from your commander. After you're are done reading, review the items you highlighted before going to the Training Drill questions.

Participate in Training Drills

Answer these questions, being open to the Spirit's interaction with your mind and heart. If you become aware of Him speaking… STOP! Jot down what you hear in the margins.

1. There are _____levels_____ of demonic forces that are assaulting the world. These range from demonic attacks on_____ __individuals___, to principalities that seek dominion over ___regions___ or __nations___, to "world rulers" that seek dominion over the _entire earth_.

2. The enemy is always seeking to __counter___ the work of God. We are close to another _Great Awakening_ _____ sweeping over America.

3. Where is the greatest opportunity for faith to be released?_____ ___In every place the enemy attacks___

4. Faith is much more powerful than __fear_____, and ___faith___ will ultimately _prevail___.

5. What should earthly governments fight against? _terror on the level of natural weapons_ Can they achieve ultimate victory over this enemy? _No, only the Church can_

6. To have a true and lasting victory, with what must we fight the spiritual battle? _Spiritual weapons_

7. FILL IN THE CHART with information from Ephesians 6:10-20.

Our Struggle is against: *powers*	Our Struggle is against: *principalities*	Our Struggle is against: *spiritual wicked*	Our Struggle is against: *rulers of Darkness*
Define this: *demons*	Define this: *powers/prin*	Define this: *Satan*	Define this: *world rulers*
Target of attack: *individuals*	Target of attack: *regions/church*	Target of attack: *the earth*	Target of attack: *the earth*
Method of attack:	Method of attack:	Method of attack:	Method of attack:
Who has authority over these: *All Christians*	Who has authority over these:	Who has authority over these: *Jesus*	Who has authority over these:

8. What type of battle do most Christians face? *A personal battle with the mind*
   How do we conduct our battle at this level? *Recognizing, Confronting & Casting out, Speaking God's word*

9. How does our promotion in spiritual authority affect the demons that we may face? *they are bigger demons*

10. Where does the battle against evil begin? *Our minds*
    Where does the battle go from there? *the Church*
    How does the Church displace principalities? *When it is victorious*

11. MATCHING: Match the beginning of the sentence with its conclusion.

a. If we have national or international authority and prevail,

b. Because Jesus is the highest authority in the Kingdom,

c. Satan has to use men to do his will,

d. As one grows in spiritual authority and powers.

i. He had to be confronted by satan.

ii. just as the Lord works through His people

iii. They will be buffeted by more powerful demonic forces.

iv. we can count on attacks from principalities.

12. Why should we not fear the greater demons who may attack us as we gain spiritual authority? *Because He that is in me is greater than he that is in the world*

    Why should we actually be encouraged by this? *Because Jesus has greater power than all of them*

13. TRUE OR FALSE:

    a. If evil events cause sweeping changes over the whole earth, we can count on a world ruler being behind them. *T*

    b. It is not right that civilized governments have made terrorism the world's foremost enemy. *F*

    c. Terrorism as an earthly enemy that can be defeated by bombs and bullets. *F*

    d. Christians must overcome the fears that dominate their own lives. *T*

    e. The Church must rise to the place of faith and authority where we confront the world ruler that is assaulting us. *T*

    f. Being called to a high position does not automatically give one authority. *F*

    g. Spiritual authority is given so we can receive more respect from people. *F*

14. What are the two mandates that we are given in Romans 13:1-4? *We are to be in subjection to Governing authority*

    How should we pray for our governments? *for their success in bringing the wrath of God on evil*

    How is righteousness and justice restored to the earth? *Through civil authority*

    Do what is good

15. If we are not here to avenge evil, what are we required to do? *love our enemies and pray for them*

    What would the greatest victory that we could have in terms of our enemies? *repentance and salvation of our enemies*

16. FILL OUT THE CHART to note the difference between the seen and unseen.

	Target of Attack	Weapons of warfare	Limits to the battle
SEEN		*guns/ bombs*	
UNSEEN		*mighty thru God*	

17. Spiritual authority is something we _grow into_
    _____. We are given more authority as we
    _mature_____ _spiritually_ and are given higher
    _commissions_____ by the Lord. This is evidenced by an
    _increase___ of _faith_____ to new levels.

18. There are two goals that we have as Christians as we fight
    effectively against evil. The first is _confront_____. The
    second is _overcome____.

19. How should our view of the end times affect or not affect our
    faith? _We should not be complacent but continue_
    _to fight against evil_____

20. The primary inroad that the enemy has into our lives is
    through _our lives, families etc._ We must _take_____ a
    _stand_____ against the enemy so that it will not
    _dictate_____ the course of our lives or our present
    actions. We are at war with _fear_____.

21. MULTIPLE CHOICE:

    A. True faith:

    1. is not an ambiguous confidence in ourselves.

    2. is not the result of a living relationship with God.

    3. is not due to the empowerment we receive from God.

    B. Everything that has been sown in man:

    1. will bring the Second coming of Christ.

    2. will come to full maturity, both good and evil.

    3. will prevent the end of the age.

    C. The light and glory is appearing upon the Lord's people:

    1. at the same time when darkness is covering the earth

    2. because the Church is becoming more pure.

    3. in place of false unity and unguarded peace.

    D. We are about to experience:

    1. the wrath of the Lord's angels.

    2. pressure from overwhelming demonic activity.

    3. the greatest fear and the greatest faith ever released on
       earth.

    E. If we are not growing in faith:

    1. we will at least have peace to calm our fears.

2. we can count on the understanding God gives us to get us through.

(3.) we will be growing in fear.

Covert Operations Yield Victory

Review what you prayed in the beginning of the chapter, the highlighted items in the book, and notes you made during the Training Drills section. Now, spend time asking the Lord for specific ways in which you need to change your thought processes, alter your daily life, and/or make adjustments to relationships you have. Write your action plan for battle and follow through with its pursuit.

PART II

THE ROOTS OF OUR BONDAGE; THE SOURCE OF OUR FREEDOM

CHAPTER 5
GOOD FEAR

Put On Your Armor

Take time to pray before you read Chapter 5 to ask the Holy Spirit to enlighten your understanding as to how you need to adjust your thinking in the battle for your mind. Jot down anything that the Lord tells you.

Work Your Battle Strategy

Read Chapter 5 and highlight anything that stands out to you. Read as if you will be tested on the information from your commander. After you are done reading, review the items you highlighted before going to the Training Drill questions.

Participate in Training Drills

Answer these questions, being open to the Spirit's interaction with your mind and heart. If you become aware of Him speaking… STOP! Jot down what you hear in the margins.

1. What is the one good fear that we must have? *the fear of the Lord*

   How does the fear of God cast out all other fear in our lives? *It is so great it casts out all other fears*

2. In your own words, describe the paradox between fearing God and trusting Him. *The two words, though opposite refer to each other*

3. COMPLETE THE BLANK SENTENCES referencing First John 4:16-19 (NKJV):

   What we know *the love that God has for us*
   What we believe *the love that God has for us*
   What happens when we abide? *When we abide in love we abide in Him*
   What has been perfected? *love*
   Who is being perfected? *I am*
   For what purpose are we being perfected? *to love perfectly & have boldness*
   What does not exist in love? *torment*
   What is involved in the experience of fear? *torment*
   How do we know we are loved? *He loves us because we love Him*

4. What is the beginning of wisdom? *fear of the Lord*
   What is the ultimate wisdom? *to perceive the love of God*
   How does our fear of God build a strong foundation for the love of God? *Only then can we comprehend His love*

5. Explain the meaning of Romans 11:22a, "Behold then the kindness and severity of God." _God is Kind in His severity and severe in His kindness_

6. TRUE OR FALSE:

   a. The Bride of Christ is going to purify herself because she is afraid the Bridegroom will find her soiled. _F_

   b. The Bride of Christ is going to be without spot or wrinkle because she loves the Bridegroom so very much. _T_

   c. The Bride of Christ will be determined to be ready for the Lord's return. _____

   d. The Bride of Christ will have a singular focus on being ready for her Bridegroom. _T_

7. Construct the steps that will bring the Bride of Christ from a position of fear to a position of love.

   STEP 1: The Bride is filthy and sees that He is appalled at her condition _dirt poor s filthy_ INITIAL CONTACT

   STEP 2: _____ FEAR

   STEP 3: _____ RESPONSE

   STEP 4: _____ LOVED

   STEP 5: _____ RESPONSE

   STEP 6: _____ DEEPENING

   STEP 7: _____ FINAL OUTCOME

8. What does it mean to be called into the very family of God?

   _____

9. How does the process of renewing our minds affect how we come out from the foundation of fear to the triumph of love?

   _____

10. How will fear and faith mingle as we grow in our love of God?

    _____

11. Describe the necessary process that we need to go through in order to transition from being filthy to being pure.

    _____

12. What happens if we use God's love and forgiveness as an excuse to sin? _____

13. What kind of marriage is Christ calling us into? _____

    _____

Describe the characteristics of that marriage._____
_____

14. Describe the way in which the apostle John learned both love and fear. _____

15. CHART THE SKELETON PRINCIPLES of Proverbs 2:1-5

Verb phrase	Direct Object phrase
Receive	My Words
Find	Knowledge of God

16. The fear of the Lord is a _____
_____ than anything else we could possess on this earth. It is worth _____ more than any
_____ _____.

17. Psalm 31:19 (KJV)—Oh how great is Thy _____,
which Thou hast _____ _____ for
them that _____. Thee; which Thou
hast _____ for them that _____ in
Thee before the _____ of _____.

18. Psalm 33:18-19—Behold, the_____of the Lord is
on those who_____ _____, on
those who_____for His_____
to_____their_____
from _____and the keep them
_____ in _____.

19. Psalm 103:11—For as _____ as the heavens are
above the earth, so_____is His
_____toward those who _____ Him.

20. Psalm 103:13—Just as a _____ has _____
on his children, so the Lord has _____ on those
who _____ Him.

21. Psalm 145:19—He will _____the_____
    _____of those who_____Him; He will also
    _____their_____and will_____them.

22. Proverbs 14:26-27—In the _____ of the Lord
    there is _____ _____, and His chil-
    dren will have _____. The _____ of
    the Lord is a _____ of life, that one may
    _____ the _____ of death.

Covert Operations Yield Victory

Review what you prayed in the beginning of the chapter, the high-lighted items in the book, and notes you made during the Training Drills section. Now, spend time asking the Lord for specific ways in which you need to change your thought processes, alter your daily life, and/or make adjustments to relationships you have. Write your action plan for battle and follow through with its pursuit.

CHAPTER 6
IDOLS AND FEARS

Put On Your Armor

Take time to pray before you read Chapter 6 to ask the Holy Spirit to enlighten your understanding as to how you need to adjust your thinking in the battle for your mind. Jot down anything that the Lord tells you.

Work Your Battle Strategy

Read Chapter 6 and highlight anything that stands out to you. Read as if you will be tested on the information from your Commander. After you are done reading, review the items you highlighted before going to the Training Drill questions.

Participate in Training Drills

Answer these questions, being open to the Spirit's interaction with your mind and heart. If you become aware of Him speaking... STOP! Jot down what you hear in the margins.

1. After tearing down the ___evil___ ___strongholds___ that keep us in ___bondage___, our goal is to ___replace___ them with ___fortresses___ of ___truth___ Every time that we can do this, we basically will be turning a ___fear___ into the ___faith___ that allows us to ___advance___ further toward our ___purpose___.

2. What are some of the results of getting rid of our bondage? ___freedom boldness and confidence in our faith___

3. There is no ___greater___ ___confidence___ that we can have on this earth than knowing that we are ___right___ with God, and that is always our ___ultimate___ ___purpose___ to be ___right___ with God.

4. What are some of the idols that keep Christians in bondage today? ___Religious idols, graven images___

5. Explain how Jeremiah 50:6 explains what is happening in our time. ___Many people today are being led astray by their pastors___

227

6. TRUE OR FALSE:

T a. The fruit from the good side of the Tree of Knowledge of Good and Evil is just as deadly as the fruit from the evil side.

T b. Good works that are not initiated by God can be a trap to us.

F c. Our goal is to graft God's love into the Tree of the Knowledge of Good and Evil.

F d. The Tree of Life has good and bad fruit, just like the Tree of the Knowledge of Good and Evil.

7. How do we distinguish between the works of the Lord and those that are motivated by men? *By following the Lord*

8. What are some of the results of walking on the path of true faith? *rejection by some & having to reject some*

9. If we are controlled by the _____*fear*_____ of man, then we will be serving _____*man*_____ and not _____*Christ*_____.

10. To be a true _____*worshipper*_____ of God is to do His _____*works*_____ _____*alone*_____ and His _____*alone*_____.

11. MATCHING: Finish the sentences.

a. Good works that have originated out of someone's good intentions

b. Many spend their entire lives doing things

c. Many who call Jesus "Lord" and did many great works in His name

d. And then I will declare to them, I never knew you;

i. that God has not called them to do.

ii. are one of the most dangerous traps.

iii. depart from Me, you who practice lawlessness.

iv. yet are not doing the will of the Father.

12. How do Christians today come up with their own image of God and worship it? *Through human idealism*
Why is this idolatry? *It is not accurate*
How is this like a graven image? _____

13. Where does human idealism have its root? *good side of Tree*
How does it appear to be good? _____
How is its fruit deadly? *It is false*

14. How can we become deceived about other people as we create our own image of who they are? _____

How does being open to those people who have a different perspective than ours help us keep from this kind of deception?

15. MULTIPLE CHOICE:

A. Everyone who does not serve the Lord

1. makes more friends on earth.

2. will be seen as a fraud by true Christians.

③ worships idols.

B. Any bond will grow into bondage if

① it surpasses our love for, and trust in, God.

2. we learn too much about it at the Tree of Knowledge.

3. we are not careful to keep our distance from others.

C. Misplaced trust will turn into

① idol worship.

2. physical abuse.

3. irrational fears.

16. FILL IN THE CHART for Hebrews 12:25-29. Go sentence by sentence or phrase by phrase and choose the key words that stand out to you. Then explain them. Use as much of the chart as you need, or add on as necessary.

PHRASE	KEY WORD	MEANING
Do not refuse Him who speaks _for if_	refuse	Reject, decline to hear

17. How can we know where our treasure is? *It's where our heart is*

How does our investment make itself known? _____

18. How can we keep our hearts focused toward the Kingdom rather than on this present world? *To Stay Kingdom minded can trust in God instead of world Systems*

19. What are the signs that can tell us what idols control us? _____ *Fear controls us*

20. What is the ultimate key to our freedom from idols? *To have faith in God - truly worship Him and love Him above all else*

21. What are the three things Second Corinthians 13:5 tells us that help us check if we are allowing Jesus to rule in our heart and affections? _____

Covert Operations Yield Victory

Review what you prayed in the beginning of the chapter, the highlighted items in the book, and notes you made during the Training Drills section. Now, spend time asking the Lord for specific ways in which you need to change your thought processes, alter your daily life, and/or make adjustments to relationships you have. Write your action plan for battle and follow through with its pursuit.

CHAPTER 7
BUILDING ON THE HIGH GROUND

Put On Your Armor

Take time to pray before you read Chapter 7 to ask the Holy Spirit to enlighten your understanding as to how you need to adjust your thinking in the battle for your mind. Jot down anything that the Lord tells you.

Work Your Battle Strategy

Read Chapter 7 and highlight anything that stands out to you. Read as if you will be tested on the information from your Commander. After you are done reading, review the items you highlighted before going to the Training Drill questions.

Participate in Training Drills

Answer these questions, being open to the Spirit's interaction with your mind and heart. If you become aware of Him speaking... STOP! Jot down what you hear in the margins.

1. What is the primary way to combat fear? _____

   How do we grow in faith? _____

   How does this build our trust in Him? _____

2. At the end of the age, how will Romans 11:22a "behold...the kindness and severity of God" be seen? _____

   _____

   Why is it important to understand this? _____

   _____

3. How have some people made their doctrines of the end times into an idol? _____

   What happens if we do this? _____

4. Deception is more than just misunderstanding _____ or _____. An even more serious _____ is not _____ in the _____ of God, or not _____ the _____ of God.

5. When the Lord gives us _____ or _____, He will not take them _____, even if we fall into _____ or _____ He remains _____ even if we become _____. That is why the gifts may still _____ even though someone has _____ from the _____ of God.

231

6. TRUE OR FALSE:

    a. Studying the biblical prophecies is the most important thing we need to do. _____

    b. We need to know how the end time will unfold more than any other issue of faith. _____

    c. It is important that we are not deceived about God's will for our lives. _____

    d. If our eschatology is not correct, it can affect us being in the right place at the right time. _____

    e. Following and abiding in Jesus will help us do the right thing in the right place. _____

7. We declare the gospel of the Kingdom as _____ on earth. This means that we are _____ whose true _____ is the country that we represent which is _____.

8. We must _____ over _____ things and not allow them to _____ over us. Any wrong or excessive _____ that we have is an open door for the _____, who will usually come through that door in the form of _____. Any wrong or excessive attachment to our _____ also will _____ _____ us likewise.

9. MULTIPLE CHOICE:

    A. To date it is rare in Church history to find anyone who

        1. can heal others.

        2. understood a biblical prophecy before it happened.

        3. bring words of consolation to the government.

    B. The main focus of our attention should be

        1. on the troubles that are coming to the world.

        2. on the glorious Kingdom that troubles are preparing the way for.

        3. on the tenets of doctrine that will convince the world of truth.

    C. The world needs to know the reason for the troubles, which is

        1. that people are oblivious to God's forms of discipline.

        2. that man is in rebellion and practicing idolatry.

        3. that no one has stepped forward to bring the Gospel to the world.

D. In order for the world to trust anyone, including God, it needs to hear

    1. about the theology of end times.

    2. about the practices of meditation and prayer.

    3. about the goodness of God.

10. Romans 2:4 tells us that it is the _____ of God that leads to _____. The world desperately needs to hear of His _____ that _____ us from sin, _____ us from sin, and then _____ us to the condition that we were _____ to be in.

11. Part of our ability to _____ the Kingdom of God is for us to _____ in it ourselves, now.

12. One of the ultimate _____ of the human heart is _____. To represent the Lord and His Kingdom without _____, we must be free of this _____. We must be financially _____.

13. According to the author what is the definition of financial independence? _____

_____

14. If we are abiding in God's Kingdom, there are unlimited _____. These are not to be drawn on at our whim, but to do His _____.

15. True faith is directly linked to _____. We _____ the one we truly _____.

16. MATCHING: First Timothy 6:10-12 (KJV)

    a. For the love of money is   i. follow after righteousness.

    b. They have erred from the faith and   ii. before many witnesses.

    c. Flee these things and   iii. the root of all evil.

    d. Fight the good fight of faith and   iv. pierced themselves through with many sorrows.

    e. Thou hast professed a good profession   v. lay hold on eternal life.

17. Why is the love of money the root of all evil?_____

_____

18. If we have _____ the true _____ of the Kingdom and beheld the true _____ of God, having a lot of _____ or a little _____ will not be of great _____ to us. We just want _____ to do His _____.

19. Why does the Lord need people with whom He can trust His resources? _____.

What are they to do with the resources? _____.

_____

What does this have to do with how the Kingdom will be seen?

_____

20. Why is the mark of the beast an economic mark?

_____

How will this test us?

21. What does fear and faith have to do with money?_____

_____.

How does our freedom of the love of money demonstrate our liberty that comes from being a slave of Christ?_____

_____.

22. Our goal is to become those who can be _____ with the _____ of the Kingdom. The wealth of the nations will be brought to the _____ of the Lord. We will be trusted with _____ _____, but we must be in the place _____ where it will not be a _____ _____ to us.

23. If we will _____ and _____ the Lord, we will ultimately _____ far more than the _____ could ever give us.

Covert Operations Yield Victory

Review what you prayed in the beginning of the chapter, the highlighted items in the book, and notes you made during the Training Drills section. Now, spend time asking the Lord for specific ways in which you need to change your thought processes, alter your daily life, and/or make adjustments to relationships you have. Write your action plan for battle and follow through with its pursuit.

CHAPTER 8
THE ULTIMATE IDOL AND THE ULTIMATE FREEDOM

Put On Your Armor

Take time to pray before you read Chapter 8 to ask the Holy Spirit to enlighten your understanding as to how you need to adjust your thinking in the battle for your mind. Jot down anything that the Lord tells you.

Work Your Battle Strategy

Read Chapter 8 and highlight anything that stands out to you. Read as if you will be tested on the information from your Commander. After you are done reading, review the items you highlighted before going to the Training Drill questions.

Participate in Training Drills

Answer these questions, being open to the Spirit's interaction with your mind and heart. If you become aware of Him speaking... STOP! Jot down what you hear in the margins.

1. Money can be the ultimate _____ of the human heart. This is why _____ is the emphasis of a substantial portion of _____. If we do not understand how to handle money _____, we will do it _____.

2. Every one of the _____ and _____ that John the Baptist gave to those who questioned him was _____ in nature. Sound, biblical _____ teaching must become an important emphasis for the _____ in our times.

3. The Lord made clear in the parable of the talents that _____
   _____.

4. What does we "cannot serve God and mammon" mean? _____
   _____

5. MATCHING:

   a. We must balance godly and wise financial management

   b. We must seek the purposes of the Kingdom of God

   c. The love of money, or poor financial management

   i. in everything we do.

   ii. will corrupt ministry as well as individuals.

   iii. than the wealthy.

    d. The poor can be more   iv. with keeping our
        controlled by the love   primary motives pure.
        of money

6. We must learn to be _____ with _____ goods before we can be entrusted with the _____ riches of the _____. Learning to properly handle _____ _____ while maintaining a _____ ____ is important for every Christian. If _____ is our primary goal, then we will _____ the one who gives it to us.

7. TRUE OR FALSE:

    a. Satan will offer us the difficult way to attain the promises. ____

    b. We need to go to the cross to receive the promises. ____

    c. Many fail to recognize when they are dealing with satan. ____

    d. Ministries can have a lot of activity and bear fruit but still not be doing the will of the Father. ____

8. Taking the mark of the beast is not the _____ that brings _____. The sin is to _____ the beast. The mark is simply _____ that one has been _____ him.

9. Will we escape judgment if we refuse to take a mark, but go on living our lives according to the ways of the beast _____

_____

   What is the only way we will not take the mark of the beast?__

_____

10. MULTIPLE CHOICE:

    A. The main reason Christians today are not free to respond to the call of God on their life is:

       1 fear

       2. debt

       3. a lack of faith

    B. Our financial condition rules us if:

       1. our main consideration is affordability.

       2. we are buying the wrong things at the wrong time.

       3. everyone seems to be better off than ourselves.

    C. We have built our lives upon the foundations of this present age if:

      1. we don't obey the will of God in our finances.

      2. we can't see the Kingdom for all the debt we have accumulated.

      3. we have less money this year than last year.

    D. When we are in Christ, once we miss a turn and start down the wrong road:

      1. we can never turn back.

      2. we can detour to the right road.

      3. we must go back to where we missed the turn.

11. Financial independence is being in a place where you_____ _____ have to make a _____ based on _____ _____, but simply on the _____ _____ of God.

12. Repentance + Obedience = Freedom. Explain this equation.___
_____
_____

13. Is the way out of a financial situation to make more money? Why or why not?_____
_____

14. What do we need in order to not make matters worse?_____
_____
_____

15. What do we have to do in order to be in good shape financially?
_____
_____

16. Explain the concept of a bond servant. _____
_____

    What is the difference between a believer and a believer who is a bond servant? _____
_____

17. Explain the four areas of what a bond servant does not have when Christ is his true Master.

    a. Money _____

    b. Time _____

    c. Family _____

    d. Life _____

18. Those who are truly _____ and _____
    in the ways of the Kingdom, do not just seek_____
    _____. They seek to be the _____ of
    the _____ _____ of the Lord. The
    Lord _____ many things that He will not
    _____.

19. What kind of Master is the Lord? _____

    _____

    What kind of life does He give His bond servants?_____

    _____

    What kinds of resources does He have to answer to our
    a. Money _____
    b. Time _____
    c. Family _____
    d. Life _____

20. When Christ is our _____, our _____,
    and the true _____ of our _____,
    He can then trust us with _____ _____
    and _____ that we are called to rule over. But if He
    is not our _____, our _____, and the
    _____ of our _____, our
    _____ and _____ will inevitably
    _____ over us.

21. When we are fully _____ to God, having
    _____ _____ all the yokes of this
    _____ _____ _____,
    He will then be free to _____ us with the
    _____ _____ of His Kingdom.

22. The only answer to the radical _____ that bind
    us is radical _____ to the Lord.

Covert Operations Yield Victory

Review what you prayed in the beginning of the chapter, the high-lighted items in the book, and notes you made during the Training Drills section. Now, spend time asking the Lord for specific ways in which you need to change your thought processes, alter your daily life, and/or make adjustments to relationships you have. Write your action plan for battle and follow through with its pursuit.

CHAPTER 9
SOCIAL FREEDOM

Put On Your Armor

Take time to pray before you read Chapter 9 to ask the Holy Spirit to enlighten your understanding as to how you need to adjust your thinking in the battle for your mind. Jot down anything that the Lord tells you.

Work Your Battle Strategy

Read Chapter 9 and highlight anything that stands out to you. Read as if you will be tested on the information from your Commander. After you are done reading, review the items you highlighted before going to the Training Drill questions.

Participate in Training Drills

Answer these questions, being open to the Spirit's interaction with your mind and heart. If you become aware of Him speaking… STOP! Jot down what you hear in the margins.

1. What was the very first thing that God said was not good? _____ Why did He say this? _____

   _____

2. Our relationship to God should be the most _____ part of our life, but we must have _____ with others, too. Relationships are _____ in our life. The _____ versus _____ principle works in _____ as well.

3. Every new believer quickly should come to know his or her _____ and _____ _____ and be given the _____ and _____ that would enable the person to take his or her _____ _____ _____. As these new believers begin to _____ as part of the _____ that they are called to be with _____ and _____, the Lord will _____ them.

4. TRUE OR FALSE:

   a. Ninety-five percent of the people who make decisions for Christ are added to the Church. ____

   b. Five percent of new Christians will be joined properly to the Body. ____

c. One hundred percent of converts in the first century were added to the Church. ____

d. We must be joined to the Head, but being joined to the Body is optional. ____

e. If we want to serve the Lord, we must be connected to the Head. ____

5. Who is at fault for the failure of many people who make decisions for the Lord not becoming members of a church?

_____

Why is this true? _____

_____

6. How is the Church supposed to fill the deepest social needs of every human heart? _____

_____

7. Explain the difference between entertainment at worship services and the anointing. _____

_____

8. What is the one most captivating, most desirable relationship that we can have? _____

How is this relationship supposed to be increased during worship services? _____

9. MULTIPLE CHOICE:

A. The army of God that marches in these last days will have

1. a fire that comes from the consuming fire of God.

2. a fire that comes because of the indignation of the saints over evil.

3. a fire that brings about the end of the world.

B. The consuming fire of God will

1. bring terror to the hearts of believers and non-believers alike.

2. break the idols of the world and consume what man has built.

3. pull the saints out of the earth to escape the flames.

C. The army of God will have

1. weapons and plowshares that will strike fear to everyone.

2. many gifts that will please the governments of the nations.

3. the Word in their mouths.

D. We must find our place in God's army, the Church because

1. it is critical to our survival.

2. we will need others to be our guides.

3. misery loves company.

E. Those in God's army

1. will be placed in government rulership.

2. will know increasing peace and security.

3. will defy the social order and create a revolution.

F. As we cast off restraints

1. we will overcome the world.

2. we will be the most bound and pitiful of people.

3. we will capture the hearts of the nations.

G. The army of God needs to know its place

1. in order that it not be found in a lost state.

2. in order to prevent the inevitable destruction of the Church by the world.

3. so that we can fulfill our purposes and experience true freedom.

10. Through interviews and conferences, the author determined that what percentage of believers know their calling, gifts of the Spirit, or place in the Body of Christ? _____

To what does the author attribute this? _____

_____

How does this low percentage affect the Church?_____

_____

11. Why is Ephesians 4:11-16 one of the most crucial biblical texts for our times? _____

12. What are the equipping ministries listed in Ephesians 4:11-16?

_____

13. What purpose do these equipping ministries have for the Church? _____

What purpose do they not have according to text?_____

_____

14. What are the four goals of the building up of the body of Christ?

   1. _____

   2. _____

   3. _____

   4. _____

15. What are the four ways that we are to build up the Body of Christ?

   1. _____

   2. _____

   3. _____

   4. _____

16. What are two reasons why churches turn away unbelievers?____

   _____

   _____

   How do these two work together? _____

17. What kind of vision of growth do we need? _____

   _____

   How is this accomplished? _____

   _____

   What does unity have to do with vision? _____

   _____

18. Compare the joints of the body with the joints that are spoken of in Ephesians 4:11-16. _____

   _____

19. How is love supposed to work within the Body of Christ?

   _____

   _____

   How does love help us become devoted to seeing everyone in the Body function? _____

   _____

20. We will never be free until we become what we were_____ to _____ and _____ what we were _____ to _____. We will never be the _____ _____ that we are called to be without the proper _____, _____, and _____ of the saints into their _____ on this earth.

21. Compare the way the Church is operating to a huge mob that has been mobilized for war. _____ _____

How is the Church like a huge sheep pen where shepherds throw food at them? _____ _____

22. We must realize that the _____ and _____ of the Spirit are for _____ _____, not just meetings. In light of this, where is some of the greatest ministry taking place? _____

Covert Operations Yield Victory

Review what you prayed in the beginning of the chapter, the highlighted items in the book, and notes you made during the Training Drills section. Now, spend time asking the Lord for specific ways in which you need to change your thought processes, alter your daily life, and/or make adjustments to relationships you have. Write your action plan for battle and follow through with its pursuit.

CHAPTER 10
THE WEAPONS OF GOD'S ARMY

Put On Your Armor

Take time to pray before you read Chapter 10 to ask the Holy Spirit to enlighten your understanding as to how you need to adjust your thinking in the battle for your mind. Jot down anything that the Lord tells you.

Work Your Battle Strategy

Read Chapter 10 and highlight anything that stands out to you. Read as if you will be tested on the information from your Commander. After you are done reading, review the items you highlighted before going to the Training Drill questions.

Participate in Training Drills

Answer these questions, being open to the Spirit's interaction with your mind and heart. If you become aware of Him speaking... STOP! Jot down what you hear in the margins.

1. Describe the paradox between the army of God and the peace of God. _____

2. What is one of the most powerful spiritual weapons that God's people have? _____

3. Describe what Romans 16:20 says about what will crush satan.
   _____

4. When we abide in the peace of God, what results do we receive for our warfare? _____

5. How does our peace work against the enemy?_____
   _____

6. TRUE OR FALSE:

   a. Most of the attacks of the enemy are intended to first rob us of our joy. ____

   b. The linchpin fruit of the Spirit that must be in place to hold all others in their places is peace. ____

   c. When we lose our peace, we fall from our position in Christ. ____

   d. The Beatitudes tell us that the peacemakers are called the friends of men. ____

   e. To overcome evil, we must overcome it with good. ____

   f. We destroy the enemy's power of destruction by standing in and imparting peace. ____

7. Why does the world view the Church as a source of conflicts?__
   _____

   What should it be? _____
8. The Church is called on to _____ the world, and as
   _____ and _____ grow in the world,
   _____ and _____ are going
   to grow in the Church to such an extent that even the
   _____ will start coming to Christians for
   _____.
9. Contrast the Church's spiritual authority to lawlessness in the
   coming days. _____
10. What is the significance of the "Jerusalem above" to the Church
    in Galatians 4:26? _____
    _____
11. Does the Church currently have peace? _____
    Explain. _____
    _____
12. Is there hope for the Church to become what she is called to do
    and be? _____ Explain. _____
    _____

13. MATCHING:
    a. Isaiah 60:1-2 says that   i. the Church will know
       when darkness comes up-   unprecedented peace.
       on the earth

    b. Peace will become a for-   ii. the true sanctuary on
       tress so that   earth.

    c. The Church will become   iii. it will be impregnable
                                              to the enemy.

    d. When human conflict and   iv. the Lord's glory will
       strife reach unprecedent   rise upon God's people.
       levels
14. MULTIPLE CHOICE:
    A. The conflict in the Middle East
       1. has to be solved in the United Nations.
       2. is bigger than anyone can imagine.
       3. has no human solution.

B. The conflict within the Church

   1. has no human solution.

   2. will be solved through ecumenical solutions.

   3. is another sign that we will never be in unity.

C. The solution for the Middle East

   1. is within the hearts of men.

   2. is only going to come from God

   3. is never going to be found until Jesus comes again.

D. The peace of God

   1. is rooted in the knowledge that Jesus is King above all other rulers.

   2. can make us walk in denial about the world's problems.

   3. is beyond a new Christian's reach.

E. When we see that God is in control

   1. we understand that we are merely pawns in the game of life.

   2. we are able to embrace the truth that God causes everything to work for good.

   3. we can believe the truth that we can change God's mind if we pray hard enough.

F. When we know in our hearts that God causes all things to work for our good

   1. we are able to believe in humanity again.

   2. there is no power on earth that can steal our peace.

   3. we can up the percentage of those who come to the Church.

15. What two things happen when we abide in the peace of God regardless of our circumstances? _____

_____

16. The Lord knows the _____ from the
_____. He already knows what He is going to do to
make things _____.

17. If we are _____ in the Lord, seated with Him in the
_____ as we are called, we too
will _____ in perfect _____.

18. Isaiah 26:3 reminds us that "The _____ of
_____ You will keep in _____
_____, because he _____ in You."

19. FILL IN THE CHART according to Ephesians 1:18-23:

BEGINNING OF CONCEPT	CONCEPT FURTHER EXPLAINED OR COMPLETED
The eyes of your heart	
So that you may know	1. 2. 3.
The working of the strength of His might Which He brought about in Christ	1. 2. 3. 4. 5.

20. Explain the concept of the "eyes of your heart" and what they will see. _____

21. How does really knowing that He is God help us to cease striving? _____

22. How will the peace of God be a contrast to the fear people will have in the days to come? _____

Covert Operations Yield Victory

Review what you prayed in the beginning of the chapter, the high-lighted items in the book, and notes you made during the Training Drills section. Now, spend time asking the Lord for specific ways in which you need to change your thought processes, alter your daily life, and/or make adjustments to relationships you have. Write your action plan for battle and follow through with its pursuit.

CHAPTER 11
THE ULTIMATE TRAP

Put On Your Armor

Take time to pray before you read Chapter 11 to ask the Holy Spirit to enlighten your understanding as to how you need to adjust your thinking in the battle for your mind. Jot down anything that the Lord tells you.

Work Your Battle Strategy

Read Chapter 11 and highlight anything that stands out to you. Read as if you will be tested on the information from your Commander. After you are done reading, review the items you highlighted before going to the Training Drill questions.

Participate in Training Drills

Answer these questions, being open to the Spirit's interaction with your mind and heart. If you become aware of Him speaking… STOP! Jot down what you hear in the margins.

1. What causes the fall of almost everyone in history? _____
   _____

   What are some of the Scriptures that speak to the problem of pride? _____

2. How does casting our anxiety on the Lord humble us? _____
   _____

3. As anxiety rises in the world, what will happen in the true followers of Christ? _____

4. MULTIPLE CHOICE: There may be more than one correct in each group.

   A. The anxiety that is coming upon the world is the direct result of

      1. man trying to do everything on his own.

      2. man trying to live without God.

      3. man bringing too many issues to the throne of grace.

   B. The original temptation of man was to get him to try to become

      1. a masterful being in charge of his own destiny.

      2. what God had called him to be, but without God.

      3. free of the worry of doing good and evil.

C. Peace can only come by
    1. our souls becoming immune to the world's woes.
    2. preaching the truth.
    3. returning to God.

D. The more humankind turns from God,
    1. the more striving and confusion there will be.
    2. the more we will need to be perfect.
    3. the more fear there will be.

E. Fear increases
    1. impatience.
    2. self-centeredness.
    3. deeds of the flesh.
    4. conflict.

F. Christians must grow in
    1. persecution.
    2. the knowledge of the Lord's authority and control.
    3. the peace of God.

5. What does "crushing satan under our feet" mean? _____
_____
_____

6. Why is the River of Life a river and not a pond or a lake?_____
_____
_____

7. What will happen when we walk in the peace of God in our home? _____
_____

8. What will happen when we walk in the peace of God at work?
_____
_____

9. What will happen when we walk in the peace of God in our city?
_____
_____

10. What will happen when we walk in the peace of God in our country? _____
_____

11. TRUE OR FALSE:

  a. God's prophetic barometer on the condition of humanity is the nation of Islam. ____

  b. External conditions will bring Israel the peace that she seeks. ____

  c. The author sent missionaries of peace to Israel to speak to the government officials. ____

  d. The best witness for Israel is having believers living there and demonstrating peace. ____

  e. Although the enemy has sent onslaught after onslaught against Israel, peace will be victorious. ____

  f. True peace is the condition of the heart that trusts God regardless of the circumstances. ____

12. There is no _____ like the _____ of God, and this alone can lead to a true _____ among the nations around Israel.

13. Explain the parable of the fig tree in Mark 13:28-29._____

_____

_____

14. Why do we need to understand Israel as a sign of the times?

_____

_____

15. What was the Church's response when Agabus prophesied a famine? _____

_____

16. What does the blessing of Abraham have to do with why the Christians took up an offering for Israel? _____

_____

17. What eternal law has God established that deals with seed reproduction? _____

_____

18. Why should we bless the natural seed of Abraham?

_____

_____

19. Why should we bless the spiritual seed of Abraham? _____

_____

_____

Covert Operations Yield Victory

Review what you prayed in the beginning of the chapter, the highlighted items in the book, and notes you made during the Training Drills section. Now, spend time asking the Lord for specific ways in which you need to change your thought processes, alter your daily life, and/or make adjustments to relationships you have. Write your action plan for battle and follow through with its pursuit.

CHAPTER 12
THE ROAD TO THE KINGDOM

Put On Your Armor

Take time to pray before you read Chapter 12 to ask the Holy Spirit to enlighten your understanding as to how you need to adjust your thinking in the battle for your mind. Jot down anything that the Lord tells you.

Work Your Battle Strategy

Read Chapter 12 and highlight anything that stands out to you. Read as if you will be tested on the information from your Commander. After you are done reading, review the items you highlighted before going to the Training Drill questions.

Participate in Training Drills

Answer these questions, being open to the Spirit's interaction with your mind and heart. If you become aware of Him speaking...STOP! Jot down what you hear in the margins.

1. What is the source of the greatest conflict in your life?_____

   Have you cast this anxiety upon the Lord?_____

   _____

2. What happens when we cast our anxiety on the Lord?_____

3. PUT THESE IN ORDER according to Hebrews 12:14-15:
   a. and by it many be defiled.
   b. See to it that no one comes short of the grace of God
   c. Pursue peace with all men
   d. that no root of bitterness springing up causes trouble
   e. and the sanctification without which no one will see the Lord.

4. Why do you think there is no reason for a Christian to ever be bitter at anyone or anything?_____

5. If we are bitter we are being _____, and we also will _____ _____ with that bitterness.

6. We are called to the _____ _____ of soul that is reflected in _____ and to the _____ _____ that comes from walking in the _____ of God.

7. What are the sources of conflict and agitation in your life?
   _____

   How should you repent of these because of a lack of faith?
   _____
   _____

8. What does it take to trust the Lord with matters of conflict and anxiety? _____
   _____

   What needs to happen in your heart? _____
   _____

9. The lack of _____ in our lives is directly related to the lack of _____ that we have in the Lord. Why is this true? _____

10. When we trust the Lord every day, what will be the result in terms of our ministry? _____
    _____

11. When we trust the Lord every day, what will be the result in what Jesus is building in our hearts? _____
    _____

12. Explain how the Lord judges the quality of a church._____
    _____
    _____

13. TRUE OR FALSE
    a. The peace of God leads us to victory over ourselves.
    b. The peace of God is our power over the strongholds of the enemy.
    c. The peace of God is the result of peaceful conditions.
    d. The peace of God results from our profound confidence in God no matter what conditions we face.
    e. The peace of God most demonstrates motivation when there are stressful or violent conditions.
    f. The peace of God is an accurate barometer of the true level of our faith.

14. How should we build our lives upon this Kingdom that cannot be shaken? _____
    _____

15. What does Romans 14:17 say about what the Kingdom of God is and is not? _____

16. Why can't joy and happiness be attained outside of Christ? _____

_____

17. What foundation is needed so that we can know true peace?

_____

_____

18. MULTIPLE CHOICE:

   A. When we are living lives that are obedient to the Lord and His ways,

     1. joy will come in the morning.

     2. no one can ever harm us.

     3. peace will be the result.

   B. When we are right with God and have peace,

     1. true joy comes that is beyond anything we can experience in the world.

     2. many people's faults will be revealed to us.

     3. we can pursue our careers.

   C. Man was created to have fellowship with God and nothing but

     1. meditating on Him for eight hours a day will bring us joy.

     2. working full time in ministry will bring us fulfillment.

     3. intimacy with Him will ever satisfy the deepest longing of our soul.

19. How is the righteousness of God lived out in our lives?_____

_____

_____

What is the best thing God desires for us? _____

_____

20. What does being armed with the peace of God mean?

_____

_____

What does this peace bring? _____

21. What does Paul's prayer in First Thessalonians 5:23 tell us about the God of peace? _____

_____

22. How is abiding in the peace of God the same as abiding in the Lord? _____

_____

Covert Operations Yield Victory

Review what you prayed in the beginning of the chapter, the high-lighted items in the book, and notes you made during the Training Drills section. Now, spend time asking the Lord for specific ways in which you need to change your thought processes, alter your daily life, and/or make adjustments to relationships you have. Write your action plan for battle and follow through with its pursuit.

CHAPTER 13
PEACE AND PROPHECY

Put On Your Armor

Take time to pray before you read Chapter 13 to ask the Holy Spirit to enlighten your understanding as to how you need to adjust your thinking in the battle for your mind. Jot down anything that the Lord tells you.

Work Your Battle Strategy

Read Chapter 13 and highlight anything that stands out to you. Read as if you will be tested on the information from your Commander. After you are done reading, review the items you highlighted before going to the Training Drill questions.

Participate in Training Drills

Answer these questions, being open to the Spirit's interaction with your mind and heart. If you become aware of Him speaking... STOP! Jot down what you hear in the margins.

1. What does the word "guard" mean in Philippians 4:7?_____
   _____
   _____

   How does peace guard us? _____

2. What are the descriptive words used in James 3:17-18 about the wisdom that comes from God? _____
   _____

3. In what areas of our lives should the peace of God rule?_____
   _____
   _____

   Why should this be a high priority for us? _____
   _____

4. TRUE OR FALSE:
   a. Difficult times will come on the world at the same time the glory of the Lord will come upon His people.____
   b. The prophecies about difficulties should bring us alarm.____
   c. The Lord does not worry about anything.____
   d. Abiding in God's perfection will be able to keep us from being shaken.____
   e. Peace will abide for us if we have built our lives on a Kingdom that cannot be shaken.____

5. How did Jesus answer every temptation of the devil in the wilderness? _____

_____

Why was this appropriate for Him? _____

_____

What does this say to us today? _____

_____

6. What does Psalm 29:11 promise to us? _____

_____

7. If we have anxiety, what does this mean about our relationship to God? _____

_____

Once we understand this, what should we do to correct the situation? _____

_____

8. What does Psalm 85:8-9 tell us about the peace and glory of God? _____

_____

9. What does First Peter 3:10-11 reveal about a primary reason many people do not have peace in their lives and are not walking in glory? _____

_____

10. How does the principle of reaping and sowing apply to sowing peace and unity? _____

_____

How do our words apply here? _____

_____

11. MATCHING: match the phrases with the Scripture passage. There will be multiple phrases for the Scriptures.

a. prepare the way for the Lord	i. Isaiah 52:7
b. government will rest on Jesus' shoulders	ii. John 14:27
c. Jesus will give peace to get rid of our fear	iii. Isaiah 9:6,7
d. guide our feet into the way of peace	iv. Luke 1:76-79

      e. peace, but not as the world
        gives

      f. our God reigns

      g. increase of government
        and peace will have no end

      h. announces peace and brings
        good news of happiness

12. What does Psalm 122:6-9 tell us about how to pray for Jerusalem? _____

13. Looking at Psalm 27:1-5, fill in the blanks to emphasize the meaning of the verses:

"The Lord is my _____ and my _____; whom shall I _____ ? The Lord is the _____ of my life; whom shall I _____? When evildoers came upon me to devour my _____, my adversaries and my enemies, they _____ and _____. Though a host encamp _____ me, my heart will not _____; though war arise _____ me, in spite of this I shall be _____. One thing I have _____ from the Lord, that I shall _____ : that I may ____ in the house of the Lord all the _____ of my life, to _____ the _____ of the Lord, and to _____ in His _____ For in the day of _____ He will _____ me in his tabernacle; in the _____ _____ of His tent He will _____ me; He will _____ me up on a rock." What does this passage mean to you?

14. Explain what Psalm 112:4-9 tells you about the person who is gracious and lends. _____

_____

15. Describe the way we should and should not seek wisdom from Proverbs 3:7-27. _____

_____

16. Describe the value of wisdom as described in Proverbs 3:7-27.

_____

_____

17. What are the results of having the Lord's wisdom?_____

_____

_____

Covert Operations Yield Victory

Review what you prayed in the beginning of the chapter, the high-lighted items in the book, and notes you made during the Training Drills section. Now, spend time asking the Lord for specific ways in which you need to change your thought processes, alter your daily life, and/or make adjustments to relationships you have. Write your action plan for battle and follow through with its pursuit.

PART III

DEFEATING THE THIEF OF HUMAN POTENTIAL

CHAPTER 14
OVERCOMING THE SPIRIT OF POVERTY

Put On Your Armor

Take time to pray before you read Chapter 14 to ask the Holy Spirit to enlighten your understanding as to how you need to adjust your thinking in the battle for your mind. Jot down anything that the Lord tells you.

Work Your Battle Strategy

Read Chapter 14 and highlight anything that stands out to you. Read as if you will be tested on the information from your Commander. After you are done reading, review the items you highlighted before going to the Training Drill questions.

Participate in Training Drills

Answer these questions, being open to the Spirit's interaction with your mind and heart. If you become aware of Him speaking... STOP! Jot down what you hear in the margins.

1. Why do you think the spirit of poverty is one of the most powerful and deadly strongholds satan uses? _____
_____

_____

In what way do you think this spirit is related to fear?

_____

2. Most evil strongholds, which are basically _____
_____ of thinking, are _____ and can be overcome _____ only as we _____ their entire _____.

3. Keeping God's people _____ and in
_____ is the intent of many of the
_____ that the enemy of our soul sends against us. Every church and every believer must _____ and _____ this spirit of _____ in order to walk in the _____ for which they were called.

4. If we overcome the spirit of poverty, what are some of the positive results for us? _____

_____

5. MULTIPLE CHOICE: (There may be more than one correct answer.)

    A. The spirit of poverty may or may not have anything to do with

        1. our grace

        2. principalities

        3. money

    B. The purpose of the spirit of poverty is to

        1. keep us from walking in the fullness of the victory of the cross.

        2. make us break from wealth.

        3. keep us from the blessings of our inheritance in Christ.

    C. The spirit of poverty can relate to the following areas:

        1. pressure points

        2. quality of our families

        3. our anointing

        4. resources

        5. ability to borrow money

    D. The goal of the spirit of poverty is to

        1. keep us from the will of God.

        2. keep us from things.

        3. keep us from believing in the power of money.

    E. Our goal for being free of the spirit of poverty is

        1. to get things we need.

        2. to do the will of God without hindrance.

        3. to be free from physical or spiritual depravity.

    F. Jesus was free of the spirit of poverty and so was able to

        1. make enough money to support the disciples.

        2. heal the sick.

        3. preach sermons in the synagogues.

        4. raise the dead.

        5. multiply food.

        6. draw on the resources of Heaven.

6. Second Corinthians 9:8 tells us: "And God is _____ _____ to make _____ grace _____ to you, so that _____ having _____ suf- ficiency in _____, you may have an _____ for every good deed." Making all grace abound must be a basic _____ of our life—to _____ in the grace of God. A key to this is knowing that it is not something we can _____. It is released by having _____ in who He is and what He has done.

7. The goal of our faith should be to _____ a life of "always having all _____ in _____." We should _____ represent the _____ and _____ that are available to _____ citizen of the Kingdom. That does not mean that we will never know _____.

8. Jesus did not meet _____ need because it was _____ the Father's will for Him to do so. However, there was _____ one that He could not meet because of a _____ of supply. When he multiplied the bread and the fish there was such an _____ that there was _____ left over.

9. One manifestation of the spirit of poverty is having_____ _____ _____ _____ _____ _____. The Lord wants our lives to _____.

10. TRUE OR FALSE:

   a. If abundance and overflow are not true in our life, we have the spirit of poverty.____

   b. A key way to break the spirit of poverty is to save for a rainy day.____

   c. Being generous to others will release the generosity of God.____

   d. If we have an attitude of just getting by, it will affect how we sow into the Kingdom.____

   e. The Lord gives just enough for us to get by.____

   f. We must be free of every financial yoke so we can make decisions based on how much money we have.____

   g. Abundance does not have to do with how much you have, but means you have more than you need.____

    h. We can expect to go through ups and downs so that we can expand our faith.____

    i. We must be content if we are abased or abounding, as long as we are in God's will.____

    j. The key for liberation from any evil stronghold is to know the technique for combating it.____

11. It is important for the Church to be prepared to handle unprecedented _____. The _____ of nations will be brought into the Church, not as a great opportunity _____ the advancement of the Kingdom, but as a result _____ the advancement of the Kingdom. Some of the greatest tests at the end of the age will be_____

_____.

12. We must seek financial _____ but it is not an _____ in itself. We also need to know our ____ in God. His will is our true _____, and therefore it should be the _____ thing that we seek.

13. Yokes represent _____. They usually appear to be a form of _____ but they result in the most terrible _____. We cannot serve two _____. We can make every claim to be a _____, but if we live our lives according to the ways of this present_____

_____ _____, we are _____ the _____ of _____.

14. We do not need to _____ any of the _____ that are coming upon the earth. The Kingdom of God cannot be _____, and if we have built our lives upon it, we will not be _____.

15. MATCHING:

    a. Judgment   i. trials produce this

    b. Crisis   ii. is not just the Lord's wrath

    c. Patience   iii. completely lacking nothing

    d. Perfection   iv. point of life or death

16. We have been called to be part of God's _____ _____, but we can be on only _____ in this battle. We must get _____ of every _____ of the enemy that causes us to _____ the ways of the Kingdom of God. The _____ we are now going through are all meant to help us do this.

17. We are on _____ now for _____ our place in His _____ force and _____ how much of His _____ we can be trusted with. This will determine whether we can be _____ with more.

18. If our positions here are taken from us, we are still_____ _____ with _____, and we will _____ Him in whatever way he calls us to _____. We must be _____ with whatever _____ He gives to us. Ultimate _____ is revealed by ultimate _____.

19. Whoever or whatever _____ over us is in fact our _____. The lordship of _____ must be more than a _____ it must be a _____ and _____ _____ in our lives.

20. Faith not combined with _____ will keep us in _____ and _____ Those who conclude that it is not _____ to be concerned about _____ are walking in _____, not _____.

21. There is a difference between being sluggish or_____ _____ and being _____. It will take _____ and _____ to inherit the _____. Patience can be one of the most profound _____ of true _____. To not combine _____ with our _____ will cause our faith to become _____.

22. We must allow the truth of God's _____ to be driven _____ into our lives. Those truths _____ will _____ the weight of our life and _____ us to go to _____ _____. We must set our _____ to walking in everything that God has called us to, including all the _____ and all the _____. However, we also want to have the _____ to know that the _____ we go, the more _____ it is not to _____ ourselves well to our Rock.

Covert Operations Yield Victory

Review what you prayed in the beginning of the chapter, the high-lighted items in the book, and notes you made during the Training Drills section. Now, spend time asking the Lord for specific ways in which you need to change your thought processes, alter your daily life, and/or make adjustments to relationships you have. Write your action plan for battle and follow through with its pursuit.

CHAPTER 15
RECEIVING THE WEALTH OF THE NATIONS

Put On Your Armor

Take time to pray before you read Chapter 15 to ask the Holy Spirit to enlighten your understanding as to how you need to adjust your thinking in the battle for your mind. Jot down anything that the Lord tells you.

Work Your Battle Strategy

Read Chapter 15 and highlight anything that stands out to you. Read as if you will be tested on the information from your Commander. After you are done reading, review the items you highlighted before going to the Training Drill questions.

Participate in Training Drills

Answer these questions, being open to the Spirit's interaction with your mind and heart. If you become aware of Him speaking… STOP! Jot down what you hear in the margins.

1. Wealth is never _____, but it often changes _____.

2. The earth will experience an even greater _____ _____ than the Great Depression. Those who are not _____ for it will be _____ by it. Those who are _____ for it will experience _____ _____. They will take advantage of the times and receive _____ over _____ _____.

3. Describe the principles that are contained in Matthew 7:24-27 and how the houses and their builders apply to what we are to do today. _____

_____

_____

4. Now is the _____ for us to _____ the Lord and to _____ our lives solidly on the rock of both _____ and _____ His Word.

5. MULTIPLE CHOICE:

   A. The reason the Lord is allowing crisis to come to His people first is because

      1. it will make us appreciate Him more.

      2. it will drive us to higher ground.

      3. it will put us to shame before the world.

B. If we have been faithful in all things

   1. sometimes the Lord still allows us to go through troubles.

   2. we are immune to the world's problems.

   3. God will grant us all the desires of our hearts.

C. The Lord allows judgment to come to us so that

   1. we can be better judges of the rest of humankind.

   2. we will inherit more than the world will.

   3. He can trust us with even more of His abundance.

D. We are being prepared to properly manage the abundance we receive so that

   1. we will be able to teach the ungodly how to manage their meager money.

   2. we will be able to rule the nations.

   3. it can save lives during the famine that will come.

6. The Lord wants His people _____ to use the _____ that are coming for the sake of His _____ One fundamental _____ that will keep us _____ by the spirit of _____ is _____. When it comes to the Lord's _____ us with more _____, _____ are crucial.

7. The Lord is _____ His people for what is about to _____. He has been _____ the Church for more than 30 years to get out of _____.

8. Those who are _____ will have nothing to _____ from what is coming; instead, they can look _____ to a godly _____ in the midst of famine. Those who continue in _____ will one day pay a _____ price for it.

9. We were bought with the _____ _____ that could be paid—the _____ of the Lamb. When we go into _____ we _____ ourselves to become the _____ of another. If we belong to _____ we are not our own to _____. When we go into _____ _____, we are actually _____ that which belongs to God.

10. Explain the principles the author shares from the Word of God as to whether we should buy a house with a mortgage or not.
    _____

11. What is the bottom line question we should ask ourselves in terms of whether we are able to borrow money for any reason?
    _____

12. How is patience necessary for climbing over a mountain of debt? _____

13. Outline the goals the author gives in order to make us financially independent:
    a. Reduce debt _____
    b. Reduce expenses _____

Covert Operations Yield Victory

Review what you prayed in the beginning of the chapter, the highlighted items in the book, and notes you made during the Training Drills section. Now, spend time asking the Lord for specific ways in which you need to change your thought processes, alter your daily life, and/or make adjustments to relationships you have. Write your action plan for battle and follow through with its pursuit.

CHAPTER 16
CHRISTIAN ECONOMICS 101: STEWARDSHIP

Put On Your Armor

Take time to pray before you read Chapter 16 to ask the Holy Spirit to enlighten your understanding as to how you need to adjust your thinking in the battle for your mind. Jot down anything that the Lord tells you.

Work Your Battle Strategy

Read Chapter 16 and highlight anything that stands out to you. Read as if you will be tested on the information from your Commander. After you are done reading, review the items you highlighted before going to the Training Drill questions.

Participate in Training Drills

Answer these questions, being open to the Spirit's interaction with your mind and heart. If you become aware of Him speaking… STOP! Jot down what you hear in the margins.

1. It would not do us much good to _____ _____ an evil _____ if we are going to allow the enemy to come right back and _____ it. It leaves us even worse off because when the enemy is _____ he will bring seven more _____ _____ even meaner than himself.

2. Our goal for tearing down every _____ _____ is to _____ a stronghold of _____ in its place so that the enemy has no _____ to _____.

3. Christian economics is the art of _____ _____ in _____ to the simple biblical _____ that the Lord has _____ to us. This is one of the primary strongholds that we must_____ _____ and _____ as Christians. Stewardship is the emphasis of a _____ _____ of the Bible because of its _____.

4. We must seek to use _____ the Lord has _____ to us in the most _____ way.

5. MATCHING: Using Luke 16:9-13:

    a. Make friends for
       yourselves

    i. is faithful also
      in much.

    b. He who is faithful in
       a very little thing

    ii. who will give you that
      which is your own.

    c. If you have not been
       faithful in the use of
       unrighteous mammon

    iii. and mammon.

    d. If you have not been
       faithful in the use of
       that which is another's

    iv. by means of the
      mammon of
      unrighteousness.

    e. No servant
       riches to you

    v. who will entrust the true

    f. You cannot serve God

    vi. can serve two masters.

6. We cannot combine the motive of _____ God with the motive of _____ _____.

7. What does "make friends for yourselves by means of the mammon of unrighteousness" mean? _____

8. Debt is probably the main reason Christians today are not _____ to _____ to the _____ of God in their lives. We must ask, "Does our financial condition _____ us, or do we have complete _____ over it?"

9. Faith can move _____, even mountains of _____. The word translated as "faith" in the New Testament also could have been translated_____ _____. Faith and _____ go together.

10. Regardless of how _____ or how _____ we have been, if we _____ the Lord will _____ us. If we call upon the Lord in _____, which is also _____, He will part an ocean to get us _____ if He has to. True faith begins with _____ _____ True repentance is _____ of the _____ _____ that compels the Lord to respond.

11. TRUE OR FALSE:

    a. The Bible is unclear as to how we are to get out of debt, stay out of debt, and become financially independent.____

    b. The Church is still wounded in many areas that satan intended to cripple her.____

c. Most of us will have to do repentance before we can even understand what we are required to obey.____

d. The Lord was wounded for us but was unable to heal Himself.____

e. When we are healed in an area, we receive authority for healing in those same places.____

f. True spiritual authority is found in judging the quick and the dead.____

g. Compassion releases the power of God.____

h. Our wounds are used to help us become sensitive to others.____

12. The Lord is going to use His Church to _____ the enemy's _____ _____ over multitudes and set them _____. He has allowed the enemy to _____ His Church in this area in order to make her _____ and _____ so we can help set others _____.

13. Our unhealed _____ keep people from getting _____ to us in those areas. This keeps us from being able to _____ for those who need our _____ Spiritual _____, therefore, can _____ us from our most _____ _____.

14. Scars keep us just _____ enough to help us _____ the wounds in others that have not yet been _____.

15. MULTIPLE CHOICE: Some may have more than one correct answer

A. The first principle to getting out of our present financial bondage is

1. break our pattern of thinking about money.

2. receive prophecy about our financial future.

3. not to get, but to give.

B. The Church has been raped repeatedly by

1. hype.

2. manipulation.

3. propaganda.

4. a controlling spirit.

C. The Lord has not allowed anything to happen to us

   1. that was against our desires.

   2. that was not for our good.

   3. that could have been averted if He had been watching closely.

   4. that was not for the higher good of His whole creation.

D. We need to quit sulking over our wounds and understand their purpose

   1. to bring humiliation to our souls and a wrenching in our hearts.

   2. so that we can receive authority over the one who wounded us.

   3. so that we can be vessels of healing for other victims.

E. Every suffering that a believer endures

   1. has a redemptive purpose.

   2. is a sign of a terrible sin in our lives.

   3. can be prevented through meditation and prayer.

F. Believers who have responded to financial abuses in the Church by refusing to give

   1. will be like goats on the day of judgment

   2. will be given fewer talents to invest.

   3. will likely stay in financial bondage.

16. Our first consideration in making any major _____ will be to determine our _____ One of the biggest open doors that the spirit of _____ has into our lives is through our own _____ _____ This is the spirit of _____ Judgments and ____ of others are the reason for many to be in _____.

17. The author has met many people with exceptional spiritual _____, but lack of spiritual _____, which is a prevailing _____ of a _____ spirit. Our _____ will bring us to _____.

18. If we want to receive grace, we had better learn to give _____. If we want to receive _____, we must start sowing _____.

19. We should not try to make _____ to the Lord until we have been _____ to our brother. We often think that our _____ and _____ can _____ for such sins, but they never will.

20. We can be the most _____ people and still stay in _____ if we are allowing the spirit of _____ access to our life through our own _____ and _____ _____.

Covert Operations Yield Victory

Review what you prayed in the beginning of the chapter, the highlighted items in the book, and notes you made during the Training Drills section. Now, spend time asking the Lord for specific ways in which you need to change your thought processes, alter your daily life, and/or make adjustments to relationships you have. Write your action plan for battle and follow through with its pursuit.

CHAPTER 17
TITHING IN THE KINGDOM

Put On Your Armor

Take time to pray before you read Chapter 17 to ask the Holy Spirit to enlighten your understanding as to how you need to adjust your thinking in the battle for your mind. Jot down anything that the Lord tells you.

Work Your Battle Strategy

Read Chapter 17 and highlight anything that stands out to you. Read as if you will be tested on the information from your Commander. After you are done reading, review the items you highlighted before going to the Training Drill questions.

Participate in Training Drills

Answer these questions, being open to the Spirit's interaction with your mind and heart. If you become aware of Him speaking... STOP! Jot down what you hear in the margins.

1. What is the first principle of stewardship? _____

   _____

2. What is tithing? _____

   _____

3. How much are we to tithe? _____

   _____

   Who was the first person who tithed and what were the circumstances? _____

   _____

4. Should legalistic tithers quit tithing? _____

   _____

   Why or why not? _____

   _____

5. What should our attitude be about tithing? _____
   How does giving firstfruits of our income demonstrate an act of faith? _____

6. TRUE OR FALSE:

    a. The Lord requires faith before He will release His power toward us._____

    b. The Lord rewards everyone who tithes with good luck._____

    c. Giving our firstfruits declares that we trust God as our Source._____

    d. We can please God with our tithes, with or without faith.

    _____

    e. Ministries and churches should tithe their income._____

    f. If you tithe this week, there will be an immediate turn-around in your problems._____

7. The Lord has told us that we are to put our tithe into the _____, which is the _____. Even if you do not agree with where your church leaders_____ _____ it, if you are part of a local body, then that is where your _____ should go.

8. God does not need our _____. The whole _____ is His. Tithing is for _____, not _____. Our excuses are only hurting _____.

9. When it was prophesied in the Book of Acts that a _____ was going to come upon the whole _____, the churches did not begin to _____; they took up an _____ and _____! If you believe that _____ _____ is coming, the only _____ place for you to _____ is in the Kingdom that cannot be _____.

10. You may think that you cannot _____ to tithe, but you cannot afford _____ to. Most of us do not really need more _____; we just need to have the _____ _____. But the Lord promises to do _____ than that; He promises that we will be so _____ that we will not have _____ _____ to hold it all.

11. If we really believe the Word of God, why would we not want to bring the _____ _____, and even much _____ ? He promises a _____ that is so great that we cannot even _____ it anyway.

12. In ancient Israel the tithe was actually the way that a family _____ in the Lord. It is an act of _____ and a way that we _____ the _____ of the Lord in our life.

13. MATCHING: Match the list of phrases on the right with one of the Scriptures on the left.

a. Luke 6:38

b. Proverbs 28:27

c. Proverbs 11:24-25

d. 2 Corinthians 9:6-8

i. one who scatters, and yet increase all the more

ii. he who sows sparingly will also reap sparingly

iii. give, and it will be given to you

iv. one who withholds what is justly due

v. God loves a cheerful giver

vi. he who gives to the poor will never want

vii. a measure-pressed down, shaken together, running over

viii. he who shuts his eyes will have many curses

ix. by your standard of measure it will be measured

x. the generous man will be prosperous

Covert Operations Yield Victory

Review what you prayed in the beginning of the chapter, the highlighted items in the book, and notes you made during the Training Drills section. Now, spend time asking the Lord for specific ways in which you need to change your thought processes, alter your daily life, and/or make adjustments to relationships you have. Write your action plan for battle and follow through with its pursuit.

PART IV

SPIRITUAL AUTHORITY

CHAPTER 18
TRUTH OR CONSEQUENCES

Put On Your Armor

Take time to pray before you read Chapter 18 to ask the Holy Spirit to enlighten your understanding as to how you need to adjust your thinking in the battle for your mind. Jot down anything that the Lord tells you.

Work Your Battle Strategy

Read Chapter 18 and highlight anything that stands out to you. Read as if you will be tested on the information from your Commander. After you are done reading, review the items you highlighted before going to the Training Drill questions.

Participate in Training Drills

Answer these questions, being open to the Spirit's interaction with your mind and heart. If you become aware of Him speaking… STOP! Jot down what you hear in the margins.

1. The Lord is going to _____ the earth, and He is going to start with His own _____. Judgments are not always _____, but they are the last _____ to _____ before the _____ comes.

2. We will be judged by our _____ and by how we have _____. To know the truth and not _____ it will only bring a more _____ _____.

3. Many presume that we can go on _____ _____ and God will _____ it. We are in the age of _____ and _____. Our salvation depends on the fact that our God keeps His _____. His people, who are called to be _____ Him, also will be a people who keep their _____, Our _____ is supposed to mean _____, and our _____ is supposed to mean _____, without _____.

285

4. To break our _____ to man is bad, but to break it
   with _____ could be the greatest human
   _____. We would be much better off never to
   _____ ourselves to being a _____
   _____ of Christ than to have made such a
   _____ and hold back part of the
   _____.

5. The bridge that every relationship is built upon is_____
   _____. Without it you can have
   _____, and even _____, but there can
   be no _____ _____. The
   _____ of the trust will determine the
   _____ of every relationship. For the Church to be
   the _____ that helped restore the
   _____ between God and man, we must be
   _____.

6. The spirit of _____ gained major inroads into the
   _____ when some public ministries were caught in
   _____, _____ or _____
   of the donations that were being given to them. Overreacting to
   this, many people stopped _____, which has caused
   some serious _____ in their lives. To break a
   _____ is a serious matter, and the Scriptures make
   it clear that there are _____ to doing so.

7. TRUE OR FALSE:

   a. Economics will be one of the major tests faced by only
      unbelievers at the end of the age. _____

   b. If we are going to be a light in the darkness, we must live
      by much higher standards of integrity in financial matters.
      _____

   c. We must examine ourselves to see if unbelievers have more
      money because God favors them. _____

   d. We must embrace correction as a sign of God's favor. _____

   e. To serve the Lord's own household and be stewards of His
      resources is a most serious matter. _____

   f. Handling money with integrity does not affect how the
      world receives the Church. _____

8. The world will look at the _____ and see a people who can be utterly _____, whose _____ is their _____.

9. The world will start to trust _____ when they see that His people are _____. The strength of our _____ will be determined first by how much we _____ God's Word and then by how much our _____ can be _____.

10. If we really believe God's _____, we will become _____ Him, and our _____ will be _____ as well.

11. MULTIPLE CHOICE:

A. There has never been a more serious business than our relationship with.

1. money

2. the Church

3. God

B. The judgment that will ultimately come upon the whole world is basically the result of the world

1. treating God so frivolously.

2. being poor stewards of the Earth.

3. making pacts with the devil.

C. God is not so harsh as to condemn us for

1. not preaching the Good News in our sphere of influence.

2. petty mistakes.

3. unforgiveness.

D. Presuming upon God's grace and holding back when we have committed to give all will ultimately result in

1. personal isolation.

2. tragedy.

3. a breakdown of society as we know it.

E. It is not enough to know God's Word—we must also

    1. keep it.

    2. write it.

    3. challenge it.

12. When _____ come, it will be _____ _____ to try to build your house on the _____. We need to take heed of the _____ of God and come to _____.

13. Psalm 34:6-10 says: "The _____ of the Lord _____ around those who _____ Him, and _____ them. O _____ and _____ that the Lord is _____; how _____ is the man who takes _____ in Him! O _____ the Lord, you his _____; for to those who _____ Him there is no _____. The young lions do _____ and _____ hunger; but they who _____ the Lord shall not be in _____ of any _____ thing."

14. The greatest _____ in the Scriptures are to those who ___ the Lord. Those who properly _____ Him, do not have to _____ _____ else on this earth.

15. John was _____ with the Lord, while Judas was merely _____ with Him. There can be a great _____. A _____ with God that breeds _____ is possibly the most _____ _____. However, _____ that breeds an increasing _____ of just how _____ He is will foster _____.

16. To know the _____ and _____ ourselves to live by it, and then not _____ it, is the very definition of a _____—a person for whom the Lord _____ His most vehement _____ _____.

17. Even though we were _____ with a
    _____ by the _____ of the Lamb, He
    will not _____ us to v Him. _____ is
    required, but we must _____ to _____
    because there is _____ not to _____.

18. MATCHING:

    a. God may not swiftly   i. it in itself is a judgment that
       judge our sin   leads to hardening.

    b. When God does not   ii. it would inhibit the freedom
       quickly discipline us   that He gives us.

    c. If God executed His   iii. by repenting before He
       judgments quicker   judges us.

    d. We prove our devotion   iv. but it does matter
       to the Lord   to Him.

19. If we knew that swift _____ was coming, we would
    most likely never _____. The same freedom that
    the Lord gives us to _____ is the freedom that He
    gives us to _____ and therefore proves our
    _____.

20. Those who love the _____ will live by
    the _____ even when it is not _____
    or seemingly, _____.

Covert Operations Yield Victory

Review what you prayed in the beginning of the chapter, the high-lighted items in the book, and notes you made during the Training Drills section. Now, spend time asking the Lord for specific ways in which you need to change your thought processes, alter your daily life, and/or make adjustments to relationships you have. Write your action plan for battle and follow through with its pursuit.

CHAPTER 19
SPIRITUAL AUTHORITY

Put On Your Armor

Take time to pray before you read Chapter 19 to ask the Holy Spirit to enlighten your understanding as to how you need to adjust your thinking in the battle for your mind. Jot down anything that the Lord tells you.

Work Your Battle Strategy

Read Chapter 19 and highlight anything that stands out to you. Read as if you will be tested on the information from your Commander. After you are done reading, review the items you highlighted before going to the Training Drill questions.

Participate in Training Drills

Answer these questions, being open to the Spirit's interaction with your mind and heart. If you become aware of Him speaking... STOP! Jot down what you hear in the margins.

1. The Lord gave two different _____ of authority on the earth—the authority for _____ _____ and the _____ authority of the _____. An important difference in these authorities is the _____ that they have been given to _____ their mandates.

2. The Church is going to move into the realm of ___ that displaces _____ and _____ over entire _____ and _____. We must understand this issue in order for us to _____ in and _____ the spiritual authority that we have been given and to _____ some devastating _____ that the enemy will try to _____ us into.

3. The mandate to the civil governments to keep _____ on this earth requires _____ or _____ weapons. The spiritual authority given to the Church is _____ by _____ weapons – the _____, _____, _____, _____, etc.

4. If the Church falls to trying to use _____ or _____ authority to accomplish our mandate, we forfeit the more _____ _____ authority. That is why we must learn to _____ between to two and keep them _____.

5. MULTIPLE CHOICE:

   A. All authority in both Heaven and earth have been given to Christ,

      1. but He has not yet directly taken His authority over the earth.

      2. but His second coming will reveal that Heaven is His choice.

      3. but He will not take charge of the earth because it is His footstool.

   B. The Lord sometimes allows the wicked to rule as

      1. a form of vengeance.

      2. a way of letting everyone know who is in charge.

      3. as judgment over regions and nations.

   C. The opposition of civil governments to the Church

      1. was part of God's plan to keep these two separate.

      2. is a direct result of satanic attack.

      3. will be eradicated in the last days.

   D. One reason the Lord wants to keep the Church and civil governments apart is

      1. because we cannot trust civil government, but we always can trust the Church.

      2. because the authority given to the Church is much greater than that entrusted to civil authorities.

      3. because no one understands the heart of God but God Himself.

   E. Civil authority is temporary and can change laws, but the Church's authority

      1. is eternal and can change men.

      2. is about to experience a great shaking.

      3. will change the civil laws one day.

    F. Christians should try to influence laws and the seating of righteous people in civil authority but they must do this as

      1. citizens of the Church.

      2. people of a Heavenly vision.

      3. citizens of our nations.

    G. Israel is a special nation that has a different relationship to God unlike any other because

      1. they were the first people on earth.

      2. Israel is to be a type of God's relationship with His Church.

      3. Israel was the only hope to bring a Messiah.

6. Spiritual authority is found in the _____ in men's _____ that _____ them to do _____ even when the lights go off and the police are not around. It is this light that keeps young people _____ _____.

7. One biblical example of a man who walked in true spiritual authority while being a civil authority was_____ _____. Explain how David demonstrated great character. _____

_____

8. The church will need to pass the test of respect for authority if we are going to reign with Christ. Why? _____

_____

9. The limit of the authority that we can be trusted with is basically dependent upon what? _____

_____

10. Why would someone who walks in true authority never undermine any authority established by God? _____

_____

11. Why must we be patient to allow the Spirit to make a way for our authority on earth? _____

_____

    What will happen if we are not patient? _____

_____

12. MATCHING:

     a. The Lord cares that conditions on this earth   i. and will not intervene until we ask Him to.

     b. The Lord has delegated authority to men   ii. have little or no authority on earth.

     c. An intercessor can   iii. move the hand of God.

     d. Many who have the greatest authority in Heaven   iv. be as good for people as possible.

13. We must distinguish which Scriptures are for the age to_____ _____ and which are for _____ age. Not doing so leaves the Church open to leaving her true ____ of _____ to impose her _____ in the _____ of _____ authority.

14. The Church's call is to be a _____ for _____, upholding God's standard of _____. She is to be a _____ to the civil governments.

15. Jesus could not be made _____ by the people, because He was born _____. The source of His _____ never came from people but from the _____. The Church's authority comes from _____. She cannot seek authority from any other _____.

16. Those who understand spiritual _____ will be very _____ of the sphere that has been _____ to them, for to go beyond it invites _____. Whenever the Church has tried to _____ her means by using the _____ appointed to the _____ _____, or whenever the _____ _____ have tried to _____ their ends by using the _____, there have been _____ and _____.

17. The sphere of _____ for civil governments is the realm of the _____, and the sphere of _____ appointed to the Church is the realm of the _____. The _____ of our sphere of authority can be easily recognized as the _____ of the _____.

18. TRUE OR FALSE:

    a. The Church is called upon to speak prophetically to governments.____

    b. The prophetic anointing is a foundation of our mandated influence with governments.____

    c. Prophetic authority is the carnal authority and power to speak of future events.____

    d. Prophetic authority is clearly articulated and established by a righteous and just life.____

    e. Moral authority is built on the foundation of the Spirit.____

    f. When men are reconciled to God, every evil will be dealt with.____

    g. Jonathan Edwards was used to help ignite the second Great Awakening.____

    h. The Church's authority is found in the power to demonstrate.____

    i. Martin Luther refused to compromise his convictions and changed the world in his own generation.____

    j. Martin Luther King, Jr. relied totally on spiritual authority and not civil government.____

    k. It is because the Church has been a silent prophet that the heathen have to wake us up.____

19. It is possible to use our influence in the realm of secular _____ _____, but good can be the worst enemy of _____. If we eat from the Tree of _____ _____ _____ _____ _____ _____, we may be able to do a lot of _____ but in the end we, and the _____ that we have done, will _____.

20. When the Church learns to live before _____ rather than _____, she will be entrusted with similar _____ to that of _____.

21. One of the ways that we can come to understand_____ _____ _____ and how we _____ to others is by _____ the existing _____ and our _____ in relation to it.

22. What are some ways that Christians can function under both mandates of authority? _____

23. God is the ultimate _____. His mandates are _____. If a government, spiritual or civil, exceeds its mandate, it is _____ place to correct it.

24. Freedom and _____ cannot last without the _____ of God as the _____ force _____ it. It is as major purchase of the Church to ____ civil authorities with our _____ authority. This can be done only by the _____ of _____.

Covert Operations Yield Victory

Review what you prayed in the beginning of the chapter, the high-lighted items in the book, and notes you made during the Training Drills section. Now, spend time asking the Lord for specific ways in which you need to change your thought processes, alter your daily life, and/or make adjustments to relationships you have. Write your action plan for battle and follow through with its pursuit.

CHAPTER 20
THE BATTLE FOR LIFE

Put On Your Armor

Take time to pray before you read Chapter 20 to ask the Holy Spirit to enlighten your understanding as to how you need to adjust your thinking in the battle for your mind. Jot down anything that the Lord tells you.

Work Your Battle Strategy

Read Chapter 20 and highlight anything that stands out to you. Read as if you will be tested on the information from your Commander. After you are done reading, review the items you highlighted before going to the Training Drill questions.

Participate in Training Drills

Answer these questions, being open to the Spirit's interaction with your mind and heart. If you become aware of Him speaking… STOP! Jot down what you hear in the margins.

1. We are not to "win" in the _____ spirit, or by going _____ our realm of _____ If we do, the consequences can be a _____ _____ for the cause of the _____ as well as for the cause of _____.

2. Regardless of how many laws are passed _____ this great _____, the _____ of _____ already have been _____ Even the beasts will instinctively _____ their own _____ to protect their _____, but we have proven willing to _____ our _____ for the most petty reasons on _____ and _____.

3. Revival is usually God's final _____ to show _____ instead of _____. The first Great Awakening came before the _____ _____. It was an opportunity to _____ this _____. The last Great Awakening came just before the _____ _____. That awakening was given as a way to _____ the Civil War.

4. Had the last Great Awakening continued on _____,
it would almost certainly have _____
_____. The political _____ of
that time, the _____, turned the revival
from its _____. They were driven to
_____ blown by the winds of _____.

5. The abolitionists had the right _____
_____, but they tried to achieve them by the wrong
_____. Such political _____ comes
from the _____ _____
_____ _____ _____,
regardless of the _____ of those who use it. The
Kingdom of God will not come that _____.

6. MULTIPLE CHOICE: (There may be multiple answers for
some of these)

   A. One of the ultimate choices now facing the Church is to
   decide

      1. whether we want the Kingdom to come.

      2. if we are the right vessel for the Lord's purposes.

      3. if we want our political goals to be accomplished more
      than anything else.

   B. There are many who pressure others to act prematurely
   and

      1. to be part of an army that can make a difference early
      before judgment.

      2. to use carnal weapons to assault spiritual fortresses.

      3. to get God's blessings after we have done the work

   C. Whenever spiritual men have tried to establish authority
   or influence in the civil realm, without being called to such
   a position, they most often become

      1. extremists who damage their own cause.

      2. rebels without a cause.

      3. prophetic instruments of God's deliverance.

    D. Zeal without humble submission to the Holy Spirit will become

      1. the way in which Christians will prove themselves faithful.

      2. a righteous manifestation of God's presence.

      3. a most useful tool of the enemy

    E. As soon as the enemy is able to push people into a realm they have not been called to, beyond the grace that they have been given

      1. he can use them as effective weapons in his hand.

      2. he can take them to places they could not have dreamed they would go.

      3. he can permanently work his plan.

    F. Prayer can bring a revival that can prevent a division in our country over abortion if

      1. we picket the governmental legislation.

      2. we go on a concerted campaign to use carnal weapons against abortionists.

      3. it is not sidetracked by zealots.

7. It is a wonderful thing to have been given _____ over _____ of the _____ of the enemy, but it is an even _____ thing to be found in God's history book—_____ _____ _____ _____.

8. We make God's history book if we _____ by the _____ of His _____, without succumbing to the _____ to live by human _____. It is much better to have _____ with God than to have _____ with all men.

9. In nature, the _____ of life is the most basic and _____ motivation. Therefore, family is a _____ _____ of life. It was no accident that the very first test of Solomon's _____ was concerning the issue of a mother's _____ for _____. The very first test of _____ for any government is its _____ to the _____ of _____.

10. True _____ is not measured simply by
_____ _____; true _____
is _____ what is _____ A civilization
that is not based on _____ will be open to
_____ and _____. Lawlessness always
results in _____. The inability to rise above ____
also results in _____. The _____ of
life is _____ to both _____ and
_____.

11. MULTIPLE CHOICE:

    A. There will be no peace of mind or peace on earth until

        1. life comes into the direct desires of the Church.

        2. life is esteemed above selfish ambition or convenience.

        3. life is renewed through hard work.

    B. Resolution of the abortion issue gives us the opportunity to provide the world with

        1. leadership in finding higher standards of morality, justice, and esteem for life.

        2. the threat of severe judgment from the redeemed Church.

        3. new enterprises for the new citizens that will be born.

    C. Failure to resolve the abortion issue with courage and honor, just not with law, will

        1. leave us penniless.

        2. leave people with a lack of understanding as to the most important issue the Church has today.

        3. leave a crack in our foundation which leads to tyranny.

    D. The Church should be involved in the battle of life

        1. whether is deals with abortion, euthanasia, or other issues.

        2. because the Church has the civil authority to do so.

        3. so that no one will accuse us of not doing our duty.

    E. An important question for the Church to address social issues is

        1. Under what authority will we address this?

        2. How should we bring our children into the discussion?

        3. Why does this issue exist anyway?

12. Spiritual authority comes from the _____
_____, and He is the _____
of _____. He will _____ with His
_____ only those who are _____,
who _____ what they _____.

13. Can we cast stones at the _____ who
_____ her child if we are _____ our
living _____ at the _____ of the petty
gods of _____ _____ and
_____ _____ ?

14. The first condition that God said was not good was for
_____ to be _____ and it is not
_____. Yet that is exactly where we will end up if
we do not give our _____ the _____
they _____.

15. Spiritual abortion is when the Church aborts the spiritual
_____ that God has planted in her. These are
_____, _____, and even the simple
_____ to our neighbors.

16. If we had not aborted the spiritual seeds, then the heathen
would not be _____ in such _____ and
would not be _____ their seed. The reasons the
Church aborts _____ seed and the heathen abort
their _____ is the same. It is because of our
_____.

17. It is time for us to quit _____ at the
_____ and put the _____ to
the _____ of the tree! Abortion is a great
_____, but it is just one of the _____
of the terrible _____ of humanity, which is
_____.

18. MATCHING:

a. Abortion must be   i. be passed that will help
   stopped but it is   fight against evil.

b. The only thing that can   ii. our government's actions
   stop abortion is   against slavery.

c. In a revival atmosphere   iii. a revival on the level of
   effective laws can   another Great Awakening.

d. Finney's revivals helped   iv. far beyond the government's
   spark   ability to stop it.

19. It is fundamental at this time for the Church to _____ of her own _____, then realize the _____ of her _____ if she is going to _____ anything of _____ regarding _____ or any other issue.

20. If we spend the _____, _____, and other resources seeking the _____ that we spend seeking _____ on the _____ _____, the world would be a _____ different and _____ place already.

Covert Operations Yield Victory

Review what you prayed in the beginning of the chapter, the high-lighted items in the book, and notes you made during the Training Drills section. Now, spend time asking the Lord for specific ways in which you need to change your thought processes, alter your daily life, and/or make adjustments to relationships you have. Write your action plan for battle and follow through with its pursuit.

CHAPTER 21
THE BATTLE FOR MORAL AUTHORITY

Put On Your Armor

Take time to pray before you read Chapter 21 to ask the Holy Spirit to enlighten your understanding as to how you need to adjust your thinking in the battle for your mind. Jot down anything that the Lord tells you.

Work Your Battle Strategy

Read Chapter 21 and highlight anything that stands out to you. Read as if you will be tested on the information from your Commander. After you are done reading, review the items you highlighted before going to the Training Drill questions.

Participate in Training Drills

Answer these questions, being open to the Spirit's interaction with your mind and heart. If you become aware of Him speaking… STOP! Jot down what you hear in the margins.

1. If we believe the Bible is God's _____, we must _____ that _____ is sin. So we must ask the question, "Should the Church _____ sin?" Most of us are still _____ with some problems that would have to fall under the _____ category.

2. Galatians 5:19, 21 includes "Outbursts of _____ " and "strife" along with _____ _____, and _____ as works of the _____. If we tried to remove _____ from the Church who had a problem with _____, there would not be many _____ left.

3. The Lord also called homosexuality an _____ and _____. Abominations are those sins which are especially _____ and _____. Paul called homosexuality a sin " _____." He promised that those who practiced it would receive "in their own _____ the due _____ of their _____."

4. Biblically, we can see that most _____ have their origin in the _____ realm, as the result of _____ _____. The characteristics of the plague usually reflect the _____ that had _____ it.

5. MULTIPLE CHOICE:

    A. How should the Church respond to homosexuals?

        1. Pretend that they don't exist.

        2. Make them feel awful about their sin.

        3. Love them because God does.

    B. How are judgment and love connected?

        1. Judgment is a result of love.

        2. Judgment is the antithesis of love.

        3. Love and judgment cannot dwell together.

    C. How does God use judgment?

        1. as a means to get revenge

        2. as a way to vent his anger

        3. as a last call to repentance

    D. When will the Church have true authority over the problem of homosexuality?

        1. when she admits that she can't do anything for them

        2. when she loves them

        3. when she helps mete out the judgment of God on them

    E. What kind of a threat is homosexuality in our nation?

        1. It threatens the foundation of our social order.

        2. It makes a way for people who are not like us to become powerful.

        3. It really isn't a threat unless it affects you.

    F. Why is our religious liberty the greatest threat to homosexuals?

        1. Because it makes claims they can't refute.

        2. Because it insists on its own way.

        3. Because we preach directly against homosexuality as sin.

G. What happens if we do not confront homosexuality
with the right spirit?

1. We add years of regret to our history.

2. We are indicted for our lack of courage.

3. We are multiplying the power of evil.

6. The growing release of _____ in society is the
result of an increasing _____ from
_____ _____ in the Church. If people
are not _____ - to the proper _____ of
the _____, they will fall to _____ the
_____ Paul explained in the first chapter of
Romans, this is a _____ _____ of
_____.

7. Music and other forms of art were _____ given to
man so we could express our _____ for God. Many
of the most _____ and _____ artists in
history were _____ because there was no outlet in
the _____ for their _____ through the
_____. Therefore they would turn to
_____ the _____ instead of
the _____.

8. The Church is called to be the _____ of the world.
If the world is falling into _____
_____, we should not _____
the _____, or even _____, but on the
_____. The answers to all society's _____
are _____, not _____. When we seek
to combat _____ and _____ problems,
we must share the _____ that will set people
_____, not just _____ and
_____ them.

9. There is a "spiritual _____" that the Church must
be _____ from if we are going to have spiritual
_____ over this sin. Spiritual _____ is
having relations only with your own _____, which
is _____.

10. A _____ of homosexuality is the fear of
_____, which pushes one toward
_____ and the _____ to stay away
from those who are _____. In the Church, it is the
_____ of much of the _____ that
causes them to _____ from any kind of
_____ with those who are _____.

11. MATCHING:

a. Perfect love casts out   i. and they felt comfortable
   fear and   around Him.

b. Jesus felt comfortable   ii. shared the truth that set
   around sinners   them free.

c. Jesus did not condemn   iii. it is fear that keeps
   sinners, but   homosexuals in bondage.

d. Jesus challenged   iv. changed them by loving
   sinners' sins with   them.
   love and

12. The Church should not _____ homosexuals
further, but reach out to them with _____
_____ and _____. We must treat sinners the way _____ did, with _____
_____ and the _____ to their
_____.

13. The author heard one politician remark that when he sees
Christians _____ _____ for the
_____ than the _____ do, they will
start _____ to the _____ more than
the _____. It is not realistic that
_____ will be _____
before the _____ comes.

14. The poor are an _____ for us to
_____ and _____ others, and it is a
great _____ to be able to do it. When we try to do
this through the _____ it becomes
_____ and _____, bogged down in
_____ and _____ that only a
_____ of the _____ will actually reach
the _____ of the people.

15. The government is likely to continue _____ into
_____ _____ until the Church stands
up to do her _____. The answer to
_____ human _____ is found at the
_____. The answer to _____
human _____ is found in _____.

16. TRUE OR FALSE:

 a. The Church has had a long history of trying to bring the
 Kingdom of God to earth by might and power, without the
 Spirit.___

 b. That which is born of the flesh is really spirit and that
 which is born of the spirit is really flesh.___

 c. Whenever men have tried to bring down spiritual strongholds with carnal weapons, it has resulted in a terrible
 defeat for the Gospel.___

 d. Time heals all wounds.___

17. In order for the Church to _____ her last-day
_____, she does not need _____
_____, _____ of _____,
_____ _____, or _____
_____. We need to _____ and
_____ of God.

18. Because God gives grace to the _____, we must
_____ ourselves. We need to _____
our historic _____ and ask _____
from those we have so _____ _____
and _____.

19. In the final days of this age, the Church will be _____
to a _____ of _____ _____
like she has never experienced before. The path to that great
_____ is in _____.

20. How will we know when the Bride has come of age?_____
_____
_____

Covert Operations Yield Victory

Review what you prayed in the beginning of the chapter, the high-lighted items in the book, and notes you made during the Training Drills section. Now, spend time asking the Lord for specific ways in which you need to change your thought processes, alter your daily life, and/or make adjustments to relationships you have. Write your action plan for battle and follow through with its pursuit.

CHAPTER 22
WHERE DO WE GO FROM HERE?

Put On Your Armor

Take time to pray before you read Chapter 22 to ask the Holy Spirit to enlighten your understanding as to how you need to adjust your thinking in the battle for your mind. Jot down anything that the Lord tells you.

Work Your Battle Strategy

Read Chapter 22 and highlight anything that stands out to you. Read as if you will be tested on the information from your Commander. After you are done reading, review the items you highlighted before going to the Training Drill questions.

Participate in Your Final Test

This chapter summarizes the main principles that Rick Joyner has introduced throughout the book. The questions here are designed to be a final drill to see how much you have learned and what you will now be able to put to use in your life.

TRUE OR FALSE:

a. Our primary goal must always be to know the Lord, to see His glory, and to be changed into His image.___

b. We must take off the armor of God when we are worshiping God in Spirit and in truth because warfare is not allowed in God's house.___

c. Our first calling is to be warriors for the Captain of the Host.___

d. If we walk in love for God and love for one another, we will win every battle.___

e. All attacks of the enemy are designed to turn us from loving God and one another.___

f. Love is not a weapon of warfare and must be kept separate and undefiled.___

g. We must walk in truth by committing ourselves to God's Word.___

h. If we do not want the father of lies to have any part in us, we must be committed to truth.___

i. God wants to reveal us as His sons and daughters, so we must exercise moral authority in all places on this earth.___

j. Integrity is important to Christians, but we need not worry if we have sinned by telling white lies to protect the cause.____

k. The biggest part of the battle is to discern the schemes of the enemy.____

l. We must resist the enemy when he attacks on a personal level or on a public level. If we do so he will not flee, but become weaker.____

m. We are always told to turn our cheeks when accusations come our way.____

n. We should never respond out of personal rejection when making a defense for ourselves.____

o. Our position in the Kingdom of God is defined by the gifts of the Spirit that have been given to us for the work of the ministry.____

p. If we attack in the wrong spirit or attitude, we multiply the evil that we are trying to cast out.____

q. Sins of our generation are due to the government abdicating their job of spiritual authority.____

r. We need to know how to respond to societal problems on the basis of the authority we have been given, and no other.____

s. Our war for righteousness is better fought by prayer and revival than by laws and statutes.____

t. We must keep a pure heart, a good conscience and a sincere faith if we are to make sure love never fails.____

Covert Operations Yield Victory

Review what you prayed in the beginning of the chapter, the highlighted items in the book, and notes you made during the Final Test section. Now, spend time asking the Lord for specific ways in which you need to change your thought processes, alter your daily life, and/or make adjustments to relationships you have. Write your action plan for battle and follow through with its pursuit.

Finally

Take an hour to rescan your notes, prayers, and action steps for each of the chapters. Specifically pray that the Lord will lead you to personal victory so that you can do your part for the Church's ultimate victory.

ANSWER KEY

Some of the answers to the questions are direct quotes from the book. Others are thoughts that are expressed within the text or implied. The answer given covers the principle but does not need to have the exact wording.

PART I

Chapter 1

1. Life and death.

2. We are either taking ground or losing it in this fight.

3. Understand the battle, fight it, and win.

4. C & D

5. The reason that He has not done this yet is because of His fundamental commitment to freedom for His creation.

6. We understand the conflict in the world, the conflict in our own soul, or even in a real sense the nature of God.

7. We cannot be who we were created to be without freedom. If all that the Lord wanted was perfect, harmonious worship, He would have done better to create computers instead of man so He could just program them to worship Him in perfect harmony.

8. This reflects one of the most basic differences between the kingdom of darkness and the Kingdom of God. In the domain of darkness there is fear, oppression, and bondage. In the Kingdom of God there is faith and freedom.

9. Tree of Knowledge— B, E,

   Tree of Life—A, C, D

10. a F

    b. T

    c. T

    d. F

    e. F

    f.T

11. Good or evil.

12. One half of the battle is won

13. *We are destroying speculations and every lofty thing raised up against the knowledge of God, and we are taking every thought captive to the obedience of Christ,*

14. a. iv

    b. v

    c. i

    d. ii

    e. iii

15. Our flesh is not binding to spiritual warfare. Satan will look at every thought we have to lead us from obedience under God.

16. It is true because we are not to sit back and ward off satan's attacks. We are to fight against satan's schemes at every turn, actively. We can stay alert to those things that sway us from what God has already shown us.

17. We know because we are all children under God, and we are to fight together. "As You sent Me into the world, I also have sent them into the world" (John 17:18). To set the captives free, to see every human soul set free of bondage to the devil and released into the glorious liberty of the children of God.

Chapter 2

1. the end of the age.

2. bride; army; worshipers; warriors

3. the Lord of hosts; the Lord of armies

4. a. F   d. F
   b. T   e. T
   c. T   f. T

5. conflict

6. of what they are doing right, not what they are doing wrong.

7. A. 2.
   B. 1.
   C. 3.
   D. 4.

8. They are inevitably overcome by it.

9. He who is in us is much greater than he who is in the world (see 1 John 4:4).

10. We must take on the full armor of God, and remain vigilant, we will not only stand, but also prevail against the gates of hell.

11. They continue to work because the Church has difficulty recognizing them.

12. free; yoke; yoke; use; set; free

13. authority and dominion

14. desecrate the sanctuary fortress

    do away with the regular sacrifice

    set up the abomination of desolation

    turn the wicked toward godlessness

    If we truly have the light, we will confront the darkness.

15. do the deeds of David.

16. a. i
    b. iii
    c. iv
    d. ii

17. worship; sword in our hands.

18. Our instruction is love from a pure heart and a good conscience and a sincere faith.

19. Love and truth

20. see the Lord; seeing the Lord

21. eyes of our hearts; worship; worship in our life

22. Set your mind on the things above, not on the things that are on earth.

Chapter 3

1. Basic gifts and talents, their knowledge and experience, as well as their fears and social wounds that affect the way they think and perceive others. Soul.

2. All the above characteristics combined to form how the group thinks, perceives, and acts. Churches, businesses, sports teams, and clubs.

3. nations; individuals; nations; minister

4. a. iii

   b. iv

   c. i

   d. ii

5. We are under the control of evil to the degree that fear is allowed to control our life.

6. faith or fear

7. One basic definition of faith might be to fight fear.

8. a. T   d. F

   b. F   e. T

   c. F   f. T

9. singular; multitude

10. simplicity; complicated

11. Fear of rejection; the fear of failure; the fear of embarrassment or humiliation, etc.

12. peace; rest; and fulfillment

13. If we were living by faith in that area.

14. release

15. A. 2

    B. 1

    C. 1

16. A continual battle to maintain position.

17. vulnerable; faith

18. faith; resists,; dominate; dominion; faith; serving,; free; dominating

19. Even so, it is natural in people that when one senses fear in another, he will almost inevitably move to dominate that person.

20. We must understand that our competitive nature must be redeemed and focused rightly.

21. We are in word by letters when absent, such persons we are also in deed when present. For we are not bold to class or compare ourselves with some of those who commend themselves; but when they measure themselves by themselves and compare themselves with themselves, they are without understanding.

22. A. 3   D. 3
     B. 2   E. 1
     C. 1

Chapter 4

1. levels; individuals; regions; nations; entire earth
2. counter; Great Awakening's
3. In every place the enemy attacks.
4. fear; faith; prevail
5. terror; but only the Church can achieve the ultimate victory
6. spiritual weapons
7. Our struggle is against: powers; world forces of this darkness; spiritual forces of wickedness in the heavenly places.

    Define this: Demons; principalities and powers; world rulers; the evil lord, satan himself

    Target of attack: individuals; regions or nations; the earth;

    Method of attack: gaining influence; gaining influence; gaining influence; gaining influence

    Who has authority over these: all Christians; Christians who are trusted with more spiritual authority; the Church as she is trusted with more spiritual authority; Jesus

    Method to combat these: recognizing, confronting and casting out; wrestle; faith and wrestling; the cross

8. a personal battle; Recognizing, confronting, and casting out demons is normal, biblical Christianity.
9. we may be called on to confront evil on a higher level
10. They both begin simply by seeking to gain influence. Seeking the liberation of a region or even a nation from the enemy's domain. We must "wrestle" with them.
11. a. iv
    b. i
    c. ii
    d. iii
12. The One who is in us is much greater than all of the power of the evil one. To be attacked on a higher level should actually be an encouragement to us.
13. a. T   e. T
        b. F   f. T
        c. F   g. F
        d. T
14. Every person is to be in subjection to the governing authorities. For there is no authority except from God, and those which exist are established by God.

Therefore whoever resists authority has opposed the ordinance of God; and they who have opposed will receive condemnation upon themselves. For their success in bringing the wrath of God on those who practice evil. Civil government is essential for keeping order to the degree that it is possible until the Kingdom of God comes to restore righteousness and justice on the earth.

15. We are required to love our enemies and pray for the repentance and salvation of our enemies.

16. Seen—Our civil governments, physical weapons, physical world

    Unseen—The Church, spiritual weapons, spiritual world

17. grow into; mature spiritually; commissions; increase; faith

18. confront and overcome our personal demons and our personal fears, to overcome the evil that is now controlling the world.

19. We may not see evil fully displaced until the King Himself returns to Earth, but there is a biblical mandate for us to do all we can to prepare the way for His coming Kingdom by overcoming evil in every way that we can now.

20. fear; take; stand; dictate; fear

21. A. 1

    B. 2

    C. 1

    D. 3

    E. 3

PART II

Chapter 5

1. The fear of the Lord; When the pure and holy fear of the Lord reigns in our life, we will not have to fear anything else.

2. The fear of God isn't a negative fear but an understanding or wisdom about who God is. Knowing Who He is leads us to trust Him.

3. God has love for us.	God has love for us.	We abide in God and love.
Love	Us	That we may have boldness.
Fear	Fear involves torment.	He first loved us

4. The fear of the Lord is the beginning of wisdom, but it is not the ultimate wisdom or the ultimate of spiritual maturity. The fear of God is the beginning, or the foundation, of wisdom. If our understanding of the love of God is not first built on a solid foundation of the pure and holy fear of God, our understanding of His love will be perverted into a subtle form of man-centric idealism that is really a form of humanism.

5. He is kind in His severity and severe in His kindness because He loves us.

6. a. F
   b. T
   c. T
   d. T

7. STEP 2: For her to be called into His great palace is an understandably fearful thing

   STEP 3: causes her to clean herself up to be near Him

   STEP 4: she is so captured by His irresistible love that she will fall in love with Him

   STEP 5: Then she will want to be pure and ready for Him because of her love

   STEP 6: As her love grows, so does this devotion

   STEP 7: But we will eventually overcome with His love

8. To be actually called into the very family of God may be doctrinally understandable to a new believer, but in fact it is almost incomprehensible. To be simply brought into the presence of the King is a fearful thought, as well it should be.

9. He is God! But we will eventually overcome with His love. It is a part of the process of our minds being renewed that transforms us into an ever-deepening lover. However, as much as we grow in love, we will never forget that He is God!

10. We realize how filthy we are, where we come from and how desperately we need the forgiveness of the cross. Then we can comprehend His holiness and His grace to accept and then change us. Realization of sin leads to a revelation of holiness which leads to the fear of the Lord.

11. being renewed that transforms us into an ever-deepening lover

12. To use God's love and forgiveness as an excuse to continue in our sin is an ultimate affront to the cross and to His love.

13. an absolute commitment to His Lordship; the most wonderful, intimate, and fulfilling relationship to the King of Glory

14. he beheld the glorified Lord Jesus whose breast he had once leaned against; he fell at His feet like a dead man

15.

Receive	My Words
Treasure	My commands
Incline your ear	To Wisdom
Cry out for	Discernment
Lift up your voice for	Understanding
Seek	Her as silver
Search for	Her as for hidden treasures
Understand	The fear of the Lord
Find	Knowledge of God

16. greater treasure; pursuing; earthly treasure

17. goodness; laid up; fear; wrought; trust; sons of men

18. eye; who fear; hope; loving kindness; deliver; soul; death; alive; famine

19. high; great; living; kindness; fear

20. father; compassion; compassion; fear

21. fulfill; desire; fear; hear; cry; save

22. fear; strong; confidence; refuge; fear; fountain; avoid; snares

Chapter 6

1. evil strongholds bondage replace fortresses truth fear faith advance purpose

2. As we proceed, we therefore should become a less fearful person and start becoming more secure and bold.

3. greater confidence right ultimate purpose right

4. Many of the idols that are keeping Christians in bondage today are religious devotions that are used to keep people in the control of the religious authorities.

5. They try to keep them moving from one high place to the next, from project to project, but they are not leading the people to their true resting place, which is the Lord Jesus Himself. We must keep in mind that one of the primary strategies of the enemy is to wear out the saints, and this is one of the most effective ways that he has been able to do it.

6. a. T

   b. T

   c. F

   d. F

7. We do this by following the Lord.

8. If we are going to walk on the path of true faith, we are going to be rejected by some, and we are going to have to learn to reject some, including their works

9. fear man Christ

10. worshiper works alone

11. a. ii, b. i, c. vi, d. iii

12. We can come up with our own image of God in our minds and worship it in place of God; a physical representation of what we think God looks like, our concept of who God is and what He is like that is born out of our own idealism rather than revealed truth.

13. Human idealism is born out of the good side of the Tree of Knowledge, all of the appearances of being good, but its fruit is deadly. Much of the teaching and theology that is prevalent in the Church today has its source in man rather than in the Scriptures.

14. It is not that we always make them out to be better than they really are; they may in fact be much better than we perceive them to be, but it is still our own image of them rather than who they really are. Therefore, if we are to have a complete knowledge, we must put what we know together with that which others have been given.

15. A. 3, B. 1, C.3

16.

Do not refuse Him who speaks	refuse	Reject, decline to hear
if they did not escape	Escape	Flee from
Him who spoke on earth	spoke	To verbalize
we not escape if we turn away from Him	turn	Go another direction
whose voice then shook the earth	shook	Move back and forth quickly
receiving a kingdom	receiving	Given to us
let us have grace	let	allow
we may serve God	serve	honor
godly fear	fear	reverence
God is a consuming fire	fire	Unstoppable force

17. there will our hearts be also, we will not have fears that this world has

18. By keeping the principles of the Kingdom, discerning idols/affections that control us

19. if something has our affections, or our attention, more than God does.

20. The ultimate key to our freedom from idols, or any other fear, is the true worship and love for God above all other things

21. To test ourselves in this way is something that we should do on a regular basis, The way that we know we pass this test is when Jesus Christ is truly the One ruling our heart and our affections.

Chapter 7

1. to grow in faith. We grow in faith by beholding the Lord and drawing closer to Him.

   The more that we are able to behold the glory of His plan, the more we will trust Him.

2. The end of this age is going to be a time of great trouble on the earth. We are deceived if we cannot see this.

3. This is what they have put their trust in even more than the Lord. it is unlikely that we will be able to understand accurately the biblical prophecies about these times.

4. doctrines or prophecies; deception; being; will; doing; will

5. gifts; authority; back; sin or idolatry; faithful; unfaithful; work; departed; will

6. a. F

   b. F

   c. T

   d. F

   e. T

7. ambassadors; citizens; home; Kingdom

8. rule; material; rule; attachment; enemy; fear; eschatology; mislead

9. A. 2, B. 2, C. 2, D. 3

10. kindness; repentance; plan; redeems; delivers; restores; created

11. preach; live

12. idols; money; compromise; idol; independent

13. "Financial independence" means different things to different people, but the way that I am applying this term does not have to do with being wealthy or poor. It means that we should never be in a place where our decisions are determined by financial considerations, but simply whether the matter is the will of God or not. We must be ruled by God's will, period. If we are abiding in His Kingdom, there are unlimited resources. However, these are not to be drawn on at our whim, but to do His will.

14. resources; will

15. obedience; obey; worship

16. a. iii, b. iv, c. i, d. v, e. ii

17. To repeat again, the love of money is the root of all evil because it can be the ultimate idol that we put our trust in by allowing it to take God's rightful place.

18. tasted; wealth; riches; money; money; concern; enough; will

19. The Lord needs people whom He can trust with resources for the great work of His Kingdom. The way His people handle money will be one of the distinguishing characteristics of the Kingdom.

20. Because it will challenge the Church's ability to use God's resources for the great work of His Kingdom. It will test where our trust is.

21. Our freedom from one of the ultimate yokes of bondage at the end of the age, the love of money, is actually to walk in the ultimate liberty that comes from being a slave of Christ.

22. trusted; resources; house; unprecedented wealth; spiritually; stumbling block

23. obey; follow; receive; tempter

Chapter 8

1. idol; stewardship; scripture; rightly; poorly

2. warnings; counsel; economic; financial; Church

3. we should seek to use everything the Lord has entrusted to us in the most profitable way.

4. we cannot combine the motive of serving God with the motive of making money.

5. a. iv

   b. i

   c. ii

   d. iii

6. faithful; worldly; true; Kingdom; unrighteous mammon; right spirit; prosperity; serve

7. a. F

   b. T

    c. T

    d. T

8. sin; judgment; worship; evidence; worshipping

9. Of course not. be concerned about how we may be serving the beast or living according to his ways.

10. A. 2

    B.1

    C. 1

    D. 3

11. never; decision; financial considerations; revealed will

12. We must start by recognizing and repenting of any ways in which we have departed from the clear mandates of Scripture. Then we must begin to obey the clear and simple biblical instructions for financial management. If we do, we will escape our present situation and begin to live a life of freedom that is better than we have ever dreamed.

13. No, That is seldom the answer to financial problems, and it can even make matters worse. What we need is true faith in God, which is always demonstrated by obedience to Him. God's plan for our financial freedom does not require us to make more money, and He probably will not give us a revelation so that we can win the lottery.

14. What we need is true faith in God, which is always demonstrated by obedience to Him.

15. Most of us would be in good shape if we just had "the devourer" rebuked from our lives so that the losses and waste are stopped.

16. The Lord created us for freedom. This may seem to conflict with the concept of a bond servant, who is literally a slave, but we can become a bond servant only if we freely choose to be one. Believers come to an understanding of the sacrifice of Jesus for their sins, but they still go on living their lives for themselves. A bond servant does not live for himself, but for his master.

17. a. money—A true bond servant does not have any money of his own, so he cannot spend freely what he has been entrusted with because it is not his.

    b. time—Neither does a bond servant have any time of his own. His time belongs to his master. A bond servant does not waste his free time because it does not belong to him.

    c. family—Our children are not "our" children, but have been entrusted to us. The Lord wants them overseen with the devotion of a governor or governess who is entrusted with the child of a king, an heir to the throne.

    d. life—To voluntarily become a slave is the ultimate commitment that can be made in this world. That is what it really means to embrace the cross. Those who are truly bond servants do not live for themselves, but for their Master. These are the ones who receive the Lord's mark.

18. wise; mature; blessings; habitation; manifest presence; blesses inhabit

19. the best Master that one could ever have; The life of a bond servant is the most fulfilling, the most interesting, and the easiest life that we could ever live on the earth.

20. life; trust; desire; heart; earthly possessions; positions; life; trust; desire; heart; possessions; positions; rule

21. yoked; cast off; present evil age; trust; unlimited resources

22. fears; discipleship

Chapter 9

1. The very first thing that God said was not good was for man to be alone. God created us so that we would need other people as well.

2. fulfilling; fellowship; crucial; fear; faith; relationships

3. calling; spiritual gifts; training; equipping; rightful place; function; Body; wisdom; grace; promote

4. a. F

   b. T

   c. T

   d. F

   e. T

5. The failure of so many who make decisions to serve the Lord to ever become members of a church is an indictment on the church, not the converts or the evangelists. When the Church becomes the Body that it is called to be, with the proper functioning of every individual part, we also will see those who make commitments to Christ become added to His Church and quickly begin to find their place.

6. The Church, as it was intended to be, fulfills the deepest social needs of every human heart like no other entity on earth will ever be able to do.

7. The real basis of many church services is more entertainment than anointing, and the best entertainment that a church can come up with is going to be boring compared to what the world can do. We are not called to compete with the world in that arena, and we do not have the grace or anointing to do it. However, there is nothing more interesting, more captivating, more desirable, or more wonderful than the Lord.

8. than the Lord; If we spent more time trying to get the Lord to come to our meetings than we did trying to get people to come, we would have more people than we can handle.

9. A. 1.   E. 2

   B. 2   F. 2

   C. 3   G. 3

   D. 1

10. around 5 percent of the believers; the equipping ministries are doing the work rather than equipping believers to do the work

11. It also should be interesting to us that this seemed to be about the same percentage of those who make decisions for Christ who become a part of the Church.

12. as apostles, and some as prophets, and some as evangelists, and some as pastors and teachers

13. but to equip the believers to do the work of the ministry; cannot be built any other way

14. We attain to "the unity of the faith." We have "the knowledge of the Son of God." We become "a mature man" (singular). We have grown up into "the measure of the stature which belongs to the fullness of Christ."

15. We speak "the truth in love." We grow up "in all aspects" into Christ. We become "fitted and held together by that which every joint supplies." It is the proper functioning of each individual part that causes the building up of the Body in love.

16. One reason some churches and Christians turn away unbelievers is because they do not speak the truth. The second reason is that those who speak the truth often do not speak it in love. Speaking the truth without love will not work.

17. up in "all aspects into Him;" First, we must understand that no one can do this alone. No one person is going to have all the gifts and ministries of the Lord. It is as a body of believers together that we can manifest "all aspects" of Christ. This requires that we come into unity. Then we are to be "fitted and held together by that which every joint supplies."

18. We must understand that some members of the body must become closer to certain members. We must allow special bonding between certain members as long as they are bonding around their function in the body.

19. is the proper functioning of every individual part that causes the building up of the Body in love.

20. created; be; do; created to do; victorious army; training; equipping; deploying purpose

21. the Church is right now more like a huge mob that has been mobilized for war, but no one is training them, much less equipping them (putting the weapons in their hands) and then sending them out to battle.

22. ministries; gifts; everyday life; His ministry took place in everyday life and in every place that He went. Ours must do the same.

CHAPTER 10

1. We may think that peace is not a weapon, but it is such a weapon that Paul did not write that it was the Lord of hosts, or the Lord of armies, who would crush the enemy, but that "the *God of peace* will soon crush Satan under your feet" (Rom. 16:20).

2. The peace of God is the linchpin fruit of the Spirit that must be in place in order to hold all the others in their places.

3. crush the enemy; but that "the God of peace will soon crush Satan under your feet."

4. it is both a fortress and a weapon that the enemy has no power against.

5. it unravels the enemy's power over that situation.

6. a. F   d. F

   b. T   e. T

   c. F   f. T

7. (personal explanation, including: the Church is broken into factions and disagrees internally; we say one thing and do another; the Church disagrees with the humanistic mindset and looks like it is narrow and brings judgment on society)

8. judge, conflicts, anxiety, peace and wisdom, help

9. the Church's spiritual authority will grow stronger and stronger as lawlessness erodes human authority.

10. Jerusalem means "city of peace."

11. No, the Church is now embroiled in almost continuous strife with war within herself as well as war against the forces of the world without.

12. Yes; When human conflict and strife reach unprecedented levels, the Church will know unprecedented peace.

13. a. iv
    b. iii
    c. ii
    d. i

14. a. 3   d. 1
    b. 1   e. 2
    c. 2   f. 2

15. it crushes satan's attempts to turn and use those circumstances, and it also allows us to see God's purpose in them.

16. end; beginning; right

17. abiding; heavenly places; dwell; peace

18. "The steadfast of mind You will keep in perfect peace, because he trusts in You."

19. BEGINNING OF CONCEPT   CONCEPT FURTHER
                                   EXPLAINED OR COMPLETED

The eyes of your heart   *heart may be enlightened, so that you may*
                                  know what is the hope of His calling

So that you may know

   1. *is the hope of His calling*

   2. *what are the riches of the glory of His inheritance in the saints,*

   3. *what is the surpassing greatness of His power toward us who believe*

The working of the strength of His might which He brought about in Christ

   1. *He raised Him from the dead and seated Him at His right hand in the heavenly places*

   2. *above all rule and authority and power and dominion*

   3. *name that is named, not only in this age, but also in the one to come*

   4. *And He put all things in subjection under His feet*

   5. *gave Him as head over all things to the church,*

20. The "eyes of your heart" refer to our spiritual eyes. When they are open, we will see Jesus where He sits, far above all authority, power, and dominion on the earth.

21. When we really know that He is God, we will cease striving. When His people come to this knowledge and walk in it, He will be "exalted among the nations."

22. The peace of God will be in such profound contrast to the fears that are coming upon the world and causing people's hearts to fail.

Chapter 11

1. Pride caused the fall of satan and almost every fall since. We know that "God is opposed to the proud, but gives grace to the humble."

2. This implies that one of the ways we humble ourselves is to cast our anxiety upon the Lord.

3. peace will rise correspondingly in those who are true followers of Christ.

4. A. 1, 2   D. 1, 3
   B. 2   E. 1, 2, 3, 4
   C. 3   F. 2, 3

5. This speaks of his power being broken through our "walk."

6. Christianity is not static; it is always moving forward, always growing. That is why the River of Life is a river and not a pond or a lake. A river is always flowing, proceeding toward its destination.

7. it will ultimately crush the enemy's influence there.

8. it will soon crush the enemy's influence there.

9. the Church there would soon come into unity, and the enemy's influence over that city would be crushed.

10. they will crush the enemy's influence over that nation.

11. a. T   d. T
    b. F   e. T
    c. F   f. T

12. peace; peace; peace

13. when its branch has already become tender, and puts forth its leaves, you know that summer is near. Even so you too, when you see these things happening, recognize that He is near, right at the door.

14. Because the fig tree is a symbol of Israel, this is an exhortation to understand this nation as a sign of the times.

15. the way the Christians prepared for it was to take up an offering for the believers in Israel.

16. They understood God's promise to bless those who bless Abraham's seed.

17. They also understood that God had established an eternal law in the beginning that a seed could reproduce only after its own kind.

18. If we want to be blessed in the natural, we should bless the natural seed of Abraham.

19. If we are seeking spiritual blessing, we should bless the spiritual seed of Abraham, which is the Church.

Chapter 12

1. (personal answers)

2. When you do this exercise of faith, it will release Him to move into the situation.

3. c, e, b, d, a

4. (personal answer that deals with reliance on God, peace, patience, and love)

5. defiled; defile others

6. ultimate nobility, forgiveness, ultimate dignity, peace

7. (personal answer that speaks of trust in the Lord in relation to them)

8. Cast this anxiety upon the Lord. Determine that, regardless of appearances or situations, you are going to trust the Lord to deal with these matters. He will do it, but usually after He has dealt with something even more important—your own heart.

9. peace; faith; A fundamental calling on our lives is simply to trust God.

10. Simply trusting Him every day will accomplish much more than many of the works and projects that we try to do for Him.

11. The Church and the Kingdom that Jesus is building are in our hearts, and they will be manifested in our daily lives.

12. The Lord does not judge the quality of a church by how good the meeting is Sunday morning, but by how good the people are on Monday morning.

13. a. T   d. T

    b. T   e. T

    c. F   f. T

14. "For the kingdom of God is not eating and drinking, but righteousness and peace and joy in the Holy Spirit."

15. "For the kingdom of God is not eating and drinking, but righteousness and peace and joy in the Holy Spirit."

16. We will never know true peace without building our lives on a foundation of righteousness, which is simply having a right relationship with God.

17. simply having a right relationship with God.

18. A. 3

    B. 1

    C. 3

19. living the way we were created to live, doing that which is in fact the best for us; is to walk with God, dwell in His presence, follow Him and be obedient in all things.

20. Those who are armed in this way will go forth conquering in His name. The peace of God is an impregnable fortress. Never, ever, lose your peace, and you will always know victory.

21. may your spirit and soul and body be preserved complete, without blame at the coming of our Lord Jesus Christ.

22. It is "the God of peace" who will sanctify us, for it is by abiding in the peace of God that we abide in the Lord.

Chapter 13

1. ." It is interesting that the Greek word translated as "guard" in this text is phroureo, which comes from a compound word that means "to be a watcher in advance, that is, to mount guard as a sentinel (post spies at gates); figuratively, to hem in, protect—keep as with a garrison."

2. pure; then peaceable; gentle; reasonable; full of mercy and good fruits; unwavering; without hypocrisy

3. our hearts and minds; Having the peace of God rule in our hearts, our families, and our churches must be a high priority if we are going to be free from deception.

4. A. T
   B. F
   C. T
   D. F
   E. T

5. He answered every temptation with Scripture. The Word of God is stronger than any power that we will ever be faced with. Now is the time to search the Scriptures, taking our stand on that which will stand forever—the Word of God.

6. The Lord will give strength to His people; the Lord will bless His people with peace.

7. If anxiety is growing in our life, it is because we have somehow become separated from Him. Therefore, we should ask the Holy Spirit to convict us of our sin, repent of what is revealed to us as the cause of the separation, and resolve to grow in both peace and faith.

8. I will hear what God the Lord will say; for He will speak peace to His people, to His godly ones; but let them not turn back to folly.

   Surely His salvation is near to those who fear Him; that glory may dwell in our land.

9. "He who would love life and see good days, let them refrain his tongue from evil and his lips from speaking deceit.

   "Let him turn away from evil and do good; let him seek peace and pursue it."

10. A primary reason many, and possibly most, are not walking in the peace of God or experiencing His glory in their lives is because of what comes from their own tongues. For this reason let us heed the words of King David in Psalm 34:14: "Depart from evil and do good; seek peace and pursue it."

11. a. iv   e. ii
    b. iii   f. i
    c. ii   g. iii
    d. iv   h. i

12. Pray for the peace of Jerusalem.

13. light salvation; fear defense dread flesh stumbled and fell. against fear; against confident.

    asked, seek: dwell days behold beauty meditate temple.

    trouble conceal secret place hide lift, it is about dealing with fear through the Lord.

14. It is well with the man who is gracious and lends; he will maintain his cause in judgment.

    For he will never be shaken

15. Do not be wise in your own eyes; fear the Lord and turn away from evil.

16. How blessed is the man who finds wisdom, and the man who gains understanding.

    For her profit is better than the profit of silver and her gain better than fine gold.

    She is more precious than jewels; and nothing you desire compares with her.

    Long life is in her right hand; in her left hand are riches and honor.

    Her ways are pleasant ways and all her paths are peace.

    She is a tree of life to those who take hold of her, and happy are all who hold her fast.

    The Lord by wisdom founded the earth; by understanding He established the heavens.

    By His knowledge the deeps were broken up, and the skies drip with dew.

    My son, let them not vanish from your sight; keep sound wisdom and discretion,

17. Then you will walk in your way securely and your foot will not stumble.

    When you lie down, you will not be afraid; when you lie down, your sleep will be sweet.

PART III

Chapter 14

1. (personal insights based on the success of the enemy in this area); (personal reflection based on how fears keep us oppressed and in poverty)

2. deceptive patterns; interrelated; completely; web

3. oppressed; poverty; fears; fight; overcome; poverty; purposes

4. advances and spiritual successes in place of spiritual authority to meet needs

5. A. 3   D. 1, 2

   B. 1, 3   E. 1, 2, 3

   C. 2, 3, 4   F. 2, 4, 5, 6

6. able; all; abound; always; all; everything; abundance; goal; walk; earn; faith

7. live; sufficiency; everything; always; life; power; every; need

8. every; not; never; lack; abundance; plenty

9. just enough to get by; overflow

10. a. T   f. F
    b. F   g. T
    c. T   h. T
    d. T   i. T
    e. F   j. F

11. wealth; wealth; for; of; economic

12. independence; end; purpose; treasure; primary

13. bondage; freedom; burdens; masters; Christian; evil age; serving; powers; evil

14. fear; difficulties; shaken; shaken

15. a. ii
    b. iv
    c. i
    d. iii

16. invasion force; one side; free; yoke; compromise; trials

17. trial; establishing; invasion; determining; authority; trusted

18. seated; Him; worship; next; content; job; faith; trust

19. rules; lord; Jesus; doctrine; profound; continuing reality

20. patience; slipping; presumption; faith

21. slothful; diligent; faith; patience; promises; demonstrations; faith; patience; faith; presumption

22. Word; deeply; support; enable; higher safely; visions; power; provision; wisdom; higher; dangerous; secure

Chapter 15

1. destroyed; hands

2. economic upheaval; prepared; devastated; prepared; unprecedented prosperity; authority; unprecedented wealth

3. (own words that describe the wise man building on the rock which shows that we are to build upon God. The rains, floods and wind come—these represent our trials. The house did not fall and we will not fall but endure to the end. The foolish man built upon sand, which shows those who build on earthly things. When the rain, floods, and winds come the house falls, which represents everything that we build that is not based on God's will…it is the wood, hay and stubble that will not endure.)

4. time; seek; establish; hearing; doing

5. A. 2
    B. 1
    C. 3
    D. 3

6. prepared; circumstances; gospel; flaw; bound; poverty; selfishness; trusting; resources, motives

7. preparing; come; warning; debt

8. obedient; fear; forward; prosperity; disobedience; terrible

9. highest price; blood; debt; sell; slave; Christ; sell; debt; selling

10. (in own words describing that it is a principle, not a law to stay out of debt. We are told to loan money and charge interest, so borrowing is not a sin. But we need a clear directive from the Lord.)

11. Did God give us this directive?

12. (in own words describing how we need to make one step at a time to overcome and rid ourselves of debt)

13. a. 5% per year; 10% the next year; etc.

   b. 10% per year and increase by 10% per year for the next 5 years

Chapter 16

1. tear down; stronghold; rebuild; displaced; evil spirits

2. evil stronghold; rebuild; truth; opportunity; return

3. good stewardship; obedience; procedures; given; confront; overcome; substantial portion; importance

4. everything; entrusted; profitable

5. a. iv   d. ii
   b. i   e. vi
   c. v   f. iii

6. serving; making money

7. to use mammon to make friends

8. free; respond; call; rule; authority

9. mountains; debt; faithfulness; patience

10. disobedient; foolish; repent; deliver; faith; faithfulness; free; true repentance; evidence' true faith

11. a. F   e. T
    b. T   f. F
    c. T   g. T
    d. F   h. T

12. break; financial power; free; wound; sensitive; compassionate; free

13. wounds; close; intercede; ministry; scabs; disqualify; important ministries

14. sensitive; discern; healed

15. A. 3   D. 2, 3
    B. 1, 2, 4   E. 1
    C. 2, 4   F. 3

16. decision; Master's will; poverty; unrighteous judgment; criticism; criticism; poverty

17. gifting; fruit; characteristic; critical; criticism; poverty

18. grace; mercy; mercy

19. offerings; reconciled; sacrifices; offerings; compensate

20. generous; bondage; poverty; criticism; unrighteous judgments

Chapter 17

1. obedience to the King
2. giving first fruits of our labors to the Lord
3. 10%; Abraham gave 1/10 of the spoil from battle to Melchizedek
4. no; They need to walk in obedience (discipline) while examining if they have the right spirit
5. act of faith; believe God will meet our needs and give abundance beyond what we need
6. a. T   d. F

     b. F   e. T

     c. T   f. F
7. storehouse; church; spend; tithe
8. money; world; us; Him; ourselves
9. famine; earth; hoard; offering; gave; economic catastrophe; wise; invest; shaken
10. afford; not; income; devourer rebuked; more; blessed; room enough
11. whole tithe; more; blessing; contain
12. boasted; faith; honor; goodness
13. a, iii, vii, ix

      b. vi, viii

      c. i., iv, x

      d. ii. v

PART IV

Chapter 18

1. judge; house; condemnation; call; repentance; condemnation
2. deeds; lived; live; severe judgment
3. willfully sinning; overlook; grace; truth; Word; like; word; yes; yes; no; no; compromise
4. word; God; folly; commit; bond servant; commitment; price
5. trust; forgiveness; love; genuine relationship; strength; strength; bridge-builder; relationship; trustworthy
6. poverty; Church; lies, unfaithfulness, misuse; giving; repercussions; pledge; repercussions
7. a. F   d. T

     b. T   e. T

     c. F   f. F
8. Church; trusted; word; bond
9. God; trustworthy; witness; trust; word; trusted
10. Word; like; words; true

11. A. 3

   B. 1

   C. 2

   D. 2

   E. 1

12. storms; too late; Rock; Word; obedience

13. angel; encamps; fear; rescues; taste; see; good; blessed; refuge; fear; saints; fear; want; lack; suffer; see; want; good

14. promises; fear; fear; fear anything

15. intimate; familiar; difference; familiarity; presumption; terrible delusion; familiarity; revelation; awesome; obedience

16. truth; commit; do; hypocrite; reserved; condemnation

17. bought; price; blood; force; serve; Obedience; choose; obey; liberty; obey

18. a. iv

   b. i

   c. ii

   d. iii

19. judgment; disobey; disobey; obey; devotion

20. truth; truth; convenient; expedient

Chapter 19

1. mandates; civil government; spiritual; Church; weaponry; accomplish

2. authority; principalities; powers; regions; nations; grow; exercise; avoid; traps; push

3. order; carnal; physical; exercised; spiritual; truth, love, peace, patience

4. carnal; civil; powerful spiritual; distinguish; separate

5. A. 1   E. 1

   B. 3   F. 3

   C. 1   G. 2

   D. 2

6. light; hearts; compels; right; morally pure

7. David; unjustly persecuted but did not raise his hand against the authority that God had placed over him

8. So that God can trust us with unprecedented authority

9. the level of our dependence on the Lord

10. Because that person trusts God

11. to show that we are led by the Spirit of God and not taking position by our own hand; we may seize temporal authority but we will rule according to the ways of the present evil age and do the devil's bidding

12. a. iv

   b. i

c. iii

d. ii

13. come; this; realm; authority; will; realm; civil

14. force; good; righteousness; conscience

15. King; King; authority; Father; above; source

16. authority; conscious; appointed; disaster; accomplish; sphere; civil authorities; civil authorities; accomplish; Church; tyranny; oppression

17. authority; law; authority; Spirit; boundaries; fruit; Spirit

18. a. T   g. F

    b. T   h. F

    c. F   i. T

    d. T   j. F

    e. F   k. T

    f. T

19. civil authority; best; Knowledge of Good and Evil; good; good; perish

20. God; men; power; God's

21. our purpose; relate; understanding; authority; place

22. When they are on the job, military and law enforcement use their civil authority with the weapons they have been given for their jobs. When they are off duty, they operate by the spiritual authority they have as Christians, using the weapons of love, truth, peace, etc.

23. authority; supreme; His

24. democracy; fear; moral; underpinning; underpin; moral; power; truth

Chapter 20

1. wrong; beyond; authority; major defeat; Gospel; life

2. legalizing; evil; laws; nature; passed; sacrifice; lives; young; sacrifice; children; convenience; selfishness

3. attempt; mercy; judgment; Revolutionary War; avoid; war; Civil War; prevent

4. track; abolished slavery; zealots; abolitionists; course; extremes; impatience

5. moral goals; means; manipulation; spirit of the evil one; motives; way

6. A. 1, 3   D. 3

    B. 2   E. 1

    C. 1   F. 3

7. authority; all; power; greater; the Book of Life

8. live; authority; Book; temptation; authority; influence; influence

9. preservation; powerful; primary drive; wisdom; sanctity; life; wisdom; commitment; sanctity; life

10. morality; legal compliance; morality; doing; right; law; despotism; tyranny; preservation; fundamental; nature; morality

11. A. 2

    B. 1

    C. 3

    D. 1

    E. 1

12. Holy Spirit; Spirit; Truth; endorse; authority; true; live; preach

13. mother; aborts; sacrifices; children; altars; selfish ambition; personal success

14. man; alone; good; families; priority; deserve

15. seeds; missions, outreaches; witness

16. living; darkness; aborting; spiritual; unborn; selfishness

17. flailing; branches; ax; root; evil; symptoms; diseases; sin

18. a. iv

    b. iii

    c. i

    d. ii

19. repent; sins; Source; power; accomplish; significance; abortion

20. time, money; anointing; influence; human level; radically; better

Chapter 21

1. Word; understand; homosexuality; tolerate; struggling; sin

2. anger; immorality; idolatry; sorcery; flesh; everyone; anger; people

3. abomination; perversion; corrupting; destructive; against nature; persons; penalty; error

4. plagues; spiritual; widespread sin; sin; released

5. A. 3   E. 1

    B. 1   F. 3

    C. 3   G. 3

    D. 2

6. homosexuality; departure; true worship; devoted; worship; Creator; worshiping; creation; primary cause; homosexuality

7. talents; adoration; gifted; talented; homosexuals; Church; worship; arts; worshiping; creation; Creator

8. light; increasing darkness; blame; government; society; Church; problems; spiritual; political; social; moral; truth; free; condemn; alienate

9. homosexuality; delivered; authority; homosexuality; kind; sectarianism

10. root; rejection; isolation; compulsion; different; insecurity; leadership; refrain; relationship; different

11. a. iii

    b. i

    c. iv

    d. ii

12. alienate; genuine; love; help; Jesus; open arms; answers; problems

13. caring more; needy; liberals; listening; Church; liberals; poverty; eradicated; Kingdom

14. opportunity; love; help; privilege; government; depersonalized; institutionalized; waste; inefficiency; fraction; resources; needs

15. degenerating; socialistic delusions; job; every; problem; cross; every; need; Christ

16. a. T

    b. F

    c. T

    d. F

17. accomplish; mandate; public opinion, force; numbers, financial resources; political power; grace; anointing

18. humble; humble; acknowledge; mistakes; forgiveness; tragically persecuted; wounded

19. exalted; position; spiritual authority; exaltation; humility

20. When healing has reached Jerusalem and touched the heart of the Jew with a grace and truth that is realized through Jesus Christ

Chapter 22

a. T	k. T
b. F	l. F
c. F	m. F
d. T	n. T
e. T	o. F
f. F	p. T
g. T	q. F
h. T	r. T
i. T	s. T
j. F	t. T

Author Contact Information

For information about the ministry of Rick Joyner and other available books and materials, call **1-800-542-0278** for a free catalog or visit the Website at **www.morningstarministries.org.**

Additional copies of this book and other
book titles from Destiny Image are
available at your local bookstore.

Call toll-free: 1-800-722-6774.

Send a request for a catalog to:

Destiny Image® Publishers, Inc.
P.O. Box 310
Shippensburg, PA 17257-0310

*"Speaking to the Purposes of God for This
Generation and for the Generations to Come."*

**For a complete list of our titles,
visit us at www.destinyimage.com**